# Rude Awakening

*The Government's Secret War Against Canada's Veterans*

by Colonel (retired) Pat B. Stogran

Suite 300 - 990 Fort St
Victoria, BC, Canada, V8V 3K2
www.friesenpress.com

Copyright © 2015 by Colonel (retired) Pat B. Stogran
First Edition — 2015

All rights reserved.

No part of this publication may be reproduced in any form, or by any means, electronic or mechanical, including photocopying, recording, or any information browsing, storage, or retrieval system, without permission in writing from FriesenPress.

**ISBN**
978-1-4602-7165-0 (Hardcover)
978-1-4602-7166-7 (Paperback)
978-1-4602-7167-4 (eBook)

1. Biography & Autobiography, Political

Distributed to the trade by The Ingram Book Company

# Table of Contents

**vii**      Foreword

**ix**      Prologue

**1**      Chapter 1: Scene Setting

**24**      Chapter 2: Meet Canada's Veterans

**35**      Chapter 3: The OVO

**87**      Chapter 4: Rude Awakening

**110**      Chapter 5: Homeless Veterans

**126**      Chapter 6: Internal Review

**133**      Chapter 7: Parliamentary Committees

**145**      Chapter 8: Lousy Leadership

**150**      Chapter 9: Institutionalized Malfeasance

**183**      Chapter 10: Going to the Wall

**229**      Chapter 11: The March Continues

**244**      Chapter 12: Conclusion

**247**      Epilogue

**249**      About the Author

*To my family: Trish, Molly and Dylan.
You made me who I am today!*

# Foreword

Tough, determined, courageous, compassionate, and outspoken. These are some of the traits that earned Colonel Pat Stogran his appointment as Canada's first Veterans Ombudsman. They are the same traits that made the Harper Government deeply regret giving him that job.

During his tenure, Pat spoke out for those who had difficulty speaking for themselves. He spoke on behalf of men and women that sacrificed almost everything for Canada. He spoke for soldiers who came back from combat changed forever.

Pat Stogran did the job he was asked to do and he did it well. People are often rewarded for succeeding on the job—Pat Stogran was fired.

There is no greater litmus test for the decency and efficiency of Government than the way it treats and cares for its military veterans. Colonel Stogran's book is an important reminder of that fact. This is a document that all Canadians and our current government should reflect upon.

I salute Pat Stogran for everything he has done for our country and for refusing to go quietly into the night.

*Rick Mercer*

*Office of the Veterans Ombudsman's Logo 2007 – 2010.*
The logo above was displayed by the Office of the Veterans Ombudsman during the tenure of Colonel (retired) Pat Stogran.

Each element was carefully chosen to reflect the relationship between the work done by the OVO and who they did the work for — Canada's veterans, their families and the people and the Government of Canada.

- The shield is significant because of its association with defending the bearer. It symbolizes veterans who have defended the interests and values of all Canadians, and the responsibility of the OVO to defend veterans and their families by ensuring that they are treated fairly.
- The thirteen maple leaves surrounding the shield are representative of each province and territory of Canada.
- The background colour of the shield is aligned with the colour scheme of the Canadian flag, and the crown-shaped top represents the Crown – the Government of Canada.
- The Latin word written across the scroll is "Aequitas", which means fairness, the raison d'être of the OVO.
- The handshake depicted on the shield extends from higher to lower, representing the Government of Canada and the citizens who have accepted the term of unlimited liability in the service of our country.
- The handshake also denotes the mutual understanding of the obligation that the Government of Canada has to look after veterans and their families.

# Prologue

In November of 2007, I hung up my uniform after serving in the Canadian Forces for thirty-one years. I had joined the military when I was eighteen and didn't really understand very much about the world around me, other than it was my oyster, as they say, and I was quite sure there was a pearl in it somewhere for me. I thought I had found that pearl in the military, throwing my heart and soul into the profession and the lifestyle. Life has its ups and downs, but for the most part my life seemed to be on the up and up. I loved my career, I had a healthy and happy family life, and in the end I can say that I had achieved the only objective I had ever set for myself in my life; in the year 2000 I returned to the Third Battalion, Princess Patricia's Canadian Light Infantry, as the commanding officer. After that accomplishment, I was ready to pursue other challenges but wasn't sure where my passions lay.

The Office of the Veterans Ombudsman offered me an opportunity to leave the military gracefully and consider my options, while continuing to serve my country and those who make such huge sacrifices on our behalf. My time as ombudsman did fulfill my desire to give back to the people in Canada's military; however, it also served as a rude awakening to me in my understanding of the very government that I had devoted my adult life to serving.

During my thirty-year career in the military, I had survived almost two full years in two separate war zones. I had been threatened, shot at, shelled, held at knife-point and detained in a makeshift cell. None of that, however, was more traumatizing than the three years I would spend as Canada's first Veterans Ombudsman. I could not believe how badly we treat some of our most seriously disabled veterans and how seriously dysfunctional our government is. This realization caused me to renounce my lifelong profession, question my country and what I thought it stood for, and lose focus on my life's journey. It also took its toll on my health.

In *Rude Awakening*, I intend to describe to mainstream Canadians how badly we treat a large number of our veterans of service in our military. I estimate that fifteen to twenty percent of those who need government assistance, often those veterans with the most serious challenges and in the greatest need of help, are either ignored or unfairly treated. My aim with this book is very simple. By describing my terrible experience, I hope to bring Canadians together to insist that our government remedy the situation that it's created. The Government of Canada must live up to the longstanding tradition we have in this country of erring on the side of generosity when it comes to caring for and compensating those loyal Canadians who accept the condition of unlimited liability when answering our government's call to protect Canadians and uphold Canadian values.

I am confident that I reacted to the gross callousness and malfeasance I witnessed in government the way that any conscientious and patriotic Canadian would have, given my circumstances. I hope my story will resonate with you to awaken your awareness of that reality and activate your opposition to the status quo.

CHAPTER 1:

# Scene Setting

My upbringing had a profound impact on me with regards to standing my ground and speaking truth to power. My parents named me Patrick Benton Stogran, and I was born on April 16, 1958 in a small town called La Sarre, in the Abitibi region of Quebec. My father worked in the mines of Normétal, and later, Matagami. The local communities were tiny, and the closest hospital to that rapidly expanding northern Quebec frontier was in La Sarre. Dad was the eldest of two sons of Ukrainian immigrants and grew up in the Dauphin area of Manitoba. His dedication, ambition, and work ethic earned him a good reputation in the mining industry and he was able to make a decent living. He set an example of loyalty and tenacity for my three brothers and me that we each emulated in our own way for the rest of our lives.

My kid brother Sheldon and I were inseparable for the first part of our lives, very much as close as twins. He was only sixteen months younger than me. Even when we were very young, we often settled our differences in all-out fights; no holds barred competitions that resembled the Ultimate Fighting Championships of today. But as often as we may have fought each other, we made a great team. My older brother, Wade, was my idol. A naturally gifted athlete, he could climb like an ape and was a high school wrestling champion. Shell and I took up weightlifting at an early age so we could be like him. Shell shared some of the right genes with Wade and became as strong as a bull, while I languished as somewhat of a pencil-neck. My youngest brother, Kc, was six years my junior. The age difference between us was enough that we had a different circle of friends, but I remember him tagging along with me and Shell quite often.

Needless to say, my mother was a special kind of lady. Like many of the military wives I came to know in the army, Mom was the glue that held the family together through everything. Where my father taught us what a work ethic and loyalty were all about, Mom showed us by example how to be strong willed and self-sufficient. Her family roots were deeply embedded in the Badlands of Alberta, in and around Medicine Hat, so undoubtedly my brothers and I were also imbued with a healthy dose of the cowboy and rancher ethos. She shovelled coal into the furnace, showed Sheldon and me how to shoot a rifle for the first time, kept us busy with all sorts of arts and crafts when we weren't out being feral, coached us in sports, mentored us through Cub Scouts, and tore us apart when a fight broke out amongst "The Brothers," as she called us.

Growing up in rural Canada was an outstanding experience, but we eventually moved to Pierrefonds, a suburb of Montreal. My parents thought it would offer us kids better opportunities. Dad was still employed in the mining field. His firm provided equipment for the mines, so his work kept him on the road a lot. Mom continued to carry the lion's share of rearing four growing boys fresh out of the bush; swimming lessons, hockey and wrestling practices, and even learning how to build bikes from spare parts. After three short years in Pierrefonds, my father was selected to open the west coast branch of the firm, so we loaded up and moved to the lower mainland of British Columbia.

Shell and I remained inseparable throughout our elementary school days in Richmond, but began drifting apart when I went on to high school. It wasn't long after that I became involved in martial arts, an interest that Shell didn't share with me. I started out taking judo lessons in Steveston, a quaint little Japanese fishing village on Lulu Island, the delta at the mouth of the Fraser River upon which the town, now city, of Richmond, is situated. That was short lived, though. I loved the grappling, but something was missing. It wasn't the kind of stuff Bruce Lee performed in his role as Kato, which I watched with fascination on the television show *The Green Hornet*.

My older brother Wade later discovered karate also, and we became equally infatuated. Together we spent every spare moment pursuing our martial arts passion. Eventually we inculcated my youngest brother Kc, who was only seven or eight years old at the time, into the cult of karate. We pushed each other through the highs and lows of a lifelong commitment to our art. At the time, there were a lot of fly by night, all-show-no-go styles of martial arts that preached a Dim Mak "death touch" kind of nonsense. Fortunately for us, we had fallen into a form of karate that was renowned in the day for pushing the envelope of freestyle, full-contact sparring. In my teenage years everything else — school, social life, entertainment, part-time jobs, sports — took a back seat to martial arts, a passion that continued throughout my military career.

## Royal Military College (RMC)

When I was young I had no idea what I wanted to do with my life, but it went without saying in our family that my brothers and I would go on to university. I eventually joined the Canadian Forces, for no other reason than I saw officer training in a military college as an easy way to get a degree and secure a job while I figured out what I would do for a living. I started off at Royal Roads Military College in Victoria, BC in August of 1976. From the very first moment, I hated every second that I spent in military college. I decided that if I was going to endure all the bullshit just to get a degree, I might as well go for one that would be really marketable on "civie street." I went down the electrical engineering path, which meant I had to move on to the Royal Military College in Kingston, Ontario in my third year. I didn't have any aptitude whatsoever for engineering, so academics were a constant stressor for me.

I was definitely not a model officer cadet either. In fact, I was actually a non-conformist of the highest order. The closest I ever came to assimilating into college life was to train occasionally with the wrestling team. I approached the sport of wrestling very much as a martial art in its own right, and have a great deal of respect for the amazing skill and strength of its competitors, but when it came to fighting I was not much into "grappling." So I went out of my way to slip out of college activities to go train with martial artists in Ontario and Montreal. The other source of enjoyment for me in college life was the annual boxing competition. The Royal Military College in Kingston was the last bastion in the Canadian Forces for the sport of boxing, which was compulsory for all first-years. As a third-year cadet I could not compete against the first-years (for good reason), so I coached our team in Four Squadron. We became a powerhouse, the team to beat in my fourth and final year. Sadly, we came in second in the finals, due to a contentious split decision that irks me to this day.

And, oh yeah, I graduated.

## Army

During the summers in between each academic year, the cadets from the military colleges would join the Regular Officer Training Programs (ROTP) in the army, navy, and air force. I spent one summer in Borden, and three in Gagetown learning how to be an infantry platoon commander. Unlike the disdain I had held for military college, I loved everything about the army. I loved the training and, if I do say so myself, I excelled at it. After RMC and my final summer of infantry training in Gagetown, in 1980 I joined the Third Battalion of Princess Patricia's Canadian Light Infantry (PPCLI) in Victoria, BC.

At the time, I still had every intention of serving my compulsory four years and then getting out. The oil patch was booming, so I began following the job postings and networking where I could to exploit the engineering degree, which I had endured so much to earn. In the PPCLI, my love for all things army continued to grow; the professionalism and ethos of the military, fitness and weapons training, the rigours of the outdoors, jumping out of airplanes, tactics and strategy, and the challenge that I perceived leading men in combat to be. Of course, unarmed combat was high on my agenda whenever I could fit it in, and when we were in garrison I would spend most evenings and spare time on weekends training in a gym or some dojo. It didn't take long for me to realize that I loved what I was doing, and I decided that I would stay in the army at least until I could command a battalion.

Although I aspired to command, I was driven solely to train myself mentally, physically, and spiritually to be a warrior — period. I wanted to master the arts of war and combat leadership. I kind of expected that if I was successful at mastering the way of the warrior, promotion and command opportunities would follow, so I never sought to cultivate mentors or apply for jobs just to get myself promoted. In retrospect, I approached the infantry like it was a martial art with a pension plan, an internal quest for self-fulfillment that also paid the bills. My first regimental tour was inordinately long, so much so that it could have constrained my career progression and ultimately prevented me from commanding a battalion. That never entered my head, though. I was completely consumed with learning everything I could about all aspects of an infantry battalion in battle.

## Family

I met my future wife, Trish, during my first regimental tour in Victoria. I had been tasked to organize the adventure training program at the Vernon Army Cadet Camp and Trish was the head of the swim program there. It may sound like a bit of a cliché, or that I am laying it on too thick, but from the moment we first met I thought there was something special about her. I was struck by many things; her kindness, empathy, sincerity, sense of humour, intelligence, competence, and dedication; however, our jobs were too demanding to socialize much during the summer. Serendipitously, Trish was majoring in education at the University of Victoria, so we were able to get to know each other better. We married in 1985, several months before I was posted for a year to the Royal Military College of Sciences in Shrivenham, England to study military technology and project management.

Our first child, Molly, was born upon our return to Canada in 1987, and our son, Dylan, was born in Calgary when I served in the First Battalion PPCLI. The army was my preoccupation, so Trish was saddled with the lion's share of parental duties. To her great credit and my good fortune, having a phantom father didn't impair Molly's or Dylan's childhoods. Garrison life in the Regiment proved to be the penultimate test of our relationship, though. The real test of our family unit was when I was sent to war.

## Bosnia

In 1993, at the height of the Bosnian war, I was seconded for a year as a United Nations Military Observer (UNMO) for service in the former Republic of Yugoslavia. This was a life-defining experience for me, witnessing war in an up close and personal way for the first time.

In the spring of 1994, I was the leader of a small team of unarmed UNMOs that represented the only UN presence in the city of Gorazde, a Muslim enclave surrounded by Serbs. In April of that year, the Serbs mounted a major offensive to close down that pocket of resistance. My team and I were instrumental in preventing this from happening, and we saved thousands of people from the same deadly fate that befell the Muslim defenders when the Serbs crushed the enclave of Srebrenica a little over a year later. It had become clear to me that the United Nations Protection Force was incapable of stopping General Mladic and the Serbian Army, so I went outside my chain of command and made a public appeal to the North Atlantic Treaty Organization (NATO) for airstrikes. NATO promptly imposed a twenty-kilometre exclusion zone and issued an ultimatum to the Serbs, who subsequently tripped over themselves to adhere to it. Ironically, I became the scapegoat for the ineptitude of the UN Commander in Bosnia, Lieutenant General Sir Michael Rose. As author David Rieff describes in his book *Slaughterhouse*, Rose and his staff began rewriting history as soon as the crisis had abated, alleging that I had "broken under the strain." Nothing could have been further from the truth. On the contrary, in fact, I actually revelled in this rich opportunity to learn about my profession.

Trish was well aware when I deployed to Bosnia that I would do whatever the job called for regardless of the dangers, but she managed to keep life at home normal for our kids. When the Serbian offensive against Gorazde was all over the news at home in Canada, she maintained calm on the home front but the stress ultimately took its toll on her health to the point that she had to be hospitalized for extreme fatigue.

For me, the most traumatic part of that experience was the feeling of abandonment that I endured when I returned to Canada. In June of 1994 I attended the Canadian Forces Command and Staff College for a year, but the influence of Lieutenant General Sir Michael Rose was pervasive. His assault on my character infected the senior ranks of the Canadian Forces, and my career was on the verge of stalling out. Adding insult to injury, that same year the Government of Canada disbanded the Canadian Airborne Regiment, an elite combat unit comprised of volunteers from across the army, particularly the three infantry regiments: the PPCLI, the Royal Canadian Regiment (RCR) and the Royal 22nd Regiment (the famed Van Doos). This was a drastic reaction to ongoing scandals in the military after the grotesque murder of Shidane Arone in Somalia. Following the release of a disturbing video depicting the gross initiation rituals practiced by members of Premier Commando — the element of the former Airborne Regiment made up of troops from the Van Doos — the Liberal government of Jean Chretien announced that the entire regiment would be disbanded. It was a rash, selfish political decision to inflict such a disgrace on a military unit in which the vast majority of members, save a very few miscreants, were steadfastly professional and loyal to the country.

What really hurt was that only one senior officer in the entire Canadian Forces spoke up in defence of the Airborne Regiment, its commander at the time, Colonel Peter Kenward. Also a member of the PPCLI, Colonel Kenward's courage and loyalty to his troops was exemplary, and made a lasting impression on me as a leader. To my dismay, the Chief of Defence Staff (CDS), Chief of the Land Staff (CLS), and several other general officers in key positions — some of whom had been prominent cheerleaders inside the Canadian Forces for the Airborne Regiment — I knew very well as members of the PPCLI. Unlike the rank-and-file who in the course of their duties risk everything in the service of country and regiment, the generals weren't prepared to risk a thing. So much for regimental loyalties and senior "leadership" in the CF. As if that wasn't enough, that same year the United Nations Protection Force in Croatia — under the command of another PPCLI general — failed to prevent the Croatians from ethnically cleansing the entire Serbian population from the Krajina. These events all compelled me to seriously reconsider the profession to which I had devoted my life.

The year 1995 was turning out to be very debilitating for me, when out of the blue I was contacted by Peter Jennings from *ABC News* in the U.S. Over the objections of my chain of command in the Canadian Forces, and on my own time, I flew down to New York to be interviewed by the renowned journalist. Jennings's documentary, *Why the United Nations Failed in Bosnia*, aired in late spring, and exposed the tactical and ethical errors committed by Lieutenant General Sir Michael Rose, which vindicated me. Many other academics and journalists followed with similar assessments of General Rose's incompetence and my role in the crisis. Gradually, my career got back on track.

## Australia

An exchange posting to the Australian Army followed next, which had always been a goal of mine. One of my role models during infantry training in Gagetown had been the Aussie exchange officer, Captain Dan McDaniels. To this day I have never met anybody as intense, fearless, knowledgeable, experienced, and downright scary — but exceedingly professional — in any army anywhere. This would be an opportunity for me to see the cloth this amazing warrior had been cut from. The timing of my posting to Australia was perfect as I could also escape the drama of the Somalia inquiry that was hugely critical of senior management in the Canadian Forces and led ultimately to the resignation of the Chief of Defence Staff, Air Force General Jean Boyle. All of this and the criminal acts of a couple of individuals in Somalia destroyed the reputation of the Canadian Airborne Regiment and severely tarnished the image of the Canadian Forces. I was glad to be away from it.

As an instructor at the Australian Land Warfare Centre in Canungra, Queensland, I was able to immerse myself in the study of leadership, tactics, strategy, and the new security environment that was emerging after the Cold War. The work allowed me to study these subjects to a depth that I could never have attained as a student or part-time on my own. The magic of Australia also allowed me to decompress and work on healing some of the physical and psychological injuries that my tour in Bosnia had inflicted on me and on my relationship with my family. Were it not for this outstanding experience, my life would never have unfolded for me the way it did, either professionally or personally. I shudder to think how I might have ended up.

## Return to the Third Battalion of the Princess Patricia's Canadian Light Infantry (3PPCLI)

I had been warned that going to Australia would be career suicide, because it was such a departure from the NATO-centric focus in the Canadian Forces. I was risking being taken out of the running for timely promotion and subsequent selection for command. But it was a bird in the hand for me at a very tumultuous period, so I grabbed it. I threw myself so into the work and the lifestyle that, despite having been so far off the well-beaten path of careerism, I was promoted upon my return to Canada. In September of 2000 I reached the zenith of my career when I was appointed to command the Third Battalion of the Princess Patricia's Canadian Light Infantry (3PPCLI), precisely twenty years after arriving there as a young lieutenant.

At that time, 3PPCLI was one of three light infantry battalions (LIBs) in the army, one each in the PPCLI, the RCR, and the Van Doos. Officially they were referred to as LIBs, but that was only window dressing. These battalions were not deliberately designed to be "light" in order to satisfy some operational imperative, like perhaps rapid deployment or specialized operations. You see, the army staff was fixated on creating an entirely mechanized force, but they could not afford to because armoured vehicles are so expensive. The resultant shortfall of armoured personnel carriers fell on the so-called LIBs, which the army staff actually considered to be "equipment deficient battalions." The LIBs were therefore slated for disbandment, 3PPCLI included. This was supposed to happen the year after my term as commanding officer expired. Needless to say, 3PPCLI was not a happy place when I arrived; it was a real leadership challenge.

During my sabbatical in Australia, I had become a staunch believer that light forces would play a very important role in twenty-first century conflict. I was convinced that elements like 3PPCLI should be tailored to meet the emerging 'asymmetric threat.' A sexy military term, it describes international terrorists, transnational criminals, and insane extremists who have been empowered by technologies such as broadband global communications, high-speed world-wide transportation, satellite imagery, and the seemingly endless stream of actionable intelligence that is available on the Internet, all of which used to be the sole domain of professional military forces. Today, these unconventional entities pose a serious threat to sovereign states. I never missed an opportunity to express that opinion to any audience, even though it flew in the face of the vision of the Chief of Land Staff (CLS) at the time, Lieutenant General Mike Jeffery.

The troops always enjoy the entertainment value of an officer doing a kamikaze run, but I think the soldiers of 3PPCLI did not see me as simply a cheerleader to bolster morale. Troops are also quite adept at tolerating — or, if need be, dismissing — the exuberance of new commanders if it appears artificial or misplaced. I think they could see that I was being genuine in sharing my vision for the importance of highly trained and motivated soldiers in the new security environment, so they played along.

And it was a good thing they did.

## Afghanistan — Round One

The tragedy of 9/11 changed everything, and 3PPCLI was ready for it, though it was not the result of some grand design. The equipment-constrained battalions were also budget constrained, and 3PPCLI was ready for war only because of the professionalism and commitment of our soldiers. We were creative in finding ways to work around the army's treatment of us as second-class citizens, and had the expertise in-house to train to the highest possible standards. In January of 2002 we were warned of the deployment to Afghanistan, and by that February I was leading a robust battle group of Canadian war fighters in southern Afghanistan, based out of the Kandahar Airfield.

At the time, we had been designated as the Canadian Force's Land Component's Immediate Reaction Force, so we had been at anywhere between forty-eight hours to two weeks' notice to deploy to crises anywhere in the world. That was a laughable state of readiness because we had neither the logistics base nor the combat elements to meet such an aggressive timeline. Fortunately we had gotten our first whiff of possibly deploying to Afghanistan in November of the previous year, so we had time to build our logistic capacity. We were so dreadfully understrength as an infantry battalion that we had to be augmented by a complete rifle company from 2PPCLI — approximately 120 infantry soldiers. We actually had to rob the entire army of any sophisticated equipment available, like night vision devices and even body armour.

The Third Battalion was reinforced with sub-units from other combat arms units — the Armoured Reconnaissance Squadron from the Lord Strathcona's Horse (Royal Canadians), a mortar platoon and battery commander party from the First Regiment of the Royal Canadian Horse Artillery, and a squadron of field engineers from the First Canadian Engineers Regiment — as well as individual augmentation by all sorts of specialists from throughout the CF. This formidable collection of talent and commitment took over the defence of the Kandahar Airfield and together we proceeded to make history. On very short notice, and thrown together on a shoestring, the 3PPCLI battle group's deployment on Operation APOLLO represented the first time since the war in Korea that Canadian ground forces were deployed on operations against a declared enemy, and they served with distinction.

## Back to Reality

When we redeployed back to Canada, I was told that my days commanding troops were over. General Hillier, newly appointed as the Assistant Chief of Land Staff (A/CLS) and responsible for managing senior appointments in the army, advised me that prior to taking command of 3PPCLI I had been assessed as a "Tier Two" officer. This meant that my potential for promotion was still good and I could expect to continue to progress in my career, but I was destined for staff appointments rather than the field command positions that were reserved for Tier One officers. I asked the general what a person had to do to make the army consider that they may have underestimated my long-term potential in the first instance, but that was a question he could not — or would not — answer. I was confused but not particularly fussed by such a prognosis, because I had achieved my life's ambition and had never deviated from my values system. The end of command prospects did, though, represent the drawing to a close of any ambitions that I might have had in the army.

I ended up getting promoted to colonel, but I was a pariah, nonetheless. I hasten to plead *mea culpa* because it was very much my own doing. Notwithstanding the dissenting opinion regarding the equipment-deficient battalions I had voiced prior to Afghanistan, upon return I again took on the system because it was mistreating, in my opinion, many of the troops with whom I had served in Afghanistan. A less than empathetic career management system was penalizing members of the battle group for our sudden deployment by not grandfathering them for career courses. Also, some commanders in parent units of troops who had augmented the battle group could not relate to what their augmentees had been through and were treating them, as I saw it, unfairly.

I considered myself to be fireproof, so on several occasions I made personal representation to the CLS, Lieutenant General Jeffery, on behalf of the troops. He wasn't terribly sympathetic toward the troops, nor was he very impressed with me, summing me up for the last time by shouting, "So do you think I should promote you to Field Marshall, now?" I knew I had crossed the line and deserved to be jacked-up, but I couldn't believe such an emotional, childish outburst would come from a three-star general. I pulled my horns in and backed away — from the office, that is, but not the issue.

*Scene Setting*

# Afghanistan — Round Two

## JOINT OPERATIONS GROUP (JOG)

Contrary to the bad news I had received about my prospects upon my return from Kandahar, in early 2004, I had one last stab at command when I was appointed Commander of the Joint Operations Group, or JOG — a formation designed to execute large-scale expeditionary and disaster-assistance relief operations. The JOG was a Canadian Forces joint army-navy-air force asset, so the position of commander was selected by the Deputy Chief of Defence Staff (DCDS) based on the recommendation of the Director of Senior Appointments at National Defence Headquarters (NDHQ) in Ottawa, not the Chief of Land Staff. As luck would have it, the Director at the time was Brigadier General Mark Skidmore, whom I had soldiered with, ironically, in the Airborne Regiment and for whom I had a huge amount of respect. I considered Mark to be a true warrior and a good officer, as well as a friend. I guess he saw some potential in me because he got me the job.

## OPERATIONAL ROLES AND UNITS

Fortunately the JOG was located in Kingston, so Trish and I didn't have to uproot the family again. The JOG's role was to maintain a command and control element, the Joint Headquarters (JHQ), capable of controlling army, navy, and/or air force assets during a major crisis. In the event of war, it was envisioned, the JOG would be task-organized with the appropriate combat elements to meet the threat. As a high readiness, land-based, joint force headquarters, the JHQ only had three units permanently under command: the Joint Signals Regiment; the Joint Chemical, Biological Radiological, and Nuclear (JCBRN) Company; and the Disaster Assistance Response Team (DART).

Because the JOG's standing operational tasks were on a short-notice contingency basis, high readiness and last minute, mission-specific training was our main focus of effort. At the same time, the JCBRN Company was being stood up to create a brand new and vital capability in the CF. In the aftermath of 9/11 we realized that the criminals and terrorists who constitute the asymmetric threat have access to the technologies for weapons of mass destruction, and that the CF had no capability to react to an attack with or the fallout from a chemical, biological, or radiological "dirty bomb." I would be responsible for overseeing the development of that capability. I was in my element, training troops for operations, and I savoured every second of it.

**CAMPAIGN PLAN**

Around the same time that I arrived at the Joint Operations Group, it was decided that the CF would be closing down operations in Kabul and moving to Kandahar. I asserted to my boss that assuming the responsibility for operations in Kandahar Province was a much more serious venture than any of our escapades under the United Nations had been or our Afghanistan operations hitherto in Kabul under NATO. Kandahar would represent a specifically Canadian military objective, much like Juno Beach was on D-Day. As such, we wanted to make sure we got it right from the get-go. We would not have the luxury of being able to blame the U.N. for their ineptitude, like we had for our previous fiascos in Croatia, Somalia, and Rwanda.

I expressed my conviction that troops were definitely going to die in Kandahar, and that it behoved us as senior leaders to be rigorous in our planning and avoid exposing our personnel to more danger than necessary by making things up as we went along, as we normally did. The CF sends their senior officers to command and staff colleges to learn campaign planning, but in my experience and research we had never applied that learning in the Canadian context. The so-called "campaign plans" that we had created in recent history had amounted to nothing more than move orders, because we merely provided contingents to plug into someone else's campaign. I was adamant that a real campaign plan was in order for operations in Kandahar.

That was one argument that I won — if one ever wins an argument with one's seniors — and they also bought into my assertion that the Joint Headquarters had the capacity to write the campaign plan for operations in Kandahar. I was pleased to have an opportunity to influence that plan. The lieutenant colonels I assigned to the task did some excellent work on the bulk of the plan, but I took on the task of drafting the Commander's Intent portion of the campaign plan personally. When we finally briefed the Chief of Defence Staff, who by this time was General Hillier, on the initial draft, I hung on every comment he made in order to have his key messages inform the content of the "Commander's Intent" section. An always-colourful speaker, Hillier made some pretty rich comments at the briefing, such as we would "lead from behind." Our job, as he put it, was to enable the Afghans to tend to their own security, and if we were seen to be taking the lead we would have failed in our mission. It was all good counter-insurgency stuff, so I included it in my draft of the Commander's Intent.

Although campaign plans are traditionally a military phenomenon, they are often multi-disciplinary in terms of scope and objectives because of the level at which they are formulated. It made sense, therefore, for the CF to coordinate our campaign plan with the other government departments who would be involved in operations in Kandahar Province, so Rear Admiral Drew Robertson, the CF's Director General of International Security Policy at the time, recruited me to represent the CF at several inter-departmental meetings. Staff at Foreign Affairs and the Canadian International Development Agency (CIDA) were very receptive to the concept of a multi-departmental plan for the "campaign" in Kandahar, so I ended up conducting a couple of sessions of Campaign Planning 101 for select senior bureaucrats and their planners.

The previous Liberal government, under Paul Martin, having recognized that success in Afghanistan would require the harmonized efforts of more government organizations than just the Canadian Forces, coined the term "3D" for the operation, referring to the defence, development, and diplomatic elements. The Harper government subsequently changed 3D to "Whole-of-Government." To soften the appearance, so to speak, of the Kandahar campaign plan, it later became known as the government's "Common Narrative" for the Whole-of-Government operation in Afghanistan.

Subsequently, I accompanied a Government of Canada contingent overseas to compare notes with our British allies. The British were extremely impressed with how coordinated and well developed our efforts appeared to be. Somewhat less impressed was Glynn Berry, the Canadian diplomat who had been selected by Foreign Affairs Canada as their representative on the first Provincial Reconstruction Team. Glynn had spent a fair amount of time as a diplomat in Pakistan, so he knew the people and the problems. Over a quiet beer at one point, he confided in me that he was very worried about our plan to go to Kandahar. That was the last contact I had with Canada's plan for our campaign in Kandahar, and with Glynn. He became one of the first Canadians killed in action; the victim of a vehicle-mounted suicide bomber.

## Beginning of the End

Canada's campaign in Afghanistan, as I understood it from the draft plan I submitted, began to go south in more ways than physically moving from Kabul to Kandahar. The first thing the Canadian Forces did once they settled in Kandahar was take part in the US-led operation, MOUNTAIN THRUST. Advertised as the biggest offensive operation to clean out the Taliban since the start of the War on Terror in Afghanistan, it amounted to little more than a massive search-and-destroy operation, taken right out of the annals of the American defeat in Vietnam some three decades earlier. Not only did Operation MOUNTAIN THRUST ignore many lessons of counter-insurgency that the US Military had had to learn the hard way in Southeast Asia, it certainly was not in keeping with the philosophy that I thought had been articulated in the Canadian Common Narrative for operations in Kandahar. Afghanistan's military was billed as taking part in this offensive, but it didn't require an expert in military affairs to recognize from the newscasts that they were not much more than window dressing, and that the windows they were dressing were at the back of the bus.

Thus began our nation's fixation on combat operations, ramp ceremonies on the airfield in Kandahar evacuating the corpses of young Canadians who had been killed in action, sorrowful receptions in Trenton, and the long, solemn drive along Highway 401 to Toronto observed by thousands of Canadians who lined the route; a stretch that became known famously as the Highway of Heroes. For me, Operation MOUNTAIN THRUST bore little resemblance to the military scheme of manoeuvre that had been folded into the Whole-of-Government

Common Narrative, and its launch signalled the beginning of the end; the last glimmer of hope for successful operations in Southern Afghanistan, and for me and my military career. It wasn't long before our Whole-of-Government orientation was displaying some very blatant inter-departmental fault lines. I became increasingly vocal in my assertion that we had lost the plot in Afghanistan, which was the wrong thing to do when Hillier-mania was at its peak. The Chief of Defence Staff, the affable and charismatic General Rick Hillier, was a very vocal and very visible proponent of the war, and at the center of everything that was happening in Kandahar. Expressing any dissension in the back corridors, cubicles, and conference rooms of National Defence Headquarters with how operations were being prosecuted in theatre was sure to be construed as an expression of non-confidence and hence a lack of loyalty to the Chief. Consequently, when it came time for another posting, none of the A-list positions for colonels were available for me.

Regardless, I was already disillusioned by the profession that I had fallen in love with once upon a time, and had long since abandoned any aspirations that might have been kindled post-3PPCLI to become a warrior general, faint though they would have been. I decided to seek something in Ottawa — anything that would provide more stability for my family while I sorted out what I would do with the remainder of my life.

## Pearson Peacekeeping Centre

Before operations in Kandahar became the major focus of the Canadian Forces, the CDS, General Hillier, had initiated a massive reorganization of National Defence Headquarters. An integral part of that reorg included the creation of the Canadian Forces Expeditionary Force Command Headquarters, or CEFCOM HQ. Under command of Lieutenant General Mike Gauthier, CEFCOM HQ would be responsible for the command and control of all operations outside of continental North America. My Joint Headquarters would form the nucleus of General Gauthier's new headquarters, and the standing units within the Joint Operations Group were re-assigned throughout the CF. With that transformation complete, I was looking for other work within the CF.

I was offered a couple of jammy postings overseas, prestigious appointments that could have led to promotion, but I had no interest in career advancement. I wanted to go home to Ottawa. The only job that was available in Ottawa at the time was a secondment to the Pearson Peacekeeping Centre (PPC) as the vice president. Small wonder the job was available; no colonel in the Canadian Forces wanted it. The work was completely distasteful to me too, but it satisfied my desire to get closer to my family and wind down my career.

Totally out of the blue one day, I received an unsolicited email from a veteran with whom I had worked many, many years before in 1PPCLI in Calgary, Petty Officer Jeff Bentley. Coincidentally Jeff had been active for many years as an advocate on veterans' issues. In his email he noted that the government was advertising the position of a Veterans Ombudsman, a function that he had contributed to the definition of. He was in the know of who had applied for the position and expressed his surprise that my name was not among them.

I was somewhat surprised to hear from him after fifteen years, and that he would have deemed me to be a suitable candidate for the job. I had never done any work that, to my mind, might have demonstrated that I was capable of, or for that matter the least bit interested in, being the Veterans Ombudsman. That made me all that much more curious about the job, so I looked it up online. The competition was closing on April 30th, and I wasn't made aware of it until the 27th. What I saw described as the work of a Veterans Ombudsman actually appealed to me. I had never looked for work outside the military, and I had never even taken the time to create a resumé, so I scribbled one out as quickly as I could and submitted it electronically, never giving it a second thought.

## Making the Jump

I had applied for the position of Veterans Ombudsman not really expecting it would come to anything, so I was completely surprised when, out of the blue, I received a call asking me to appear for an interview. I had even forgotten that I had applied for the job, having parted ways with the PPC prematurely and since started working with Defence Research and Development Canada(DRDC). The prospect of being the ombudsman for our veterans was interesting to me, but I still had absolutely no idea that I was actually on the verge of leaving the military.

I was advised that to prepare for the interview I should familiarize myself with the programs and services that were available for veterans and their families, confirm my understanding of the machinery of government, and consider how I might approach the task of setting up the Office of the Veterans Ombudsman. I really had to cram to learn the programs; there were a ton of them available to veterans of service in the wars, and there was also the New Veterans Charter (NVC). I narrowed the focus of my preparations to developing an understanding of both. The NVC is extremely complex and convoluted and Veterans Affairs had not done a very good job of marketing it, so I spent more time with it.

Contrary to what I had expected and prepared for, the interviewers demonstrated very little interest in quizzing my understanding of the programs and services that Veterans Affairs Canada offers — they were mainly interested in how I would go about setting up the office. They asked a few questions about my past experiences and my feelings towards veterans, and then they drilled down into how I would interact with the bureaucracy. I had given this virtually no thought, but was actually grateful for their line of questioning. I viewed the position of Veterans Ombudsman as simply another command appointment, so I could speak to the requirement to build a headquarters with some degree of confidence. Fundamental to my approach would be to hire a chief of staff well versed in public service whom I could trust and communicate with well. In my responses to many questions, I kept coming back to this. This resonated with one member of the panel, the Minister's chief of staff, Jacques Dubé, or so he said later after I got the job.

## Joining the Public Service

Nothing happened after the interview, so I was quite sure that I hadn't gotten the job. I hadn't, in fact. I later found out it had been initially offered to someone else who had turned it down. I had no idea who this person was, except that he too was from the Canadian Forces. I didn't know about any of this when, in early October — almost a full six months after I'd applied — I received a phone call from someone asking me if I was still interested in the job. I couldn't say yes fast enough. Before I knew it I was in Minister Thompson's office for the final check. Minister Thomson was so impressed with my background that all he said was that he fully expected I was the right person for the job.

Not long afterwards I received a call at DRDC asking me to appear at a press conference with the Minister Thomson in Ottawa, where he would announce my appointment. No problem, I told them, and I immediately made my way to 66 Slater, the address for the department's office in Ottawa, to coordinate the details with the Minister's people and Veterans Affairs Canada staff. The notice was so short that I had the impression that this was some kind of an impromptu press conference and my dress-of-the-day, CADPAT camouflage, would be acceptable. But the staff had been expecting me to attend in my dress uniform with my medals. Being very polite they almost apologetically asked me if I could rush home and change. And no wonder.

The press conference was held in the Crown Plaza Hotel with a special gathering of war service veterans decked out in their best bib and tucker with medals. My guess was that there were easily fifty veterans and family members present, and there was also a very good turnout of media. The room was packed. As I took my seat beside the Minister, a panic-stricken staff member whispered in my ear that they had forgotten to inform me that I would be making a speech. Too easy. The Minister was first, and when my turn came I was short and sweet. I told everyone what an honour and privilege it was to be Canada's first Veterans Ombudsman and I pledged that I would go to the wall if need be to make sure that our veterans and their families were being treated the way they deserved to be by a grateful nation.

After thirty years of service, I could leave the CF on thirty-days' notice, and those dominoes started falling barely a month before Remembrance Day. I proposed November 11 as my official start date, thinking the symbolism would be rather fitting, but it would require me to immediately set about taking my release from the CF. Even so, a couple of signatures on some of my release administration paperwork had to be backdated in order to get everything done in time.

## Condition of Employment

Things started to pick up really quickly, and it wasn't long into the rushed recruitment process that I met with a Ms. Druscilla Flemming, a very nice lady who was the Assistant Director of Compensation and Classification in the Privy Council Office. She wanted to make sure that I understood the pay and benefits' side of things before this went too far. As it turned out, the Veterans Ombudsman salary was barely that of a full colonel in the military. The lack of rank and stature of the Veterans Ombudsman was a shocker, not because I needed the money, but because I recognized that it meant it would be unlikely that the senior bureaucrats would take the ombudsman position seriously. The financial aspect of the job became even more disconcerting when Ms. Flemming "reminded" me that, as a veteran, I could not collect my pension when I assumed the appointment. Someone confided to me after I became the ombudsman that the first-round draft choice for the role had rejected the offer because he was unwilling to make that sacrifice. I wanted to be the ombudsman for our veterans, so I took this reminder in stride as I left Druscilla's office.

Out of the blue one day, not too long after my initial meeting with Druscilla, I received a phone call from the prime minister's office (PMO). The young man on the other end of the line asked me why I had donated $1,000 to the Liberal Party. I was taken aback for two reasons. First of all, I didn't know what that had to do with the job, but I didn't say much because I wasn't so naïve as not to know what people in politics are motivated by. Secondly, I had never donated anything to any political party. As it turned out, it was fees that my son Dylan had paid as a delegate at Liberal Conventions, or rather, fees that I had paid on his behalf. I was excused, as the PMO didn't think that was bad enough to be denied the job. While I had this person on the line, though, I asked him why I wasn't allowed to collect my military pension. He didn't know but promised to get back to me with an answer.

True to his word he got back to me with an answer: Veterans weren't allowed to collect their pensions because Members of Parliament aren't allowed to collect theirs if they take on any other government job. I thought that was odd, so I compared the two pieces of legislation; the Canadian Forces Superannuation Act (CFSA) and the Members of Parliament Retiring Allowances Act. In the latter document, it very clearly specifies that former members who are in receipt of this "allowance," and subsequently make over $5,000 in another capacity in government will have their so-called allowance reduced by one dollar for every dollar they make in that subsequent employment. Nowhere in the CFSA is there any such restriction. This was being arbitrarily imposed by the very government who at one time referred to the parliamentarians' so-called allowance as "a gold plated pension," and at the same time liked to pronounce how important veterans were to them.

Once again, as a disciple of the likes of Machiavelli, Sun Tzu, and Captain B. H. Liddell Hart, I didn't take them on directly. I waited until I met with Druscilla again to discuss pay and benefits to challenge the idea of losing my pension. This time I explained that nowhere in the CFSA did it direct that the pensions that veterans had bought and paid for would be reduced by one dollar for every dollar they make in subsequent employment with the federal government. She summed me up by saying, "Consider it a condition of employment." Indeed! I wanted the job so I could help vets, and so I left it at that. The next time I met with Druscilla was when I had to sign the contract. I told her that I considered relinquishing my pension to be an unfair condition of employment. I also informed her that I would make a note that I signed the contract under duress and would be challenging the legality of the pension condition.

When I went to sign — surprise, surprise — no mention anywhere in writing about me having to relinquish my pension. I quickly queried this, and she replied that they weren't allowed to put that in the contract. I asked then how the money was clawed back from my pension, and she replied it wouldn't be. She added that I was expected to donate the money to a charity. Seriously. I am not making this up. I told her that I was ready to make a legal challenge, so please get their legal people engaged. Do you think that ever happened? Of course not.

I contacted Druscilla twice after this, and was promised a meeting, but both times the meetings were postponed. No reasons were given. I stopped asking, and in my three years in office they never challenged me legally or even asked for receipts from the charity of my choice. To me, charity begins at home. Surprisingly, I found that many veterans, some senior in rank and therefore presumably smarter than me and with much larger pensions, gladly but foolishly paid the equivalent of their pension to take up prestigious appointments for no other reason than the government told them it should be so.

## Becoming An Ombudsman

I took over as Canada's first Veterans Ombudsman on Remembrance Day, November 11, 2007. Poetically, laying a wreath at the prominent ceremony at the National War Memorial marked my first official duty. I viewed the position of Ombudsman as an extension of my military service, an opportunity to leave the CF gracefully and give back to the soldiers, sailors, and air force personnel I had served with. It also offered my family the stability they deserved and needed after following me around the world for thirty years and enduring my prolonged absences while I trained for war and served in two war zones for almost two full years. Little did we know that my becoming Ombudsman would be one of the most traumatic episodes in our life together; having to bear witness to our very own government blatantly abusing and exploiting some of Canada's most disadvantaged citizens.

CHAPTER 2:

# Meet Canada's Veterans

Despite my thirty-year career in the military, during which I had a deep empathy for veterans, when I came into the Ombudsman job I knew very little about the veterans' community in Canada. It was a steep learning curve — very steep indeed. I quickly learned that we must not underestimate how ubiquitous our veterans are, nor the magnitude of the influence they have had, and continue to have, on our culture.

Historians will tell you that Canada's military heritage is a rich one, having first deployed troops overseas as a fledgling nation in the late nineteenth century for the Boer War. Approximately 7,000 Canadians fought in that action, and several hundred were killed. That was a significant act for such a new nation, albeit a token effort compared to the conflicts that followed shortly thereafter in the next century.

Canada's contributions to the World Wars were nothing less than monumental. Around ten percent of our population served in uniform: more than 600,000 in WWI and over a million in WWII. Those numbers are huge by any standard, and on a per capita basis, the number of casualties we suffered was also of the highest order for any of the Allied Nations. There were few regions of Canada with any appreciable concentration of population in the early twentieth century that didn't have at least one reserve army unit to their credit. There aren't many families with any history in Canada that won't find at least one ancestor in their clan who served in Canada's military.

## Military Legacy

Our military accomplishments in the World Wars were as extraordinary as the relative sizes of our contributions, and for decades these firmly established Canada as a world player. Our conquest of Vimy Ridge in WWI and the tenacity with which the Canadian Army fought the key battles subsequently earned us the title of the "Shock Army of the British Empire," heralded by historians for having been instrumental in achieving the Armistice in 1918. In World War II, Canada earned the distinction of being assigned one of the five landing beaches of D-Day — Juno Beach. The other four landing sites were divided equally between the massive military machines of Great Britain and the United States.

Many Canadians may have difficulty comprehending the magnitude of these accomplishments. Equally compelling, but often overlooked, is the pivotal role our small navy played in the North Atlantic and the crucial support our tiny air force gave to the British Royal Air Force throughout WWII. In a similar fashion, as part of the multinational efforts in the Korean War, our minuscule-by-comparison Canadian contingent again punched well above its weight. All this tenacity and commitment was from a tiny, relatively new nation that had never known any natural enemies at home.

## Veterans Charter

Canada's tradition of magnanimous care for her veterans returning from war rose up out of the ashes of the First World War. Just prior to the Battle of Vimy Ridge in April of 1917, then-Prime Minister Robert Borden affirmed the Government of Canada's duty to care for its veterans:

> "You can go into this action feeling assured of this, and as the head of the government I give you this assurance: That you need not fear that the government and the country will fail to show just appreciation of your service to the country and empire in what you are about to do and what you have already done.

> "The government and the country will consider it their first duty to see that a proper appreciation of your effort and of your courage is brought to the notice of people at home that no man, whether he goes back or whether he remains in Flanders, will have just cause to reproach the government for having broken faith with the men who won and the men who died."

Borden's statement was never enshrined in legislation or our constitution, but it set the tone of the relationship that would exist between the People and the Government of Canada and our veterans for generations. Canada established a robust tradition of caring for her veterans, and the perception that we were so obliged was never publicly challenged. In fact, as Canada was entering into WWII, the Government of Canada reinforced the notion of there being an obligation to care for our veterans.

It seems that after the First World War there had been many problems with the programs that had been set up for veterans and how they had been administered, so the planning for the repatriation of the expeditionary forces after the Second World War, and their reintegration into civil society, began almost as soon as the first troops deployed overseas. In keeping with Prime Minister Borden's pledge more than twenty years earlier, what resulted was a generous collection of services and benefits that would treat veterans of service in WWII as a valuable asset to fuel the Canadian economy. The various acts that generated these programs became known as "The Veterans Charter."

## Culturally Influential

To this day, the people of the Netherlands celebrate their liberation in WWII at the hands of a Canadian Army that was fiercely combative yet innately compassionate. Such a military disposition was definitely the product of the pioneer spirit of the Canadians of the day, which was fused with the very robust culture of the military. Subjecting those service personnel to a righteous cause and the forge of war would have had a profound and enduring effect on their personal characters.

The half-life of that military experience would have lasted well after soldiers' return to civie street and their service-before-self ethos would have rubbed off on members of their families and communities. Veterans of war service went on to form the backbone of virtually every field of our fledgling private and public sectors: the educators, the producers, the protectors, the healers, and indeed, the leaders. Notwithstanding the obvious skills and knowledge they transferred from the military into Canadian society, the sense of faith, loyalty, teamwork, commitment, and self-discipline that military service had instilled in them subsequently would have been woven subtly but steadfastly into the fabric of the Canadian way. I submit that military tradition has been extraordinarily influential on our culture.

That military ethos and tradition has been kept very much alive in our Canadian Forces, and it still exerts a significant yet subtle influence on the culture of our nation. The number of Canadian families who have or have had kin serving in the Canadians Forces is not insignificant. Mainstream Canadians would probably be surprised to find how many of their neighbours, co-workers, and friends have served or may still be serving. Veterans are everywhere. The number of veterans of service in the Canadian Forces today stands at around 800,000, and this institution continues to produce thousands more vets every year.

## Defining Ethos

Our society is truly a militaristic one; not the Rambo-style militarism that the mind conjures today, but one that is uniquely Canadian and reflects all that is good about our veterans. The tenacity and selflessness they demonstrated in responding as a nation to crises characterized the elusive quality of the Canadian way. The benevolence that Canadians bestowed on our veterans of service in the World Wars led to the provision of social programs for the benefit of all Canadians, such as the Family Allowance and Old Age Security. Tommy Douglas, first leader of the New Democratic Party and lauded as the mastermind behind social medicine, didn't have to look very far to see a veterans' hospital and reason that the government should rightly extend such services to all Canadians. Indeed, benevolence has become one of the defining features of this nation. However, Canadians today know very little about their veterans.

## Lapses in Care: Early Limitations

Despite the early commitment of our nation to provide comprehensive and generous services and benefits for our veterans, lawmakers still had to address limitations within the Veterans Charter as they became apparent. One of the biggest obstacles that had to be overcome was a reticence to acknowledge all sacrifices objectively and fairly. A common sentiment amongst many of those who had served in the so-called Great War (the First World War) was that the hardships and horrors suffered by their successors in World War II didn't measure up to their own, so they shouldn't be afforded the same treatment as their predecessors. Eventually, the broader differences were overcome and the majority of veterans of World War II were treated fairly. That was not the case for certain identifiable groups of combatants within the World War Two cohort.

## Merchant Navy and the War in the Atlantic

One such group of veterans who were treated extremely unfairly were the members of Canada's merchant navy. When I became the Veterans Ombudsman I had no idea of the crucial role that our merchant navy had played in the war that was waged in the Atlantic. As a career ground-pounding grunt in the army, I had wrongly assumed that the bragging rights for the Battle of the Atlantic belonged to the Canadian and British Navies proper, but came to learn it could not have been won without the valiant effort of the merchant navies of the Allied nations.

One story told to me by a veteran merchant seaman characterized how close to home World War II actually was, the dangers that our merchant navy faced, and the critical role that they played. This veteran told me how his vessel was part of a patrol escorting a captured German U-Boat into Shelburne Harbour, Nova Scotia. (If I make any technical errors in relating it here I hope my naval brethren will excuse my army ignorance.) As the prisoner convoy was about to enter the harbour confines, the Canadian escort vessels received a radio message from the enemy U-Boat commander. He asked if they had any experience in the harbour, but none of the Canadians had gone alongside in Shelburne before. The U-Boat commander suggested that he take the lead because he had a lot of experience navigating inside the harbour.

## British Commonwealth Air Training Plan

I had a pretty good feel for the role that our air force played in Europe during World War II, and was also familiar with the British Commonwealth Air Training Plan (BCATP), but only superficially. Of the 131,533 aircrews that graduated from the Commonwealth and France, Belgium, Holland, Norway, Czechoslovakia, and Poland, 72,835 were Canadian. While the impact that BCATP had on the air campaign is obvious, I had no idea how the enormity of that program must have influenced Canadian society.

Canada provided the base for the bulk of the training, and evidence of that initiative remains today in the form of airfields spotted across this land from Summerside, PEI to Patricia Bay, British Columbia. In addition to the airfields, the number of BCATP facilities that popped up across the country is truly staggering. The appearance of BACTP infrastructure in many remote Canadian locales across the country played a big role in bringing the reality of the war in Europe home to Canada. Until then, Canadians saw little evidence on home soil that the rest of the world was embroiled in a devastating war. As Norm Shannon describes in his 2005 book *From Baddeck to the Yalu: Stories of Canada's Airmen at War*, the appearance of BCATP facilities in communities across Canada became a home-grown symbol that the *phony war* (italics added) was over.

Notwithstanding the enormity of their contributions to the war efforts, WWII veterans who had been assigned to the war-winning contribution of the BCATP here in Canada were treated as inferior to those who had served in Europe, regardless of how pedestrian the latter employment may have been.

# Hong Kong Prisoners of War (POWs)

Another demographic of the veterans' community that was discriminated against consisted of Canadians who had been imprisoned by the enemy. Following the war, Veterans Affairs Canada denied former prisoners of war any special differentiated treatment for the unique maladies and disabilities that would have been the result of the more severe conditions that they had to endure during their incarceration. It wasn't until 1976 that the Government of Canada made good on their obligations in this respect when they passed the Compensation for Former Prisoners of War Act.

One group of POWs who suffered particularly gruesome abuse but were refused the benefit of this legislation until 1998 were the so-called Hong Kong POWs. Almost 1,500 Canadian soldiers had suffered intolerable conditions of torture, starvation, deprivation, and exposure to the elements at the hands of their Japanese captors. For forty-four months following the Battle of Hong Kong, the POWs were also forced into slave labour; a gross violation of the Geneva Conventions.

As late as 1987, Canada's Hong Kong veterans still hadn't been compensated adequately, fairly, or otherwise for the unlawful exploitation they had endured. At that time, Major (retired) H. Clifford Chadderton and his War Amps of Canada took on their cause. In order to bring about change, Cliff had to go so far as to bring a complaint to the Human Rights Commission of the Geneva Conventions against the governments of Japan and Canada. Finally, in December of 1998, Canada agreed to pay the 350 surviving veterans of the Japanese prisoner of war camps and 400 of the widows token compensation for having been illegally forced into slave labour.

# Cliff Chadderton

This is a good place to draw closer attention to Major (retired) H. Clifford Chadderton, a true Canadian hero. In my opinion, Cliff was the most dedicated and successful advocate for disadvantaged and mistreated veterans and groups of veterans in Canadian history. Before the war he had hailed from Winnipeg where he was known around town for his work as a journalist and as an all-star in junior hockey. He served with the Royal Winnipeg Rifles, starting off as a soldier during the D-Day landings and rising to the rank of acting major as officer commanding, when he lost his right leg below the knee.

After the war Cliff became known as a curator and storyteller for the legacy of the Royal Winnipeg Rifles and the Canadian Army, but more importantly as a champion for veterans who were being disadvantaged by the Department of Veterans Affairs. As Chair of the National Council of Veterans Associations (NCVA), an umbrella organization that brings bargaining power to some fifty-eight distinct veterans associations, for decades Cliff Chadderton was the *de facto* veterans ombudsman before such a post was ever conceived of formally. In 1965 he became the chief executive officer of The War Amps and gradually expanded his activism to other sectors of Canadian society. Cliff became not only an icon for the fair treatment of veterans, but for all that being Canadian stands for — helping others. He earned a myriad of honours and awards, and was made a Member of the Order of Canada in 1977.

Within days of the announcement that I had been appointed Veterans Ombudsman, I was provided with a transcript of a radio interview with Cliff about my appointment. We had never met, but despite his obvious scepticism towards the office that the government had created, he expressed unbridled confidence that I was the right person for the job. At the time I only knew of "Cliff the Veterans' Advocate" and understood little detail of his accomplishments, but that expression of support had a profound impact on me. Throughout my term as Ombudsman I would try to live up to the faith that Cliff had placed in me.

## Korean War Ignored

Today we honour our Korean War veterans the same way that we pay homage to those who served in the World Wars, but that was not always the case. Back when Veteran Affairs Canada was still reeling in the aftermath of World War II, Orders in Council were used to respond swiftly to the immediate needs of the Korean War veterans. By 1952 Korea veterans were full beneficiaries to the Veterans Charter, but officially they were never really veterans of war. Technically they had only participated in a mere "police action" with the United Nations. This distinction wore heavily on the veterans who fought in that war. Dr. Peter Neary is a historian and author/editor of several authoritative works on the history of veterans in Canada. As he put it in his discussion paper, *Honouring Canada's Commitment: "Opportunity with Security" for Canadian Forces Veterans and Their Families in the 21st Century*, this was "a hollow distinction that belied the brutal reality of service in a bitter conflict."

As more than one veteran of the Korean War explained to me, in the early days following the Korean conflict, even the Royal Canadian Legion, which the public at large perceives as the embodiment of Canada's veteran fraternity, failed to welcome Korean War veterans as full members in their own right. As late as 1974 veterans of the Korean War were still feeling slighted, so much so that they formed an association of their own, The Korea Veterans Association of Canada, to promote their status. On their website they describe how in 1975 the *Calgary Herald* published a four-part special to commemorate Calgary's centennial that included a tribute to that city's proud tradition with the military. The feature celebrated Calgary's resident military's contributions to the First and Second World Wars but failed to mention the Korean War even though the Second Battalion of the Princess Patricia's Canadian Light Infantry had been from Calgary when it was awarded the United States' Presidential Citation for its role in the Battle of Kapyong.[1] The Presidential Citation is the highest commendation that country awards to military units and 2PPCLI remains today as one of very few foreign units ever to be a recipient. To add insult to injury, that regiment's Home Station, their First Battalion, was still garrisoned in Calgary when the feature was published. And while the United Nations and the British

---

1   In April 1951, just west of the village known as Kapyong, 2PPCLI was defending on Hill 677, and the Third Battalion of the Royal Australian Regiment was on their right on Hill 504. As the last line of defence they blunted a major Chinese offensive towards Seoul that could have been a turning point in the war in favour of the Chinese. For this action they were awarded the US Presidential Citation, a rare honour for any non-American military.

Commonwealth awarded a medal to everyone who had served in the Korean War very soon after the conflict, it took until 1992 for our own government to issue a uniquely Canadian one, the Canadian Volunteer Service Medal for Korea.

## Reaffirming/Reinforcing the Commitment

The late 1950s and early 1960s represented a crescendo of sorts of a social upheaval in Canada. Social programs became viewed as an entitlement for Canadians, not simply charity. I am neither a historian nor a sociologist, but as I suggested earlier, I believe much of this was due to the benevolent way in which the Government of Canada had been treating her veterans. Canada and Quebec Pension Plans and Medicare were introduced, which were similar to the kinds of benefits that many of Canada's veterans were already receiving. In 1962, the Report of the Glassco Commission, the Royal Commission on Government Organization, led to the transfer of veterans' hospitals to provincial healthcare authorities.

It was also recognized that the demographics of the veterans' community had changed considerably. The focus of Veteran Affairs Canada's efforts had begun to shift from caring for disabled war service veterans to providing chronic and nursing home care for the aging demographic.

At the same time it was thought that the bureaucracy charged with caring for our veterans and their families had strayed from the obligations that had been affirmed by the people and Government of Canada. So in the face of the rapidly shifting landscape of social programs in Canada, it was decided that a total overhaul of Veterans Affairs was in order. In September of 1965, Justice Mervyn Woods of the Saskatchewan Court of Appeal, himself a veteran of service in the Royal Canadian Navy in WWII, was appointed chair of a tiny, three-person committee that reported to the Minister of Veterans Affairs and was mandated to review the Pension Act and the work of the then-Canadian Pension Commission. The Woods Committee would scrub out much of the rot that had infested the bureaucracy at Veterans Affairs since the Korean War.

Additionally, Clifford Chadderton was appointed as Secretary of the Woods Committee, the same year he became the chief executive officer of The War Amps. Cliff's conviction is exemplified in the little-known committee, which completed its three-year study and submitted its final report in 1968. That report chronicles what was an exhaustive review of all things veteran, from every source imaginable. A huge document of about 800 pages, it captures the very essence of the origins, the ethos, and intent of the way the people of Canada expect our government to treat our veterans.

The committee found a system that was thoroughly dysfunctional in so many ways — too many to list here. They made 148 recommendations to correct this deplorable situation, about eighty percent of which were adopted by VAC verbatim. These recommendations eventually morphed into the system that we have today, with the Department conducting the first level of pension adjudication, the formation of the Veterans Review and Appeal Board (VRAB), and establishment of the Bureau of Pension Advocates as an independent entity to assist veterans in the review and appeals process.

The Woods Report is, in my view, the *magnum opus* on veterans in Canada, and it was fundamental in shaping my outlook on the way veterans should be treated. It is comprehensive in the extreme and took me, as a simple soldier, several months to read and really understand. I had it flagged with dozens — no, probably hundreds — of post-it notes and constantly referred to it in the conduct of my duties as Ombudsman. I swear, I almost had it memorized. This timeless masterpiece should be compulsory reading for anyone who has anything to do with our veterans and their families.

## Loyal/Faithful Canadians

Many, if not most, of Canada's veterans have made significant personal sacrifices in the line of duty for our country. Some have had their lives tragically and traumatically altered forever, and in many cases, their families have too. Many of these great patriots continue to serve their nation by quietly trying to repair or manage on their own the damage done to their lives by military service, because, despite the best of intentions of the assertions in the Woods Committee report in 1968, the Government of Canada has largely abandoned them.

CHAPTER 3:
# The OVO

## A Primer

The *Department of Veterans Affairs Act* charges the Minister of Veterans Affairs with the "care, treatment, or re-establishment in civil life of any person who served in the Canadian Forces or merchant navy."[2] Veterans who believe they have become sick or been disabled in the line of duty are required to submit a claim to the Department with evidence establishing the existence of a malady and its connection to such service. Should the Department deny the claim, the veteran may obtain additional evidence and resubmit the claim for what is known as a "Departmental Review."

Alternatively, the claimant may make representation to the Veterans Review and Appeals Board (VRAB). Operating at arm's length from the Department, the VRAB has full and exclusive jurisdiction to "hear, determine and deal" with all applications that have been denied by VAC adjudicators. Applicants have the right to present evidence and make oral testimony in review hearings before two co-chairs normally appointed by the VRAB from their stable of approximately twenty-five members. Appeals are normally held in Charlottetown without the claimants being present, but if they wish to attend they must do so at their own expense.

The Bureau of Pension Advocates (BPA) maintains a cadre of lawyers nation-wide charged with providing free advice, assistance, and

---

2   http://www.veterans.gc.ca/eng/about-us/mandate

representation to veterans who seek to have unsatisfactory decisions of VAC redressed. If a veteran is not satisfied with the outcome of an appeal submitted to the VRAB, that veteran may present the case to the Federal Court of Appeals (FCA). The Court has the power to have the VRAB reconsider their decision, although the VRAB is under no obligation to accept the findings of the Court. BPA is prohibited from representing the claims of veterans before the FCA, and veterans are required to pay the court costs themselves, which average around $30K.

## The Mandate

The Office of the Veterans Ombudsman (OVO) was established on April 3, 2007, under the authority of Order in Council 2007-5301. The Order directed the Ombudsman to review and address complaints regarding the Veterans Bill of Rights and systemic issues related to departmental programs and services. It specifically prohibited the Office from reviewing legal proceedings or judgments and the individual decisions of the Veterans Review and Appeal Board. It is, though, important to note that this did not prevent the Office from investigating problems associated with the procedures, policies, or conduct of the Board, although the Chair of the VRAB at the time made it very clear to me that, in his opinion, they were beyond our scrutiny.

## Detractors

There were many people who were critical of the Office and our mandate. Their criticisms included:

- As a veteran myself, it was a conflict of interest for me to assume the position.

- Veterans should not be required to exhaust all other forms of redress before the Ombudsman could intervene.

- The Royal Canadian Legion argued vehemently that they were already acting in the capacity of ombudsman, so the Office was unnecessary.

- The jurisdiction of the mandate was too narrow and it did not convey sufficient power to the Office to carry out the duties of an ombudsman.

I disagreed, dismissing the conflict of interest allegation out of hand. The Office of the Veterans Ombudsman quite correctly had no executive authority to redress issues; our role was to hold the system accountable. Otherwise, the OVO would have simply become another party to the problems. Veterans still had to follow the extant redress procedures that I played no part in, and I would have recused myself from any OVO activity that could have been construed to be serving my personal interests in any way. There was a desperate need for an empowered, impartial honest broker to mediate between the expectations of veterans and the realities of government, but the Royal Canadian Legion had lost the trust and confidence of the veteran community a long, long time before.

I thought any lack of jurisdiction and power that may have been inflicted on the OVO was more than compensated for by the moral authority we enjoyed from the overwhelming compassion the people of Canada have for their veterans. Also, the Order in Council allowed the OVO to intervene on behalf of a stakeholder before all redress mechanisms had been exhausted if I felt that one or more of the following circumstances applied:

- the complaint gave rise to a systemic issue;
- the redress mechanisms might take too long; or
- stakeholders were suffering undue hardship.

To me these were powerful provisos, authorizing us to act whenever I believed immediate action was required.

## Bill of Rights

The first imperative enshrined in the mandate for the Veterans Ombudsman was "to review and address complaints by clients and their representatives arising from the application of the provisions of the Veterans' Bill of Rights." The Department advertises this so-called

Veterans' Bill of Rights as a comprehensive declaration of rights for all war-service veterans, post-Korean War veterans, serving members of the Canadian Forces (Regular and Reserve), members and former members of the Royal Canadian Mounted Police, spouses, common-law partners, survivors and primary caregivers, other eligible dependents and family members, and other eligible clients.

To the uninformed, and many faithful veterans, that so-called bill represented a major coup on the part of veterans. However, as a declaration signed by then Minister of Veterans Affairs Greg Thompson and Prime Minister Stephen Harper, it was never intended to be put before the legislature to become law or to convey any special rights to veterans. The deceitful intent of this declaration is obvious in the "rights" enshrined therein. They amount to nothing more than what every Canadian citizen should expect of the government. Specifically, the bill describes the rights of veterans to:

- be treated with respect, dignity, fairness, and courtesy;

- take part in discussions that involve them and their families;

- have someone with them for support when they deal with Veterans Affairs;

- receive clear, easy to understand information about programs and services, in English or French, as set out in the Official Languages Act;

- have their privacy protected as set out in the Privacy Act; and

- receive benefits and services as set out in the published service standards and to know their appeal rights.

Who in Canada should not be able to expect their government to treat them in this manner? Notwithstanding, the provisions of that so-called Bill of Rights have failed to mitigate the gross systemic mistreatment that many veterans and their families have been suffering for decades at the hands of the bureaucracy. I challenged the bureaucrats and some well-placed advocates who had a hand in this grand act of deception. They acknowledged the veracity of my claim, arguing in their own defence that it was a quick-and-dirty solution. A real bill would have been mired in political wrangling for years before it ever saw the light of day as legislation.

## RCMP

Many veterans of service in the RCMP were eager to avail themselves of the services of the Veterans Ombudsman; however, our official mandate with respect to the Mounties was very limited. The only formal authority we had to act on their behalf emanated from our requirement to review and address their complaints arising from the provisions of the Veterans' Bill of Rights. In the main body of the Order in Council itself, there was no mention of the RCMP anywhere except Article 5, where it described limitations on the Ombudsman's authority. There it said the Ombudsman shall not review "matters within the exclusive jurisdiction of the Royal Canadian Mounted Police, apart from those matters that have been expressly assigned to be administered by the Department."

The problem with providing our services to RCMP veterans was that the majority of the responsibility for them lies with the HR Directorate at Force Headquarters in Ottawa, not VAC. Also, their veterans' issues were already being championed by RCMP Staff Relations Representatives (SRR). In the final analysis, the Office was not established to be an ombudsman for Canada's veterans but as a departmental ombudsman for clients of Veterans Affairs Canada and the Veterans Review and Appeals Board. Try telling that to a bunch of frustrated RCMP veterans. Even their SRRs refused to accept our limited mandate when it came to Mounties. I empathized with them, however, and agreed to take up that challenge as best I could. Fortunately, the key players at the RCMP Headquarters were committed to helping their veterans and working with the OVO.

## Corporate Services

Veterans Affairs Canada was charged with the responsibility to provide the OVO with logistical and administrative support, presumably to avoid the cost of generating the capabilities fully within the Office. The Department was apportioned directly $1.3M of the $6.3M the government budgeted for the Office of the Veterans Ombudsman to cover such things as financial control and accounting, letting contracts, infrastructure, security, and human resource (HR) management. This would prove to be another way that the Department could and would interfere with OVO operations.

The government refers to these functions as "corporate services," which I felt was an inappropriate term. True, government is like a corporation that takes money from "clients" in exchange for goods and services, but huge corporations often will think nothing of screwing their clients as long as they can keep the books looking attractive to their board of directors and shareholders. I feel that citizens are more analogous to those shareholders than they are clients, and elected officials are but directors on a board who can be voted out by disgruntled shareholders. I so object to the public service's warped sense of duty that I insisted we use the term "support services" instead.

From the get-go I had applied virtually my full attention to starting up operations, but as the military taught me, logistics are the lifeblood of any campaign. Without a good support system, any operation is doomed to failure. Eventually the ad hoc arrangement we had with the Department to provide support services began to encumber our progress, so I took the matter up directly with the Deputy Minister. Trying not to come across like I was telling the DM how to do her job, I proposed a short and simple, three-phase plan for how we might be able to work towards a more effective logistical and administrative interface with the Department. She appeared to take no interest in my proposal, and just delegated the whole thing away to her Assistant Deputy Minister (ADM) of Corporate Services and Director General (DG) of HR. I already enjoyed a very cordial professional relationship with these folk, but the informal collaboration was of marginal utility in terms of improving the provision of support services.

## Ombudsman In The Trenches

I approached the position of Ombudsman as I would have approached any command appointment in the military. From the outset I was determined that my place was not going to be in an office somewhere in Ottawa; it would be in the trenches with the veterans and their families. I felt that meeting and speaking with veterans was my primary responsibility. My very first act, after laying a wreath at the War Memorial on Remembrance Day, was to attend a meeting in Richmond, BC that the Western Region of VAC was having with players in the veterans' community. The issues raised at that meeting were my first taste of the subsequent three years, which were going to prove to be a tornado of travel, trouble, and turmoil.

## Meeting Mr. Babcock

It is a short hop from Richmond to Coeur d'Alene, Idaho, where Canada's last surviving veteran of World War I lived, so I took advantage of the inaugural trip to make a pilgrimage to pay homage to him. I was quite sure that he did not require the services of an ombudsman, but I felt the need to make a physical connection with that part of our history, as tenuous as it may have been. As it turned out, this visit was another key "a-ha moment" in my journey as Ombudsman. For the first time, I was struck by the great humility with which Canada's veterans go about their lives.

Mr. Babcock was 106 years old when he and his wife Dorothy welcomed us into their home. He was amazingly spry and animated, graciously sharing his war stories with yet another ensemble of admirers. What really struck me was that Mr. Babcock was adamant he was not worthy of any special recognition whatsoever as a veteran. His denial was in deference to his brothers-in-arms who had fought in the trenches, because as Mr. Babcock described it, he had never set foot out of England into the actual trenches of Europe, nor seen a bullet fired in anger. When young Private Babcock first arrived in England the army discovered he was not yet seventeen. He was close enough, however, to post temporarily to a training battalion in England until he came of age and could be deployed forward to the fight. Much to his regret, Mr. Babcock reached the age of majority just when "the Hun" capitulated, so he was never able to join his comrades and close with the enemy. Consequently, Mr. Babcock humbly but assertively rejected any suggestion that his service in WWI was noteworthy, and even refused the Government of Canada's repeated requests to honour his passing with a state funeral.

So here was a World War I veteran being heralded by VAC and the Government of Canada even though, by his own admission, he hadn't seen much of the war. There is absolutely no doubt in my mind that Mr. Babcock would demonstrate the same deference to the hardships that so many of our Peacekeepers had to face in Africa, Bosnia, and many other war zones that he did to the troops in the trenches of the Great War. That comment is not meant to detract from Mr. Babcock as a World War One veteran or to diminish the praise he so rightly deserves. Mr. Babcock was highly worthy of the state funeral proffered by the government, but his example taught me that veterans are humble to a fault.

At this very early point in my tenure I adopted the mantra of "One Veteran." I realized that the commitment of our service personnel and their families is timeless, whether in fighting Canada's wars or in standing between belligerents of someone else's wars on Canada's behalf. Moreover, the sacrifices that our veterans and their families make today for Canada are just as real, just as painful, and often just as tragic as the sacrifices made by veterans of any other era. What is missing today, however, is the sensitivity that a nation at war had for their veterans, and the protection that public awareness afforded their veterans from the callous, selfish, and parsimonious propensities of the government bureaucracy. For the most part today, our veterans have had to fend for themselves.

## Learning the Ropes

At the same time that I was learning about the veterans' community, I set out to learn the ropes in what I like to call "ombudsmanry." That is a noun I believe was coined by André Marin, the notorious ombudsman for the

Department of National Defence and the Canadian Forces (DND/CF), and subsequently for the Province of Ontario. Point of fact: everything I knew about ombudsmanry prior to becoming one was from the work Marin had done in the CF.

That said, however, I was never particularly impressed with his grandstanding, and what I perceived to be advocacy work that lent the impression of advancing a personal agenda. Marin used to publicly admonish the "chain of command" with such zeal that I, as a member of that chain of command, resented being implicated in what I perceived to be his broad brush of blame. I thought certain issues he championed, presumably on behalf of the troops, were either politically motivated or revealed his lack of empathy for, and shallow understanding of, the military culture.

As much as I may not have been a fan, though, I recognized that the role of the Office of the DND/CF Ombudsman was, as such, to be a champion for the troops, and I actively supported that. When I commanded Operation APOLLO in Afghanistan, Marin requested to pay a visit just as we were getting ready to come home. The Chief of Defence Staff had refused the request, understandably, because the timing was terrible. I went back to the Chief and asked him to reconsider that decision. I thought it would be advantageous for the troops later if their Ombudsman witnessed first-hand what the troops had gone through in theatre.

The Chief relented, so we set up a tour of Kandahar Airfield for Mr. Marin, and a private meeting with the troops. That did not go well. The troops expressed their displeasure with his presence to him personally. They resented his imposition at such a busy time, and were critical of him wearing a military uniform, even though he wore no rank or unit insignias. One must acknowledge that patience was running thin as our journey home neared but, still, I did not expect the troops to react that way.

Back at home later, and before becoming an ombudsman myself, I was interviewed by Marin's investigators regarding our snipers in Afghanistan. One (or more) of the snipers had accused me of having treated them unfairly during an investigation into an allegation that one of them had interfered with the corpse of a Taliban fighter. I was later absolved of any wrongdoing. The investigators' questions were so obviously biased I knew exactly where they were going with the investigation. One investigator even had the audacity to ask me if I would support a recommendation to give the snipers a Meritorious Service Medal in lieu of the Mention In Dispatches, which the Battle Group had recommended and that the CF subsequently awarded to them. I was incensed and I let them know it. How dare they second guess the decision-making process of the Battle Group, in a combat zone no less, or downplay the prestige that is associated with the Mention in Dispatches?

At the eleventh hour, when they were just about to release their long-awaited report, journalist Michael Friscolanti did a heart-tugging article in *Maclean's* news magazine about the plight of those poor snipers. This caused a flood of emails telling him and others how wrong he was, and describing how and why the criminal investigation I had inflicted upon them was completely justified. Friscolanti distanced himself from the article and the DND/CF Ombudsman suddenly postponed the release of the report. When I challenged Marin's investigators on their shoddy work, they lamented how the soldiers had refused to speak with them.

Those experiences had a profound impact on the way I was going to approach the business of ombudsmanry. If an ombudsman loses the trust and confidence of his or her stakeholders, that ombudsman has failed.

## Prepping for Ombudsmanry

Early on in my tenure I enrolled in a couple of short professional courses sponsored by the likes of the Forum of Canadian Ombudsman, the International Ombudsman Institute, and the International Ombudsman Association (IOA). I found them very unfulfilling. It quickly became apparent to me that there wasn't a common doctrine or approach to ombudsmanry. I came away from these courses with the impression that the profession is being invaded by lawyers, which I think is wrong. An ombudsman does need legal counsel, and lawyers definitely have the skills and aptitude for the work, but in my opinion, ombudsmanry is not about assessing lawfulness. Ombudsmanry is about fairness, and when an ombudsman comes across issues of possible illegalities, these are normally referred to the appropriate authorities forthwith.

During a session with the IOA I finally threw in the towel regarding the conventional wisdom of ombudsmanry. They spent a half-day debating whether they should change the name ombudsman to the gender-neutral term "ombudsperson" or simply "ombuds." I thought that was ridiculous. It was clear that while most of the people in the ballroom where the discussion was taking place may have been experienced in their work, whatever that may have entailed, they had a very shallow understanding of the concept of ombudsmanry. The term ombudsman has nothing to do with the gender of the person. In its original form, "*jusiteom-budsman*," it was a Swedish word meaning procurator for civil affairs, but loosely translated it means "citizen's defender." Hence, the word ombudsman is gender neutral, and we didn't need to turn it into an exercise in political correctness any more than we needed to refer to the "mandate" for the Office as a "person-date." I wouldn't waste our time sending our people on courses to take part in debates like this one.

## Research

I gained my best understanding of ombudsmanry by meeting one-on-one with and reading the work of people who studied or worked in the practice. The writings of Donald C. Rowat, an icon in the field, and studies done by Dr. Stewart Hyson at the University of New Brunswick, were particularly useful. Dr. Hyson studied provincial and territorial ombudsmans and published a book on the subject. I also met with as many provincial ombudsmans and federal commissioners as I could, to pick their brains.

Of course, that included André Marin. Despite the personal feelings I had developed when I was serving in the CF, Mr. Marin is world renowned for the work he did as an ombudsman in the Department of National Defence and subsequently as Ontario's Ombudsman. In setting up the Office of the DND/CF Ombudsman he did some tremendous research and wrote some excellent reports that helped me in my understanding of ombudsmans and ombudsmanry. He was also very generous to me, graciously agreeing to meet with me several times to help show me the ropes.

## Seeking Advice

**YVES CÔTÉ**

As much as I shunned the notion of setting up the Office of the Veterans Ombudsman as another lackey of the federal bureaucracy, to ensure the legitimacy of the Office I examined the practices of organizations and sought the advice of the appointees with similar functions in our nation's capital. One of my first such courtesy calls was to the incumbent DND/CF Ombudsman, Yves Côté. Mr. Côté had noted a concern with something I had said during my short speech when I was introduced as the new Veterans Ombudsman. Apparently I had announced my intention to collaborate with VAC to ensure that the system treated veterans and their families fairly.

In retrospect I was probably trying to distance myself from the confrontational approach to ombudsmanry that I had experienced in DND. This notwithstanding, Yves warned me that veterans would not want to hear that their Ombudsman was collaborating with the very organization they might feel was not treating them fairly. He advised me that it was beneficial to work with the Department, but that must be kept behind the scenes. His point was well taken, and a good lesson early on about the fine line that I would have to tread between championing the fair treatment of veterans and maintaining a constructive relationship with the Department and the VRAB as a catalyst for change.

Coincidentally, I had been using the word "bureaucrat" with the same acidity that Marin had uttered "the chain of command." My senior staff quickly picked up on this and told me that some people did NOT share my view that bureaucrat was a bad word. I guess I should have known that public servants are often proud to use the term to describe their profession. Since I didn't want to insult the many proud and dedicated bureaucrats the same way I had been insulted as a member of the chain of command, I thought I should restrain my use of the term in the negative.

I asked the opinion of Yves, himself a career bureaucrat, and was surprised by his reaction.

Yves encouraged me not to let up on my condemnation of bureaucrats. He explained that Anglophone Canadians have a beautiful term to describe employees of the machinery of government: public servants. He believed that title described the ethos that government employees had to embrace. In his opinion, anyone who becomes a servant to the bureaucracy is properly referred to as a bureaucrat and has no place in government. He lamented that there was no term in French that was so appropriate and so descriptive as public servant.

I was extremely impressed with this piece of wisdom. In the military I recognized that distinct from the true warriors there were many bureaucrats in uniform, for whom I had little professional regard. I would continue to focus some angst towards the kind of bureaucrats that I held in such disregard, but when I did so was quick to qualify with my audience my differentiation between bureaucrats and public servants.

### SHEILA FRASER

I was especially interested in the Office of the Auditor General (OAG). I have always had a great deal of respect for the work they do, and had even more respect for the Auditor General herself, Ms. Sheila Fraser. Fearless, forthright, articulate, and measured, Sheila was gracious enough to meet with me several times and tolerated the dopey questions of a neophyte such as myself. Early on we secured some of the OAG's training and doctrinal publications with a view to one day perhaps folding them into our own practices.

### ROBERT MARLEAU

I am particularly grateful to one commissioner for the animated, informed, and notably critical advice that he offered me from the get-go. Mr. Robert Marleau had enjoyed a very successful career in the government, as Clerk of the House of Commons from July 1987 to July 2000, and as Senior Advisor to the Speaker of the House of Commons from July 2000 until his retirement at the end of January 2001. In my opinion, that made him somewhat of an outsider *vis-à-vis* the public service mainstream. I was reminded that, as Clerk, he had been the most recent co-editor of *House of Commons Procedure and Practice*, a highly respected work on Canadian parliamentary procedure. His knowledge of parliamentary affairs and good governance and experience are not only beyond reproach, I would submit they were extraordinary for any single person in the public service at that time. Robert's insight and advice bolstered my confidence regarding my understanding of the systems at play and how I should fit into them.

## Brilliant At The Basics

As much as I read voraciously about ombudsmanry and sought out the advice and guidance of academics and those who had "been there and done that," I had no intention of trying to take on an air of being flashy or overly sophisticated. At the end of the day, ombudsmanry is about natural justice and treating people fairly, and all I tried to do was learn the very basics of the profession, and become brilliant at them.

I think my military background was a very useful influence for the fledgling Office. I understood the contemporary security environment and the extraordinary things that some Canadians are prepared to do for queen and country. I knew from my own service that so many tasks we demand of our service personnel in the course of their duties to maintain operational readiness, notwithstanding when deployed on operations, are just plain stupid-dangerous.

Soldiers need to know that if they are injured in the conduct of their duties, they will still be able to provide for themselves and their families what they reasonably would have expected of a full and successful career in the Canadian Forces. In places like Afghanistan, our young soldiers work alongside private military contractors who earn more in a month than many of our troops earn in a year. An army could never afford to pay the troops such salaries, the de facto fair market value for the kind of work they do, so some kind of *quid pro quo* is most certainly in order. That is where the services and benefits of VAC come in.

So with my chant of "One Veteran" echoing down the halls of our offices in Ottawa and Charlottetown, I urged my team to consider their work to be every bit as crucial in maintaining the security of Canada as that of the trigger-pullers in Afghanistan. It remained our job to demonstrate, with each and every complaint that we acted upon for the stakeholders of the OVO, that the services and benefits the Government of Canada provided were commensurate with the potential liability our veterans and their families accept and the sacrifices they make.

Coming from a military culture I was very familiar with the role and importance of developing and training everyone in a common doctrine as soon as possible, so I endeavoured to ensure that everything we did or said was well conceived and deliberate from the beginning. I basically followed standard battle procedure to set up this operation, although where I could, I tried to dumb-down the procedures and terminology to be outwardly less militaristic.

"Selection and maintenance of the aim" is the first principle of war, so it was very important for me, I reasoned, that we got the aim for the OVO correct right from the beginning. As a good military planner, the very first thing I did was to conduct a comprehensive Mission Analysis. This military technique is a mind-clearing exercise whereby a commander appreciates the context of a mission in a more intuitional, inductive way. I included my current senior staff in the process, which I learned later still confused the hell out of them even though I thought I had successfully 'civilianized' it. Nonetheless, I found it to be extremely useful.

Two qualities that I felt had to be engrained deeply in the OVO's culture were critical thinking and a readiness to challenge the status quo. We could not accept anything at face value, and we had to make sure that there were legitimate reasons for everything. As a combat leader I learned that these are not easy for human beings to do. Despite our best of intentions as a race, we often do some things for no other reason than everybody else seems to be doing it or because it is the way it has always been done. In fact, the human mind has developed powerful defence mechanisms to resolve the dissonance that we experience when our actions contradict our beliefs — or vice versa. Old habits die hard, as they say, and from the first day in the OVO I made sure that the habits we developed organizationally were harmonious with our *raison d'être* and the culture that I wanted to nurture.

Very early on I challenged our use of the term "stakeholders." VAC used it in reference to organizations such as the Royal Canadian Legion, The Army, Navy, Air Force Veterans Association (ANAVETS), Cliff Chadderton's NCVA, and myriad other players of varying stature and legitimacy. My team fell into the rut of assuming that our stakeholders would be the same, but I set out to eradicate this notion. The Department could quite rightly claim those entities as their stakeholders, but it did not make sense in our context. Several of those institutions had a huge stake in their relationship with government, but to the contrary in our case, had little "stake" in a Veterans Ombudsman *per se*. In fact, at least one prominent veterans' organization objected vehemently to the establishment of a Veterans Ombudsman. Our stakeholders, therefore, when we used that term, were understood to be veterans and their families.

I wanted a culture in the OVO that was as creative as it was critical. Whenever I could, I would promote a spirit of innovation. In order to mitigate the impediment that the distance between Ottawa and Charlottetown imposed on our internal communications, I sought to introduce the use of a wiki, à *la* Wikipedia. Each person would record best practices they discovered and individual lessons learned, in order to expedite everybody's learning curve and develop a common doctrine. Back in those days we had to fight departmental bureaucracy to introduce our wiki, but wikis were destined to become a leading-edge practice in the public service.

To further set the tone of critical and creative thinking in the Office, I announced that I wanted a unique logo. André Marin had enshrined a logo on the Office of the CF/DND Ombudsman, but my idea met with local resistance. Government's regulations for common look and feel prohibited anything but the "Canada" trademark. I felt this kind of gesture was symbolic of our arm's-length status with the government and the courage of the Office, so I pressed for it. Internally, our staff brainstormed an appropriate logo for the OVO and I unveiled it officially in our second annual report.

## Not Advocacy

As much as the OVO had been modelled on the Office of the CF/DND Ombudsman, there was a subtle but very important difference between us. Although the CF/DND Ombudsman's mandate has relatively few restrictions on the type of investigations they can embark on, that office's primary function is labour relations. In the case of the OVO, our function was more that of program analysis. Another important difference between the two ombudsmans is who their respective stakeholders are.

If I were to project how I defined our stakeholders, veterans, and their families, into the world of the CF/DND Ombudsman, their stakeholders would be the Canadian citizens, or the people of Afghanistan, who would have a beef with the CF or DND. While some of the complaints we received were grievances by our stakeholders expressed towards VAC staff, contrary to what it says in the Veterans Bill of Rights, the OVO could neither review nor address them because those issues must be handled by departmental management, the respective employee, and the appropriate union. The majority of the stakeholders and the chain of command that the CF/DND Ombudsman's investigators deal with are not unionized , so their ombudsman has a legitimate and very important role in their 'labour relations.'

I expected our investigators would be doing as much or more research into the traditions, best practices, legislation, regulations, and policies impacting on the veterans' community. So, I decided the Directorate would be referred to as "Investigations & Research." In addition to more accurately reflecting the work of our investigators, I thought the new title might relieve some of the anxieties of the public servants with whom they would interact.

Very early on I decided that the OVO would not be in the business of advocacy. That market was already fully saturated. By my interpretation, advocacy groups are not necessarily as attuned to the realities of government, or as constrained by any requirement to be balanced and pragmatic in their initiatives as we had to be. Select groups may indeed abide by those constraints in the conduct of their affairs, but many don't. Conversely, some advocates and advocacy groups are so connected to the

Department that many vets accuse them of being in a conflict of interest, if not conspirators in the government's malfeasance. Other groups go too far the other way, engaging in blatantly partisan politics.

I was concerned that such associations could compromise the independence or the credibility of the Office of the Veterans Ombudsman. Also, a formal association with an advocacy group might end up being construed as an open endorsement of subsequent agendas or actions that might discredit the OVO but over which I had no control. I was also concerned that a formal association that I might have agreed to with any particular advocate might have put us at odds with others. There is a lot of rivalry and antagonism in the veterans' community, and I didn't want to exacerbate or become a party to it. So we simply treated all the groups at arm's length, as we did the government.

I saw my job simply as helping veterans and their families by righting wrongs. If somebody could reasonably demonstrate to me, and by extension my team, that they had answered our nation's call and, in doing so, "took a bullet" for the cause, figuratively or literally, I was going to go to bat for him or her. As I used to say repeatedly, "It may be policy, and it may be legal, but is it fair?" Fairness, of course, is often a judgment call, but as a former military officer, I was very comfortable with making balanced and ethical decisions in volatile, uncertain, complex, and ambiguous situations. I was also conversant with such things as the principles of natural justice and administrative law. My challenge was going to be to set the conditions that would enable everyone on our team to use their best judgment on a case-by-case basis.

Our job, in simplest terms, was to identify where and how the system was broken and recommend how to fix it. I recognized that the government and the military had once done things differently and faced different constraints and freedoms than we do today, so they may have treated some veterans differently than we would expect today. I resolved to go to bat for any veterans of any era who we believed were being victimized by mistakes, lazy decision making, unfair policies or practices, or systemic limitations. The challenge would be to make a convincing and balanced case in every instance.

I did not see our job as assigning culpability or blame, I believed our role to be more one of mediation. As much as possible, my marching orders would be written by the complaints that we received from our stakeholders, and the OVO would serve as a catalyst to allow the system to correct itself. Of course we scanned the veterans' community broadly to make sure we had the right priorities based on the relative severity of the harm being caused, the number of victims, the degree of urgency, and the relative potential of expediting a timely resolution.

The Order In Council specified my job as "Special Advisor to the Minister," and I took it upon myself to educate the Minister on what issues the veterans' community was faced with and the efficacy of the work the Department was engaged in. However, neither Minister — not Thompson nor Blackburn — was at all interested in addressing issues with me. It seemed that if an issue was not going to make it past the bureaucracy, the Minister blindly stood behind the DM and the status quo.

I also took it upon myself to educate all the other parliamentarians about veterans, although I was always very careful not to divulge the Minister's business or comment on politically sensitive issues. I really wanted to build the sensitivity of parliamentarians regarding the service and sacrifices of what-I-called the "modern veteran," but was careful not to fuel political shenanigans.

## Culture

A culture of empowered decision-making such as I hoped to develop in the OVO cannot exist in a bureaucracy driven by obsessive supervisors promulgating restrictive policies and imposing prescriptive practices. It requires a set of shared principles, and leadership at all levels to model those principles and coach others on their relevance. I therefore set about writing what I called a "Charter," which described the ethos that I intended to introduce into the Office of the Veterans Ombudsman. I also set about inculcating my brand of combat leadership within the OVO, one that I had come to understand in the military and, in my opinion, is very much ethics and effects focused. The OVO proved to be an epic example of the efficacy of such an approach to leadership.

I wrote the first draft, including the organizational "values," trying to package my brand in such a way that it would be palatable in a peacetime civilian context. I circulated it for comment several times with increasingly large groups, culminating with a retreat for all staff in Summerside, PEI, once we were approaching our full complement of staff members. Even then, I considered the Charter to be a living document, and amended it several times to be more concise or to more accurately describe the culture that I wanted in the OVO.

I talked about the Charter all the time. Early on I could see some people were resistant or patronizing me hoping the idea might blow over, but I persisted. Over time, the majority of our staff seemed to develop trust and confidence in the philosophies presented in that document. Occasionally someone would even refer to the Charter in the course of his or her daily business, if for no other reason than to challenge me on it. That was certainly a healthy sign in my books. More to the point, very early on our team clearly embraced a deep sense of commitment to our stakeholders and a "make it happen" attitude in dealing with their complaints.

## Action Orientation

Although it didn't make the cut in my first draft of the Charter — my mistake — one value that very quickly floated to the top and was subsequently enshrined in the Charter was "action." Throughout my military career I was action oriented, and in the OVO I often repeated Patton's famous quote that "a good plan violently executed now is better than a perfect plan executed next week."

I had learned that the OVO would be dealing with life and death issues, both figuratively and factually, so we had to act in a timely fashion. Therefore, I wanted everyone to feel a sense of empowerment and commitment to the wellbeing of veterans and their families. We would never shrink from acting on behalf of our stakeholders when we thought it was the right thing to do. My team had no problem at all embracing that principle.

## Transparency

One of the pillars of my approach to business has always been transparency. One often overlooks one's own errors, if unintentionally, so as Ombudsman I resolved to enable our stakeholders to scrutinize our work and intentions. For the same reason, I worked with my colleagues in VAC and the VRAB on the basis of full disclosure. At the same time I encouraged everyone in the OVO to challenge me on my own actions or intentions, a fundamental ingredient for my approach to ethics and ethical leadership.

I believe in total accountability for acts of malfeasance, malice, negligence, and incompetence that are verified as deliberate, acute, or recurring. That is not to say that I have what is called a "zero defect" mentality. Nobody is perfect, and I fully expected mistakes to happen, especially anytime something new was tried. Errors of commission are excusable if they are for the right reasons and the common good. Errors of omission are less so, but concealing one's errors is never acceptable.

I never balked at taking the time to explain to our stakeholders why we might have done something that was seemingly not in our stakeholders' interests. I considered myself to be fully accountable to them for anything and everything my team did, and resolved to apologize if an apology was warranted, or resign immediately if we did something that I felt betrayed the trust of our stakeholders. We were dealing with peoples' lives, so we would treat them with the empathy and fairness that they deserved.

I encouraged all of my staff, from the youngest, most inexperienced person on the telephone with our stakeholders, up to my Deputy Ombudsman, to do whatever they felt a situation demanded as quickly as they felt they had to act, even without seeking higher authority if they thought it was urgent. I emphasized that I would far sooner apologize to the Minister, the system, and/or Canadian taxpayers if we did something wrong for our stakeholders for the right reason than have to explain to our stakeholders why we failed to act when should have. Little did I know that I would one day be apologizing for my naïveté regarding the persuasive power of what I perceived to be my moral authority.

## Hands-On Operations

Because of my military background my approach to operations was very much hands-on, which meant I spent the majority of my time and effort actually communicating with and in the company of our stakeholders. Frequently I conducted open town hall meetings across the country. That was not the only way I exposed myself personally to the ire of veterans. As often as I could, I would make phone calls to individual stakeholders. I found this personal touch was so valuable that we developed a practice of reserving every Friday afternoon for me to contact individual stakeholders personally.

Within the Office I never hesitated to express my empathy for our veterans. I felt a need to counterbalance any contradictory vibes that my front-line workers might have been exposed to in their dealings with the Department and the VRAB. I recognized that I could have been accused of being biased, and would probably admit as much, but I always insisted that everybody on our team should feel free to offer their own opinion on anything we were doing as an Office.

In keeping with my approach to ethical and effective leadership, our Charter specifically charged each and every person in the OVO to challenge me, directly and honestly, on anything I did if they felt it was not in keeping with the philosophies articulated therein. I understand I have frailties like any other human being, and sometimes my walk might not match my talk. So if somebody, anybody, is able to point that out to me, I am fully prepared to reflect and make a course correction as necessary.

Also, if I asked someone on our team for an opinion, I expected — no, I demanded — that he or she tell it like it is. As a practice I really wanted to understand everyone's perspective on how things were going in the Office. That was unsettling for some, because they might feel they were tattling on their immediate supervisor. However, once they realized that I am not by nature a zero-defect dictator, or somebody who reacted impulsively or unduly harshly to the receipt of what might be perceived to be bad news, I think I am safe in saying that we fostered a very focused and self-correcting work environment.

## Building Bridges

I was almost as consultative with the bureaucracy as I was with our stakeholders, having spent nearly as much energy connecting with departmental and board staff. Human nature being what it is, I knew that I would alienate some people simply for being critical of the system for which they worked, even if I didn't have a vendetta against bureaucrats. An adversarial relationship with VAC and VRAB staff would not have been constructive, so I tried to bridge the "us/them gap" by meeting with them very early on in my tenure and often.

I was grateful that Deputy Minister Tining found time to meet with me very soon after I was appointed. She graciously agreed to meet for lunch at one of the quaint little restaurants that one finds in the downtown core of Charlottetown. I expected that I would be working a lot with Suzanne over the coming three years and I hoped to put her at ease from the get-go. I impressed upon her that my priority was the trust and confidence of the veterans so we might not agree on everything, especially in public. Nevertheless, I expressed my sincere intention to be as transparent and collegial as possible with the Department. I walked away from the meeting with a feeling that we could certainly work well together.

I would reinforce the same message with Directors, Directors General, and Assistant Deputy Ministers by making regular courtesy calls to their offices when I was in their neighbourhoods. On several occasions I was invited to speak at senior staff meetings and conferences for both the Department and the Board. They seemed to be very sincere about their work and appreciative of my words. It goes without saying that I got on well with the Bureau of Pension Advocates. As lawyers who are paid by the government to assist veterans with their claims against the Department and the VRAB, I found them to be very eager to hear how I intended to serve their clients. More importantly, they became a valuable source of intelligence regarding what was wrong with the system.

I also endeavoured to meet with as many VAC staffers as I could, in the front lines of regional and district offices and even the headquarters in Charlottetown. In fact, one of my first "fireside chats" with VAC staff took place in the atrium in the Donald J MacDonald building in Charlottetown. My message was to encourage them to have a thick skin. They had to understand that my first priority was gaining and maintaining the trust and confidence of our stakeholders, which meant that there was going to be some tough talk, and the media would probably pick up that type of locker room language. I asked them to take all that with a grain of salt and view me like Hulk Hogan; I had a ring persona, and I had a business persona.

I shared the veterans' sense of urgency and even their anger, but at the same time, I spent enough time at the National Defence Headquarters to know how a bureaucracy works and that you can't turn an institutional cargo freighter on a dime. I urged the VAC staff not to take it personally. I assured them that as long as the commitment to do right by our veterans that I perceived amongst VAC employees was genuine, we would work well behind the scenes together to improve the plight of disadvantaged vets. That message seemed to resonate with everyone. They all seemed empathetic, expressing their understanding of the dilemma I faced and their willingness to work with me. Of course they reiterated their commitment to veterans and their families. I was buoyed by their reaction. That day several people even approached us for a job.

Every time I was in the vicinity of a VAC office for a town hall meeting with veterans, I made a point of meeting with their frontline operators. It was clear to me that I was gaining their trust and confidence also. Often, they would confide in me on serious problems they perceived to exist within VAC or the Board, but they were so concerned about retribution from their superiors that they did not want to be seen visiting our office or even talking privately with me. In so doing, it was apparent that frustrated frontline staff in VAC held as much a stake in the OVO as the veterans and family members they endeavoured to serve. The rank and file in the Department, like the lawyers at the Bureau of Pension Advocates, would prove to be another great source of intelligence for us.

## The Central Agencies

I am quite sure that senior bureaucrats were surprised by the stature that I assumed for the OVO, particularly when I reached out to the central agencies and asked to pay a courtesy call to the Clerk of the Privy Council Office (PCO) and Secretary of Treasury Board. I reasoned that as the head of a new agency, presumably one empowered by the prime minister to provide oversight at arm's length from government, it was appropriate that I introduce myself, seek any advice they might have to offer and give them an idea of how I intended to develop the OVO.

Peter Lynch, Clerk of PCO at the time, and the Secretary, Murielle d'Auray, blew me off. When Wayne Wouters replaced Lynch, we resubmitted our request to pay him a courtesy call and he acceded. He granted me a half hour of his time. Wouters was very professional, told me how important veterans were to him, and asked me to tell him about the OVO. By then my commitment to veterans and their families was public knowledge, so what I hoped to convey to the Clerk was that I fully intended to be a team player, if the team was willing to play. Mr. Wouters summed up the meeting by thanking me for my service and saying that he was sensitive to the needs of veterans.

## RCMP

In order to satisfy the expectations of RCMP veterans for the Office of the Veterans Ombudsman, I had to nurture an informal working relationship between the OVO and the force's HR Directorate in Ottawa. Its commissioner, Bill Elliot, the civilian senior bureaucrat who was installed to clean up Commissioner Zachardelli's mess, wanted nothing to do with me. I met, instead, with the senior uniformed member, Senior Deputy Commissioner Bill Sweeney, and his staff.

Bill had been my neighbour in Edmonton. He had commanded K Division there when I was in command of 3PPCLI. I have a huge amount of respect for Bill, whose "Aren't I Great" wall in his office was adorned with artefacts celebrating the career of a "gunfighter." Bill was one of those few cops — very, very few — who had spent his career in the front lines of crime fighting and still managed to rise to the very top of the organization. As such, he had a great deal of empathy for the cop on the beat and the veterans of the force. I think it is safe for me to say that while I was there, the OVO enjoyed a very open and action-oriented relationship with the HQ in addressing the concerns of RCMP veterans and their families.

## Staffing

Before I arrived in the OVO, I envisioned being handed a steno pad and stubby pencil and being directed to a cubicle somewhere to start planning the Office. Thankfully, shortly after the government introduced the Veterans Bill of Rights and announced their intention to establish a Veterans Ombudsman, the Department put together a project team to lay the groundwork for these initiatives. One person from that project team, Louise Wallis, agreed to stay on with the OVO until I could get it up and running.

Louise was a career public servant with Veterans Affairs in Charlottetown. She was well known and highly respected in the veterans' community, and of course well connected within the Department and highly regarded by her colleagues. The continuity and expertise that Louise brought to the OVO expedited our preparations, and her quiet, thoughtful demeanour was the perfect contrast to my "pitter, patter let's get at 'er" attitude. As a team, we would foster an action-oriented, empathetic, and balanced culture in our fledgling office that would serve our stakeholders well.

From the day the government announced their intent to have a Veterans Ombudsman, the Department — Louise and her tiny project team — was flooded with complaints, so they had to hire a skeleton staff on contract. Anne Langlois was in the front office, and everywhere else for that matter. For lack of a better public service term, Anne was the Ottawa office manager, or Jack of all trades, acting on behalf of Louise when Louise was at home in Charlottetown. In the public service, industrious, reliable, and loyal people like Anne are in big demand, so sadly, we only had the pleasure of her talents for a short period of time. That set the scene for a subsequent cavalcade of temporary administrative staff that marched through our offices in a steady stream.

David Snook, who had recently retired as a Director of Investigations with the DND/CF Ombudsman, was juggling almost four hundred cases by the time I arrived. He was aided by some investigators that he had brought in on contract: very experienced people who dipped their toes in the pool of complaints from Canada's veterans for no other reason than their loyalty and commitment to people who have served in uniform for Canada.

Despite the thorough research and planning of the project team, nobody had any idea of the volume and type of complaints we would receive or what we could do to redress them. So without any doctrine or operating procedures, this small cadre of professionals had to rely on their wits and experience to fill a badly needed niche, virtually "on the march." Thanks to them, the OVO established a degree of credibility with our stakeholders right from the get-go.

Louise hired Julie Harris as her interim Director of Communications: a young, enthusiastic public affairs officer from the Canadian Forces Reserves. With a history of military service in her family, Julie's commitment to veterans was unquestionable. Unfortunately, as a contractor her time with us was also limited. However, her open mindedness and creativity would prove to be a stark contrast to the narrow-minded and dogmatic public affairs people from the public service that I had to deal with after her.

## Hiring A "Deputy Ombudsman"

My first priority was to find a Director General (DG), or what I would have known in the military as a chief of staff, who would be God's gift to, and fount of all knowledge about, everything to do with the public service. I referred to my DG as the Deputy Ombudsman, but consternation rippled through our Office and our supporting counterparts in the Department's HR directorate. "There is supposed to be only one deputy in the Department," they said, "the deputy minister!" This was exactly my point: we weren't the Department. Rather than argue the point, we incorporated the Deputy Ombudsman title colloquially and never sought to have it changed officially.

What I did argue was that my deputy had to be an EX 2, a brigadier general equivalent, as a minimum. I had been hired as a GCQ 4, barely the equivalent of a colonel, my past rank in the CF, and my deputy was supposed to be an EX 1, roughly a full colonel equivalent. However, I envisioned my deputy dealing regularly with the ADMs and DGs in the Department, possibly even the DM in my stead. I viewed my rank as Ombudsman as inconsequential, but for my deputy to have any credibility in the eyes of other public servants, the position had to be an EX 2.

This was our first real showdown with the Department. Perhaps I should say it was Louise's first great challenge as my senior public servant, and I was reassured when the Department granted our request without any bloodshed. I had a couple of people in mind with whom I had worked in the CF, but their current ranks, employment, or French language profiles posed problems. It looked as though we were going to have to launch into a lengthy and exhausting competition for the job but that was alright with me. My deputy was going to be a keystone position in this Office, so I wanted to make sure we had the right person for the job.

All of a sudden, and seemingly out of nowhere, a person was identified for the job who was the appropriate rank and who, at first blush, appeared to have a wealth of experience in another ombudsman-like organization in the government. I was told this person's previous position had been made redundant and he was available immediately.

During the interview I found this person friendly enough and very eager to please. The reference check I made with the previous employer met with the most glowing account of his performance. The departmental Director General of HR advised me that this candidate's credentials were so fitting for the job that I would actually have to justify for the system why I would not take him on my staff. So the job of finding my "master of all that is the public service" turned out to be much easier than I had ever anticipated, but it would prove to be a huge setback in setting up the Office.

Unfortunately, my first deputy did not work out. He was a "yes-man" of the highest order, so grossly preoccupied by doing exactly what I wanted him to do that he never thought for himself. He would rarely if ever ask a question, presumably for fear of revealing a personal weakness or flaw. This would cause him to waste countless hours of everyone's time by overachieving on tasks and projects that, in the end, entirely missed the mark of my desired intent. How he ever made it to the rank of EX 2, or whether he was actually highly competent and just following orders to sabotage the development of the OVO, I will never know.

HR was hugely reticent to start building a case to fire anybody. In the military, where the consequences of incompetence at any rank level can be life or death, I would have built a case and had this person thrown out of the CF. But this was the public service, and nobody's life was directly at risk by this person so I was not going to fall on my sword over this. I was not there to fix the public service; I was there to help vets. I ended up following their advice and put my first deputy on French training, a government imperative for senior Anglophone bureaucrats and a dignified excuse to mask the real reason I was relieving him of his duties.

## Other Staffing Issues

Notwithstanding the preliminary work that Louise and the project team had done to stand up the Office, there was a massive amount of HR work to do in creating the permanent positions. The skill sets that we required in our people had to be identified and matched to the appropriate classifications and ranks within the public service. Then job descriptions had to be created and advertised, competitions run, applications collated, interviews planned and conducted, the selection process documented, successful applicants hired, and then the competition had to be closed and reported on.

We met regularly with worker bees from HR who confided in us that they had to balance this huge task with their regular departmental duties. We received assistance when and where we requested it. The operative word is "requested." In order to ask for something you have to know what you are asking for. Neither Louise, nor I, nor any of our skeleton staff were experts in all the aspects of human resource policy and practices in the public service. Consequently, we would get advice on the skill sets, classifications, and ranks our people should have and help in filling out the required paperwork to get positions established. The next thing we knew someone else would weigh in and contradict the advice we had already received.

## Principal Staff

I was very fortunate to have recruited from the get-go the colonel and chief warrant officer who comprised the Canadian Forces Liaison Office at Veterans Affairs. Liaison officers have the distinct benefit of being part of the inner sanctum of the organization to which they are attached, but with little or no responsibility for any major deliverables other than to report what they learn to NDHQ. Conversely, as representatives of the CF they must be highly professional, industrious, and clear thinking. They are expected to possess a thorough understanding of their parent organization, an eagerness and adeptness to learn about the organization to which they are attached, and to give sound advice to both.

Colonel Charlie Cue, or "Q" for short, had been the CFLO to VAC. Charlie was a Sea King pilot with Search and Rescue, a real operational kind of guy as most pilots are (but never tell a pilot I said so). Thanks to the kind of guy Q is and his previous employment, Q had an absolutely incredible understanding of all things veterans. We hired him as my Special Advisor to avoid tying him down to any specific task or issue. That was a wise move because Q was dipping his oars into all sorts of emerging issues. He decided to work with the OVO rather than the Department because, thanks to his military experience, he felt he could make a bigger impact influencing the formation of a small tactical unit like us rather than being a cog in the Department's bureaucracy. Charlie's passion and commitment was phenomenal, and he alone accomplished so much for veterans in the short three years that I worked with him. I have no hesitation in saying Q was the centre of gravity of the OVO, and should have been the Ombudsman.

Q's wingman in the CF Liaison Office was Chief Warrant Officer Michel Guay, chief warrant officer (CWO) being the highest rank in the CF for non-commissioned members. Michel retired from the CF at the same time as Q and agreed to become my Director of Early Intervention. I would swear Michel, like Q, knew more about Veterans Affairs Canada and the issues confronting veterans than anyone in government, which is why they were so effective as liaison officers. Thanks to his knowledge and leadership our Directorate of Early Intervention was operational very, very quickly, producing some outstanding results on behalf of disadvantaged veterans and their families.

Because of the great success we had enjoyed with the work that Michel Guay was doing in Early Intervention, I felt that I had accomplished yet another major coup by luring another retired CWO to the OVO to become our Director of Investigations and Research. Guy Parent came to us from Marin's stable at DND, where he had taken up employment as an investigator after having retired as the Canadian Forces Chief Warrant Officer, the highest appointment for a CWO in the Canadian Forces and sort of the 'right-hand-person' to the Chief of Defence Staff. Afterwards in the Office of the CF/DND Ombudsman Guy had worked his way up to become their Director of Investigations.

## Operations

Early on, OVO operations consisted of three efforts — Early Intervention, Investigations, and Public Affairs. As a director, Michel Guay demonstrated extraordinary skills, knowledge, and creativity in setting up the operating procedures in Early Intervention. He also proved to be a masterful supervisor, which is exactly what someone from the CF expects of a chief warrant officer. His team would do whatever they could to help stakeholders who approached our Office. The early intervention analysts were mandated to spend as much time on the phone with a person as needed to ensure they understood the stakeholder's situation completely. If they determined that our help was not required, they would provide advice and information to troubled stakeholders, once again taking as much time as the stakeholder needed. Oftentimes there was nothing that could be done for a stakeholder, but just having a sympathetic ear on the other end of the phone was hugely beneficial.

Other times we would just refer our stakeholder to the organization that would satisfy his or her needs. If our intervention analysts detected the frustration that so many of our stakeholders were enduring, and sensed that perhaps the stakeholder was at the end of his or her rope, they would do what Michel referred to as a "hot transfer." In other words, they would initiate contact with the office of primary interest in the case of a stakeholder, and once the conditions had been established for the stakeholder to become engaged, our analysts would edge themselves out of the situation. A key to our success was that our folks would not simply "fire and forget"; they would actually follow up with the stakeholder afterwards to ensure the matter had been resolved.

After having gained keen insight into a stakeholder's perspective over the phone, our intervention analysts would go to the Department's files to round out their understanding of the situation. Then, with a fully informed view of the situation — void of the emotion, frustrations, and other baggage that stakeholders were known to accumulate over years and sometimes decades of fighting with a system that was anything but efficient or empathetic — the analysts would decide if and how they would approach the Department on the issue. I gave them full authority to do so. Once again, they understood that I would much sooner apologize if they did something wrong for the right reason than to explain why we failed to respond appropriately to someone who was in need.

I never had to. Their job became one of mediating with the Department on behalf of our stakeholders, and they grew very adept at it. More often than not, simply having an intervention analyst weigh in on an issue would see it resolved. At other times, the analysts would hand issues off to Michel to mediate at a higher level within the Department.

## Investigations and Research

This low-level mediation was working so well that mediation and escalation became the central theme for all OVO operations. I preferred to use mediation with the appropriate decision maker in the Department to make the system at all levels responsive to the needs of veterans and their families. When Michel and his team were not able to mediate timely solutions to issues with the people in the front lines of the Department, they would hand the case off to our investigators.

Investigators were assigned to particularly complex or sensitive issues, or clusters of complaints that were centred on certain broader systemic issues. They had more experience so we afforded them greater freedom to dig into issues in greater detail, becoming virtual subject-matter experts and mediating solutions with higher levels within VAC. Any time that an investigator felt an issue would benefit from a little leverage from a higher level of management, one of my senior managers or I would weigh in. For more complex issues, the plan was to form special dedicated teams as required to conduct formal, more expansive investigations. In this way we developed what I saw as four levels of potential mediation:

- Level 1: EIAs or investigators confirming the facts associated with a complaint and mediating a successful outcome between the stakeholder and service provider.

- Level 2: Conducting additional research and analysis in order to improve the processes or practices.

- Level 3: Extensive research and analysis conducted by dedicated teams on broader systemic issues that result in findings or recommendations for significant changes within the Department or the Board.

- Level 4: Influencing amendments in complex systemic issues requiring regulatory or legislative changes.

I felt it was important to discriminate between the levels of intervention for the purposes of our annual reports. Clearly Level 1 interventions were an important function, but something that the Department should already have been handling as a matter of course — but they weren't. On the other hand, Level 1 complaints were useful to us because clusters of a given issue could give rise to systemic problems that would require Level Two, Three, or Four interventions. Identifying and dealing with such systemic issues, I thought, was how an ombudsman really earned his or her pay. I thought that specifying the levels of our interventions would give

Canadians a better idea of the complexity and level of effort involved in our interventions and allow them to determine more accurately whether they were getting value for money in the OVO.

To effect changes to government processes, policies, regulations, and legislation, we had to gather all of the facts and data related to an issue, analyze it, and feed it back into the system as pragmatic, coherent recommendations. Such recommendations normally constitute the contents of formal full reports.. As much as I did not want to be seen by our stakeholders to be collaborating with the bureaucracy, I thought we might resolve major issues more efficiently behind the scenes working closely with the Department and the Board. I had hoped that we would have to publish full reports only as a last resort but, sadly, I learned my lesson to the contrary too late.

We did try cutting our teeth in creating a report, and selected an issue that was fairly cut-and-dry and would be relatively easy for the government to deal with, if they wanted. Our first investigation was into the issue of funeral and burial benefits. It was not a particularly contentious or broad issue, but it was a good starting point. The Last Post Fund, an independent organization that administrates the funerals and burials programs on behalf of the Department, basically handed us a list of issues with the programs, their own analysis, and a bunch of recommendations on how to resolve these shortcomings.

I was disappointed to the point of being shocked with the first draft of the report. Not only was it poorly structured and rife with grammatical errors, but it basically just consolidated information provided by the Last Post Fund. There had not been any follow-up research or interviews with departmental staff to confirm or corroborate the information we received from the Last Post Fund, or any analysis to validate their recommendations.

When I inquired about it, Guy told me that it was never intended as an investigative report, it was what he called an "administrative review." Not so in my books. The suggestion of an administrative review never entered into our planning activities, nor had we ever discussed the concept of publishing what Guy called "administrative reviews" as opposed to full-fledged investigations. I sent them back to the drawing board.

Things weren't going to get any better in the Directorate of Investigations & Research any time soon. While they were working on the Funerals and Burials Report, Guy convinced me that we should initiate an omnibus investigation into the excessive red tape that our stakeholders were subjected to. Excessive red tape was a ubiquitous problem that had severe consequences in the veterans' community. Not only does it cause claims to be drawn out literally over many years, but all too often veterans will finally throw in the towel and abandon claims out of sheer frustration with the process.

Whereas I had been shocked by the poor quality of the work on the first draft of the funerals and burials report, I was genuinely alarmed at what was submitted to me, after months of work, as an early draft of the red tape investigation. The report was light on evidence, and riddled with all sorts of hearsay, unsubstantiated claims, and unfounded recommendations. It was verbose and repetitive and once again, it lacked a coherent trail from evidence and analysis to findings and recommendations. Something was really, really wrong, so I just left the draft report to simmer on a back burner.

## Public Consultation

Many veterans work tirelessly and often in virtual anonymity to advocate on behalf of their comrades, and some have made themselves subject-matter experts on the issues. An example is Corporal (retired) Ken Young from the west coast. He had been advocating for decades on behalf of victims of Agent Orange at CFB Gagetown and, despite being largely ignored by VAC and the Government of Canada, he has become sought after internationally for his understanding of how the use of that chemical has poisoned people. I wanted to harness the skills, knowledge, and energy of folks like Ken.

As a result, we pioneered a concept of public consultation in the Canadian public service, enshrining it as the cornerstone of our operations. Other branches of government were dabbling with a form of public consultation, most notably Foreign Affairs at the time, but it was done in a very constipated fashion. I intended to build our entire operation around it and get subject-matter experts like Ken, who were actual agents to the issues, much more involved in our work.

In doing so, we would not treat the evidence we gathered in our reviews the way the legal system does in criminal investigations, keeping it embargoed from disclosure to the counsel for the defence until such time as there are sufficient grounds to press charges. We would, rather, do exactly the opposite. I intended to disseminate all of the data we gathered on issues that were of concern to our stakeholders, via what I called Observation Papers. These accounts were not to contain any conclusions or make any recommendations, but were published on our website as works-in-progress, updated regularly as we learned anything more about an issue.

Observation Papers were to be the nucleus of a full-blown public consultation process. My intention was to develop what I called "fact-finding frameworks" for each issue we were tracking, and simply consolidate the data we collected in these Observation Papers. These were posted to the website with an open invitation to our stakeholders to contribute to our understanding of issues.

Like our experience I will describe with homeless veterans, issues affecting veterans that have not been registered in the public consciousness are all but ignored by the Department. When such issues do emerge, they capture the attention of government mainly so they can manage the political fallout. In the corridors of power, the wellbeing of veterans and their families seems virtually irrelevant relative to damage control and spin. VAC plays into that deceit, hammer and tongs, so any of the statistics they generate are highly suspect to the point of being untrustworthy. By hanging out for public scrutiny all of the major issues we encountered in the community, both substantiated and as yet unconfirmed, I hoped to attract the attention of other stakeholders who might be suffering in silence so that we could make an accurate estimation of the magnitude of the deleterious impact the issues were having.

By way of full disclosure, Observation Papers also invited the Department and the VRAB to participate in the process of discovery. The questions posed in our "Fact Finding Frameworks" and the information discussed in the Observation Papers allowed the government to proactively shape and fill gaps in our understanding of issues. In this way I hoped that our ultimate findings and recommendations would be as well informed and balanced as possible.

## "Comm Ops"

My attitude towards public affairs matured greatly during my very short time in the OVO, assuming a level of importance that was a significant departure from what it had been when I was employed in the CF. While serving in the military, I had considered the media to be an encumbrance; a tedious distraction from the real work but one that you dealt with in a matter of fact, no bullshit fashion. Initially in the OVO I assumed that our main effort was going to be the conduct of formal investigations. Indeed, the key to making substantial improvements in the lives of our most severely disabled and distressed veterans would be the quality of our investigations. That was certainly dependent upon gathering quality information from complainants, the Government of Canada, our stakeholders and the general public, but the investigations were useless unless we were effective in communicating our findings and recommendations to whom they may have concerned. In my opinion, that did not mean just cataloguing them in reports — it meant working the issues with the relevant decision makers, helping them any way we could, in fact, to make sound decisions that would better serve the veterans' community.

I envisioned our main effort to be more than auditing the need for change, but being a catalyst to stimulate change. Public Affairs was but a part of the public consultation process as I saw it, albeit an important one. So I introduced the title "Communication Operations," or Comm Ops, to describe the nexus between classic public affairs and other functions like parliamentary affairs, my town hall meetings, our web presence, and our interventions.

I wanted our Office to be the rallying point for all veterans; the clearinghouse for all issues that impact on the veterans' community. As such, I aspired to make our presence on the web the main communications hub for that community. While it was important for us to have a website to transmit our Ombudsman message to our stakeholders in the electronic brochure fashion characteristic of the government's approach to the web, our communications had to be duplex, which is technical talk for two-way. Our ability to hear from our stakeholders — or more importantly, the ability for our stakeholders to be a part of the solution — was more important a challenge than communicating our position on anything. I envisioned the OVO to be the conduit between the grassroots and the decision makers.

The two-way communications theme was a common thread through everything we did, at all levels including mine. My first occasion to speak with a veteran about his concern happened very early on when an ex-physical training instructor in his eighties called me. He sounded like he was in tears describing to me the various injuries he had endured in the military instructing unarmed combat, high-box gymnastics, confidence courses, etc. He explained how severely crippled he was due to the injuries he'd sustained in the line of duty, but how his applications for care and compensation fell upon the deaf ears of the system. He wasn't asking me to take on the system on his behalf, though. All he was hoping for from me was that I might be the one person he connected with before he died who could relate to his claim and reassure him that he wasn't a liar or a cheat.

I thought that was such a constructive encounter that I used to pick up the phone and speak with veterans out of the blue. Another veteran facing a very serious and complex situation was at his wits' end with the Department and the VRAB. His situation required a great deal of time and effort to review. The Ombudsman does not have the authority to meddle with individual decisions, so whatever the outcome of that review would have been, it would still have been incumbent upon this person to resolve the claim with the government. Understandably, this man was increasingly agitated with what he perceived to be our callousness, our ineffectiveness, or both. He decided to make his beef with us a public one.

I contacted him, knowing full well his personal predicament. I had to tell him that, just like we did in the military when we lacked the capacity to treat all our casualties, in the OVO we had to triage our complaints. It wasn't easy for me, but all I could do was to balance the seriousness and complexity of the individual issues and emergencies we were confronted with in relation to our resources, the probability of timely success, and the impact it would have on the community at large. I assured him I was involved in his case and understood the seriousness of his personal situation. I also confided that in many cases we were dealing with veterans whose conditions were terminal, but I could only do what I could do. I never heard this person complain publicly again about us, but I live with the regret that I couldn't do more for him and others like him.

In another case, I had become personally acquainted with a veteran who was suffering financially. A service-related injury had left this particular veteran unable to work at his civilian place of employment. At the same time, he was a victim of the unfair claw back of benefits from the government's Service Income Security Insurance Plan (SISIP), specifically their Long Term Disability (LTD) plan underwritten by Manulife, and the Department's own Earnings Loss Benefit. I took a personal interest in the case because I thought it might serve as an excellent example of the unnecessary hardships these unfair claw backs impose. I thought it might be a good test case for Communications Operations doctrine and allow us to formulate some approaches to crisis intervention. Our aim was to help this person stabilize his crippling financial predicament and then to deal with the more complex problem of reversing the system's unfair claw back of benefits. I had made sure this veteran understood that redressing the claw backs was going to take time.

Before too long, this disgruntled veteran went to the press and complained that not only were the system's claw backs cheating him, the Veterans Ombudsman had failed to help him out. His accusations were all over the map, and he even went so far as to admonish me for seeking out homeless veterans that the system should have been caring for when they couldn't even afford to offer him the service he believed he was entitled to. I didn't care to defend our position publicly, but at the same time, I wasn't going to take this man's complaining lying down. I phoned him personally and told him that I was fully apprised of his personal finances. We had done what we could to alleviate his immediate financial crisis, and he knew the government would not be eliminating any claw backs any time soon, if they were going to do anything at all.

I could say with a high degree of confidence that if this person had still been in the Canadian Forces they would probably have had the grounds to release him for being an administrative burden, and I reminded him of that. I even went so far as to warn him that he should hope that I would be successful in my efforts to make VAC accommodate the special needs of homeless veterans, because if he didn't straighten out his personal finances he might have to take advantage of those programs. I summed up by warning him to stop abusing my staff and suggesting he would be well advised to stop being so critical of VAC for a problem he had been less than committed to clearing up for himself. We never heard from him again.

Louise happened to witness that particular conversation and was literally dumbfounded to hear such a matter of fact explanation of reality offered to a "client." Such a thing would never have happened in the public service. I think the impartiality and dedication demonstrated by the OVO staff and the fact that I was a veteran myself proved to be beneficial for frank two-way communications and cooperation between our stakeholders and us. I thought that if we could cement the legitimacy of the Veterans Ombudsman as an honest broker within the community that had some sway with government, there might be some potential for the OVO to facilitate Alternative Dispute Resolution in the adjudication of some issues confronting veterans. The tough part, however, was going to be having any sway with government.

## Social Media

I wanted to establish an OVO presence on social media via Facebook, Twitter, and a personal blog, but given the pushback I received on that initiative you would have thought I had asked to take over a multinational mega-corporation. Academics and pundits might tell you that the Government of Canada has been working with the concept of e-government since the turn of the millennium, but I am here to say that by the time I arrived in the OVO the concept hadn't progressed much beyond allowing 24/7 access to e-brochures of government services, placations, platitudes, and outright propaganda.

Purebred public affairs officers gave me all sorts of excuses why it couldn't be done, not the least of which was that the Department would not allow it on their server. I did not relent. When I forced the issue they insisted it had to be done their way. Due to all this internal friction, our initial presence on Facebook was, well, stillborn. We were there, but it was "communications" in the form of yet another e-brochure. It was all we could do at the time to develop the content; we were yet to set up an effective system to engage in actual dialogue with our stakeholders like I wanted. Twitter never really happened in my time, but we had at least planted a flag on social media for all to see.

The only reason we had any success at all in social media was because we had Mary Anne MacEachern, Ricardo Angel, and Heidi Lund in Charlottetown who were creative self-starters. Both Mary Anne and Ricardo were new to the federal public service and Heidi was seconded from the Department. Under Q's innovative mentorship, they bought a couple of Mac computers and rented an Internet connection from local broadband cable providers in Ottawa and Charlottetown. They put us on the map online, and I daresay set a trend for the rest of the public service.

## Resistance To My Blog

And then there was my blog. As if all my other bright ideas weren't hard enough to force upon a stagnant, unresponsive, and dysfunctional system, this was damn near impossible. First of all, it was unheard of in the public service that an executive would produce copy for a personal blog. Moreover, the processes to have amendments made to a web page in the Department were so tedious it would be difficult — nearly impossible — for me to publish entries in real enough time to make them relevant.

Unlike Facebook and Twitter, where I did not have the time to oversee their implementation, the blog was mine and I just did it. I think I am safe in saying that it very quickly became a hit amongst our stakeholders. VAC and other departments have since followed our lead, but I daresay that their PR-driven, clinical approach was readily apparent and not nearly as well received as my scrawls with a grease pencil.

There was risk, admittedly, but I felt that any hazard from something stupid that I might have said was offset by the utility of honest, open communication with our stakeholders, and my belief that my commitment to full and open communications and a genuine, deeply rooted desire to serve the common good would mitigate any risk. I always circulated my drafts to my key trusted staff for comments that I would carefully consider.

More often than not, I pretty well went with my own words. I was always very cautious not to violate personal privacy, commercial confidentiality, or information security and I avoided assigning blame in the cases I discussed. I tried to restrict comment to fact reporting. That said, I knew that I would still be making some people very uneasy.

Many of my blog entries were contentious, but I think only one caused some real blowback. That entry was entitled "It's Just Dumb," and in it I was critical of some of the ridiculous decisions we had been witnessing on dental and medical claims. It goes without saying that I riled the medical and dental advisors to VAC. Louise told me one morning that the dentist that VAC had on contract to advise them on dental issues was really pissed off and threatening a harassment complaint or court action. That was very disconcerting.

I had many thorough reads of that particular entry, and while it certainly could have been interpreted as a reflection on the people involved in the decision making, my words were very clearly focused on the impact these decisions were having on our stakeholders. I therefore asked Louise to invite the person I had insulted to come and meet with me. My senior staff expressed all sorts of concern. We didn't yet have a full-time lawyer on our staff to be present at the meeting, but I didn't want any part of that. I just wanted to explain to the offended party that I really hadn't intended to cause any harm by my blog post. I thought if I couldn't remedy his angst I would not hesitate to issue a full apology.

So arrangements were made for me to meet with one pissed-off Maritimer dentist, Dr. Brian Barrett. I let him speak first, as if I had a choice in the matter. He was obviously proud of the work he did for veterans. He had friends and family who served and did not take his responsibility lightly. When I asked him to explain how decisions were made, he offered me an unrepentant but matter-of-fact description of the reality in his workplace. What I saw, in turn, was an excessive workload, ridiculous constraints on his professional judgement, and unreasonable policies that prevented him from doing what he felt needed to be done.

I told him as much. Together we revisited my blog to see if my words referred to the complaints of stakeholders regarding their dental claims or him personally. Clearly it was the former, but I heartily acknowledged that if I had known there was only one person advising VAC on dental issues I might have worded my post differently. I hastened to add that the post had attracted considerable comment, so it was working as I had intended. I told Dr. Barrett that in the fullness of time I hoped to make his working conditions more conducive to serving the veterans the way he would have liked.

Dr. Barrett left our office satisfied that my criticisms were not aimed at him or his work, but that I was critical of the system. He also arranged for me to meet with VAC's medical advisory team, which I discovered was shockingly small considering how central their mandate was to the *raison d'être* of the Department. It was clear to me that they faced the same limitations and obstructions that Dr. Barrett endured on the dental side. I managed to avert any crisis of a personal nature, but the confrontation gave me much better insight into an even more serious crisis; the one within VAC.

As I expected, the blog did make people uneasy, but it wasn't the doctors in the Department whom I was hoping to draw out in the open with my posts. Bureaucrats are too clever to fall for that. Despite the controversy, I think our stakeholders appreciated my "tell it like it is" approach, and such open and candid communications actually enhanced the credibility of our Office.

## Going Outside

I was having such bad luck with the senior public affairs people I hired from the public service that I decided I had to cut my losses ASAP. I approached a lady I had worked with at the Pearson Peacekeeping Centre whose creativity, drive, and compassion had really impressed me.

Lee-Anne Peluk arrived at the office with a basketful of new concept proposals, one of which was the suggestion that we institute a "Story Bank." This bank would be a public record of complaints that came to the OVO that we had validated, and may or may not have been in the process of investigating to arrive at formal findings of our own. This Story Bank was to be available to anybody — our stakeholders, journalists or any concerned citizens — who might have a story to tell about the problems our veterans and their families were confronted with.

That was very much the kind of tool I was hoping to develop for my public consultation approach to ombudsmanry, so I had to wonder why it had been too much to ask the public affairs people before Lee-Anne came on to the scene to come up with them. Much of what I had hoped to achieve in terms of the empathetic, proactive culture was already taking shape; the trick was going to be to create an effective Communications Operations interface to inform and be informed by stakeholders, decision makers, and a broader audience at large. One thing that was becoming abundantly clear to me was that my Comm Ops cell served too important of a function to be headed by a public servant with a public affairs background.

## Outsourcing Public Affairs Expertise

Lee-Anne moved on, but my experience with her in communications was so productive that we focused on building our Comm Ops capacity from outside the public service. One of our first contractors was Brad Mann, who had enough experience as a public servant to understand the system, but it was his depth of experiences in other forums that proved to be hugely advantageous. He helped us identify other people for our Comm Ops cell who had the right skill sets, temperament, and work ethic to build our capacity to learn and influence. His heart was also in it because he had a son who had served in Afghanistan. He knew what was at stake.

We built our presence on social media, increased the tempo of my town hall meetings and the effectiveness of our data collection from those events, created a parliamentary affairs function, enhanced my interface with our advisory committee, and integrated the processes of Early Intervention and Research and Investigation to share information and produce and track communications deliverables suitable for the intended audiences. Finally we were beginning to pick up momentum, everywhere except with our Directorate of Investigation & Research.

## The Cavalry Arrives

After my first deputy ombudsman I vowed that if it was going to be too much of a distraction I did not want to waste any more energy searching for a replacement. I was just about to roll up my shirtsleeves and assume a more hands-on approach internally with the day-to-day supervision of my directors, but Louise knew of a VAC employee who she thought was well qualified to be my deputy and might be interested in the job. Donna MacDonald ended up agreeing to take on a six-month secondment to the Office to see if it was a good fit. Because we were so new, most of what I could explain to her about what we did was still conceptual. It was an incredible challenge for her.

Donna quickly gripped the day-to-day operations. Her very presence in the OVO restored the working relationship with the Department that her predecessor had poisoned. Donna was highly competent and a self-starter who, refreshingly, could get things done without detailed instruction from me. In short order she introduced some very efficient processes and protocols. At the same time, she had considerable difficulty getting any quality work out of the Director of Investigations & Research. Donna's assessment of the Red-Tape Report was every bit as critical as mine.

Sadly, Donna left the OVO when her six-month deployment expired to pursue greater opportunities in the Department. By this point I had a little over a year left in my mandate. Time was of the essence and I did not want to fiddle around with the public service hiring practices. I therefore promoted Louise to Acting Deputy, and Louise arranged to get another warrior from the Department to fill in behind her.

Colleen Soltermann came to us with a wealth of policy experience in VAC. As I would expect of any loyal warrior, she often challenged me in defence of the Department and, at times, she was even critical of the OVO. Through it all, though, I could readily see that she was a good operator and I hugely appreciated her forthrightness. Together, Louise and Colleen could have run the OVO exactly the way I wanted without me, which is exactly how it should be. That freed me up to spend my time out of the office in the trenches with our stakeholders.

Another recruit we benefitted from so much, although rather late in my term, was Paulette McNally. Paulette came to us to function as what I would call our operations officer, a position that Donna had identified as lacking in our organization. What a godsend. Paulette was every bit as committed and knowledgeable about all things veterans as Louise, Donna, and Colleen, and she was also a wizard with work breakdown structures and process flow.

Paulette was a relentless taskmaster, and I mean that in a good way. Her attention to detail and deadlines was just what our organization needed. She took on a myriad of projects but was most instrumental in coordinating the activities of our front line operations — Early Intervention, Investigations & Research, and Comm Ops.

We also recruited another white knight from the Department, Wilma Hanscombe, to sort out our support services from the ground up. With over twenty years' experience, Wilma was no stranger to the departmental maze and with her professional contacts with their staff she was able to effect some timely and significant improvements. A loyal and hardworking VAC employee, Wilma too found the look at the Department from the outside to be enlightening. All this to say, I was beginning to see how a tour with the OVO could have become a valuable contribution to the professional development of potential senior managers in VAC.

## OVO Committees

The Order in Council "permitted" me to form an Advisory Committee, and the project team had drafted up some terms of reference and a proposed composition of the committee based on the approach of the CF/DND Ombudsman. The CF/DND Ombudsman's Advisory Committee was comprised of a group of subject-matter experts. The project team had suggested that, in a similar fashion, members of the OVO Advisory Committee should be also be subject-matter experts, but in the context of veterans those people were already members of the Department's various advisory and stakeholder groups.

Why would I want to constitute the same or similar group to those that were already contributing to the formulation of the policies that I had under review? I regularly sought all sorts of advice from those people, the likes of famed veterans advocate and self-styled ombudsman Clifford Chadderton (founder of War Amps and the National Council of Veterans Associations), Senator Roméo Dallaire, Colonel (retired) Don Ethell, Dr. Norah Keating, Dr. Muriel Westmorland, and even the famed historian and colourful commentator on just about everything — J.L. (Jack) Granatstein. The OVO had access to all the "beautiful minds" and respected Canadians we needed, when and where we needed them. Without exception, they were very gracious in providing their frank and unfettered advice to my team and me.

In keeping with my quest for consultation with my stakeholders, I sought to make the advisory committee more akin to focus groups in marketing rather than a gathering of coaches, mentors, and/or institutional icons. I was interested in soliciting opinions and advice from people who represented the various demographics in the actual veterans' community, in order to obtain feedback on how the work we were doing in the OVO might be received by our stakeholders.

I was fortunate indeed to secure as the chairperson for my first advisory committee Admiral (retired) Larry Murray. I remembered Admiral Murray from the Somalia inquiry, when he was the only person on the list of CF senior management appearing before the commission who openly challenged some of the ridiculous statements the commissioners were saying *vis-à-vis* the state of the Canadian Forces. I had a great deal of respect for him, and his chairmanship brought a lot of credibility to the OVO.

After leaving DND, Admiral Murray had been the DM for Veterans Affairs, among other public service jobs, so he knew the veterans' community very well. He helped me select the members of the first advisory committee, and he was inclusive almost to a fault. To me, a large committee was not a drawback at all, though, because I was not seeking a consensus. On the contrary, in fact, I wanted to hear the cold, hard truth from all parties to enhance the quality of the decisions I made. Through the committee I also hoped to enhance my *fingerspitzengefühl*, or intuitive grasp, of the situation I was facing.

Members of the committee had a hard time figuring out exactly what their role was. They wanted to work. They wanted me to present them with issues to analyze and then give me advice on possible solutions. While we may have evolved into that in the longer term, at the outset I didn't need that. That was the job of the early intervention analysts and investigators. I wanted to use my advisory committee as a sounding board, as grass roots veterans whom I could bounce our findings off to ensure that we were in touch with our stakeholders.

Of course, I would also have them consider my wild assed ideas, such as public consultation and Comm Ops, before investing in them too heavily. I would gauge their response in order to extrapolate the impact my initiatives might have on the community at large. Admittedly the mechanics of the solicitation of advice from the committee was a work in progress, but the very act of being inclusive of the veterans' community on the advisory committee was achieving my aim.

I wrote a little pamphlet trying to explain my approach, summing the whole thing up by identifying a phrase that I wanted them to say: "Pat, if I personally were the Ombudsman I would/wouldn't do that!" It took a while for it to register with them, if it ever did, but I often received phone calls and emails from a few of the members about issues that concerned them.

Some of them even complained about what we were doing in the OVO, which demonstrated to me that my approach to the advisory committee would be a worthwhile investment. I knew them to be knowledgeable and passionate about veterans' issues, and I got to know them well enough to recognize their limitations. If one of them didn't like something about the way I was doing business enough to talk candidly with me on or off-line, then it was something well worth my time to discuss with them and actually consider.

## Strategic Council

While I was creating the OVO Charter and the Comm Ops strategy I envisioned what I called our "Strategic Council," a board of directors kind of organization, comprised of very influential people in their own right. I thought it might even open some doors and minds in the corridors of power that would enable us to redress some of the more serious issues. This council was not a huge priority for me, but when I bumped into influential Canadians whom I respected and admired, I would introduce myself and ask if they might be willing to assist in such a capacity. I was very gratified by the extremely supportive and empathetic responses I received from some very noteworthy Canadians who need not be identified. The concept for the composition of my strategic council would change drastically, however, before it was finally stood up.

Several of the major advocacy groups whom the Department referred to as their stakeholders were put out that I didn't want them on my advisory committee. They acted almost as if it was their vested right. On one occasion I was speaking with a good friend from one such group about some policy developments that the Minister had shared with the Department and *their* stakeholders, but neglected to advise our Office of. I was not upset because I recognized our relationships were still in their infancy. This person made it quite clear that VAC's stakeholder groups were very much up to date and in on the process, which he used as justification for having them represented on my advisory committee. Somehow I saw it from a completely different perspective. If there is even a perception that the advocacy groups may have played any part in policy development, they were the very last people I wanted to be hard wired to *vis-à-vis* obtaining advice.

That said, I didn't want to offend any of the advocates. On the contrary, from my first day in office I was a strong proponent of unity within the veterans' community, and went out of my way to prevent the introduction of a Veterans Ombudsman from fragmenting that community any more than it already was. I maintained open and frank communications with all of the agencies, and was very quick to oblige when asked to attend an event or make an address as the Ombudsman. I met privately with the heads of these groups as often as I could, and genuinely valued any and all of the sage advice and, at times, constructive criticisms they offered me. In order to avoid alienating them, I eventually decided to modify my plans for the membership on our strategic council from power brokers and influential Canadians to advocacy groups and advocates.

## Ombudsman's Commendation

An Ombudsman's Commendation was in the project team's plan, and their draft terms of reference described who would be eligible for such a commendation to be awarded annually by the Veterans Ombudsman. Something about their analysis bugged me, so I took my time going ahead with the OVO Commendation. It took me about two years to finally realize what it was. The selection criteria that that the project team had proposed for the Veterans Ombudsman's Commendation were basically the same as those for the Minister's Commendation. The last thing I wanted to do as the Veterans Ombudsman was acknowledge the same efforts that the Minister's office did.

There were all sorts of champions in the veterans' community who were working very hard for veterans, hoping that one day the Minister would embrace and support their efforts. I knew that many such initiatives could have helped a lot of people in the veterans' community, but in reality didn't have much chance at all of succeeding. I felt these were the people who deserved special acknowledgement, people who persevered in the face of daunting odds, who expended huge amounts of personal toil to try and improve the lives and well-being of our veterans and their families, but for whatever reason might not ever receive any acknowledgement from the Government of Canada. I decided I would focus my commendations on these hapless heroes, although eligibility for the Minister's Commendation would not eliminate them from consideration for ours.

Cliff Chadderton was to become the recipient of the first Veterans Ombudsman Commendation even though he had already received the Order of Canada and the Minister's Commendation for his extraordinary contribution to the well-being of veterans and their families. Admittedly, that contradicted my wish to avoid duplication with this award, but Cliff's contribution to the veterans community is so compelling that I too just had to acknowledge his lifelong achievements. Cliff made no compromises when it came to advocating for veterans, which I admired greatly. I hoped to present our commendation to him personally and to seek his approval to name our commendation after him, but I left office before I could follow through with that initiative. Cliff was a resident of the Pearly Rideau Hospital by that time, so we met privately with him to make the presentation.

We put together a bit of an award ceremony for the first cadre of recipients for the Veterans Ombudsman Commendation. They included: Dennis Manuge, the lead plaintiff in the Service Income Security Insurance Plan class-action suit against the government; Harold Leduc, a long-time stalwart advocate, principal of the Canadian Peacekeeping Veterans Association and a member of the Veterans Review and Appeals Board, the nefarious practices of which he would later expose to the public; John Labelle, a long-time advocate for a more generous superannuation for veterans of the CF and RCMP; and Peter Stoffer, the New Democratic Party's Veterans Affairs Critic and an extraordinarily committed and genuine champion for Canada's veterans.

My advisory committee played an active role in recommending people for our commendation, and at times the varying opinions almost caused my committee to disintegrate. One such debate erupted over the nomination of Sean Bruyea, a retired captain who is a high profile advocate in the veterans' community and, I would submit, has as many detractors as he had fans. Several of his fans were on the committee, and they not only nominated him for the OVO Commendation, they argued vehemently on his behalf. Bruyea's nomination was well within the broad criteria we had established for the award, but some of my advisors were dead set against it. Personally, I didn't have the time of day for Bruyea because on several occasions he had tried to discredit me and the OVO. In best conscience, however, I sought the advice of my committee. Once again, I wasn't seeking a consensus. In the end, the choice would be mine alone and I would suffer the consequences should it come to that.

After a somewhat heated meeting on the subject, several very upset committee members individually confronted me in private to reaffirm their disquietude with Bruyea being considered for the commendation. They were of such conviction that they threatened to resign from the committee. Now, nobody is indispensable in any capacity and I do not cater to threats, but this kind of feedback was exactly what I hoped to receive from my advisory committee. If this nomination was so divisive within the confines of my committee, and notwithstanding my personal opinion of this person, which I felt should have little bearing on how the OVO treated him, I could well imagine the distress it could cause in the veterans' community at large if Bruyea were to receive the Veterans Ombudsman Commendation. It was therefore easy for me to make a decision, and I advised my committee members before they went home.

For the most part that was the end of the discussion. I was prepared to live by my decision and most committee members were too — except one. This member was so wed to her association with Bruyea that prior to our next meeting, which was ultimately going to be my last, she attempted to organize some kind of boycott or protest. As soon as I got wind of it I made it clear to this woman that she was not welcome on the committee anymore.

She had been recruited with the full knowledge that the committee carried no executive authority, I was not seeking a consensus on any issue within the committee, and I wasn't going to take any advice I did not agree with. My decisions were my own, and if there was any chance my decision to exclude Bruyea was going to discredit the Office then I would hold myself accountable to our stakeholders and nobody else. The issue died, and I actually received positive feedback from some other committee members who respected my rationale and decisiveness. This kind of "market testing" was exactly what I hoped to achieve with my advisory committee.

CHAPTER 4:

# Rude Awakening

It did not take long for me to start seeing how truly rotten our government actually is. Interestingly, the earliest and most blatant demonstration of the lack of sincerity or sense of service towards our veterans that permeates the Government of Canada took place at the very, very top, in the office of the Minister of Veterans Affairs.

## First Annual Report

One of the requirements the Order in Council placed on the Office was to produce an annual report. I was appointed in November, so I naturally assumed that my first annual report would be due to government the following November. I was not at all confident in the ability of my deputy to produce a document that I would put my name to, so rather than develop a writing plan for him, I decided to create the first draft myself. In keeping with my commitment to gain and maintain the trust and confidence of my stakeholders, I decided to write it as if it were an introduction for them to their Office of the Veterans Ombudsman.

As it started to take shape in draft form, I decided that I would call it "Securing the Start Line." The title came from a SOP ground forces practice immediately prior to launching a ground attack. A start line is defined as the leading edge of a safe area located as close to an enemy position as possible where assaulting troops form up immediately prior to commencing a coordinated attack. All timings for supporting fires and ground manoeuvre are based on when the lead elements will first cross the start line. For all intents and purposes, our activities up to the time of writing this first report were in preparation for an attack, an attack on the Government of Canada's mistreatment of our veterans and their families. I thought it was a fitting metaphor for where we were in standing up of the Office, and one that military veterans would relate to.

The first draft described my proposed structure, intended operating procedures, and Q's environmental scan, a catalogue of the frustrations and issues that the veterans' community was confronted with. This environmental scan, as I called it, was intended to be as exhaustive a list as we could marshal, but with no claims or suggestions regarding the validity of the issues as legitimate complaints. In fact, we made that very clear in a disclaimer that was prominently displayed in the scan. The document was intended to allow us to establish work priorities, to conduct cursory investigations to determine legitimacy, to triage the seriousness of the various issues, and importantly, to assign timelines and apportion resources for OVO operations. I envisioned the environmental scan as a living document, one that we would update and modify as we developed better clarity for the climate and complexity of the veterans' community.

Out of professional courtesy to the Minister, we provided Thompson's chief of staff an advance copy and arranged a meeting to discuss it with him. Even though I had allowed enough time for him to have thoroughly considered it in advance of our meeting, it was clear to me that he had not looked at the document by the time I was in his office to discuss it with him. He flipped from page to page, taking only a cursory look at the information, and with a sweeping stroke of a red pen he rejected the majority of the content of the document out of hand.

When it came to the environmental scan, he became incredulous. He challenged the legitimacy of some of the issues, defended the government's perception of others, and outright dismissed many because they were government policy and I had no business challenging them. During the course of the meeting I reminded him several times of my intent for the document and its intended audience, and when it came to the environmental scan I repeatedly reiterated the document's role as a compendium of the issues, legitimate and perceived but as yet not reviewed by the OVO, which gripped the veterans' community — nothing more, nothing less. None of that registered with the COS, and he was adamant that the document was not acceptable to the government.

I really resented the way he treated me, like a junior officer, discarding my work so handily and admonishing me in the process. I know many people from my past reading this would find it difficult to believe that I sat there and took it. Nobody should be subjected to such treatment; it revealed a very unprofessional lack of tact, but I was actually receptive to the feedback. At the conclusion of that meeting I conceded that I had written our annual report for the wrong audience and should have focused on other information that would have been of greater interest to parliamentarians.

I agreed to rewrite the document that I would submit to the Minister as an annual report. At the same time I asserted that "Securing the Start Line" would still be published the way I wrote it, but it would be an OVO-initiated report as my mandate permitted me to create, rather than my official annual report. We agreed that my first annual report, a different one, would be allowed to slide from November of 2008 to the summer of 2009 in order to bring it into line with the fiscal year. That would enable us to report on finances more accurately. In retrospect I should have gotten that agreement in writing, because Minister Thompson would later criticize me publicly for having failed to submit my first annual report on time.

## First Formal Meeting with The Minister

I had little if any interaction with the Minister during my first year in the job. I interpreted this hands-off approach as the Minister's commitment to the independence of our Office, and really appreciated the freedom to manoeuvre. By February 2009 I thought I had a good feel for where we as an Office were going and felt it was time for me to update the Minister in person. I knew he was very busy, so in the best tradition of a conscientious and loyal staff officer I wanted to make sure I didn't waste his time.

The Minister was very cordial when Louise and I met him and his COS in their conference room. I had prepared a very short, four-slide PowerPoint presentation — three actually, because the first one was a title page — very simple slides that I also handed to the Minister in hard copy so he could make notes. The last slide was entitled "Minister's Guidance to the Veterans Ombudsman," with three bullets describing what I was hoping to get from the Minister. That was the key slide for me:

- The first bullet was to seek clarification as to how he perceived the working relationship that I would have with him personally.

- The second bullet was a request for the Minister to tell me if he had any specific expectations of, or tasks for, the OVO.

- The third and last bullet sought some direction on restrictions; those things that he specifically did not want me to do.

As a professional courtesy I had sent a draft of these slides informally to his COS so they could consider them prior to our discussion, like I did with "Securing the Start Line." Beforehand, I had rehearsed my very simple and short speaking points many, many times to come across a professionally as possible. This was my first formal encounter with the Minister and I had to do well. As soon we arrived at the Minister's office, I handed out the slide decks and prepared my nifty little extendable pointer to help me through the presentation. I was all set.

The Minister was reassuringly congenial. We made small talk, during which time he reflected a little about his journey to that point in politics. He mused how Parliament is, in point of fact, the only prison in Canada where the inmates (i.e. the government of the day) were free to make the rules. That statement kind of creeped me out. Feeling uncomfortable I tried to steer the meeting away from the small talk by delving directly into my presentation. In my introduction I told the Minister what the purpose of my brief was, as I perceived it, which was to clarify for him the service that I envisioned providing to the veterans' community. I added that what I hoped to take back from the meeting was an understanding of the relationship that the Minister envisioned the OVO having with his office, which was summarized by three bullet points on the fourth and final slide. I then advised him that we were at about eighty percent of our staffing level, adding that the support services being provided to us by the

Department were rough. I summarized our overall operational relationship with the Department as guarded but functional.

Next I highlighted very, very briefly, what we had learned about the veterans' community. The last thing that I described for him before getting into an explanation of our work flow and processes was my definition of independence. The exact turn of phrase I used in that briefing was "decision-making ability without undue influence or constraints." So far, so good.

Then I intended to show the Minister a couple of flow charts. The first described the internal processes that we had developed — pretty cut and dried. The second was a more philosophical operational model that depicted the interface that I intended to develop between the OVO and the veterans' community, the Minister, his Department and the Veterans Review and Appeals Board. I say "philosophical" because I was seeking the blessing of the Minister to implement it, or so I thought.

Just as I flipped to the first slide with a flow chart, Minster Thompson interrupted me. He said he wasn't interested in flow charts and processes and all that administrative mumbo-jumbo, or words to that effect. He made it very clear that he didn't really care what I did or how I did it. He really just blew us off. I couldn't believe it — he clearly was not interested. Instead of returning to my last slide that captured the takeaways I was hoping to receive from him, I just concluded my presentation prematurely, and Thompson had no objection.

Louise was shocked by his *laissez-faire* attitude, and dare I say, a tad disheartened. I tried to reassure her, telling her that while I was surprised by Thompson's lack of engagement, I was encouraged at the same time. One of my personal operating principles, which I had held for a long time, is that a lack of direction is an opportunity not a constraint. To me, this meant it was full steam ahead for us. After all, everybody in senior management — the Minister and his staff included — had expressed to us in the staunchest of terms their sincerest commitment to do right by the veterans. With that as a common bond, I was sure that we were on the right track.

## Victims

One of the first complaints that came across my desk for my personal consideration showed me how inflexible the Minister's office was going to be. The complaint was from one Mr. McLeod, who had served as a RCAF flight instructor with the British Commonwealth Air Training Plan (BCATP) in Canada. McLeod had felt he had been discriminated against because he had not served in Europe, but he had long since accepted that fate. His complaint was that he was a victim, as he perceived it, of another form of discrimination.

Like Mr. Babcock, Mr. McLeod had been fully committed to the cause of winning the war at any cost, but unfortunately, the enemy surrendered too soon. Despite Mr. McLeod having volunteered for service and served where he was ordered, victory was declared and he was released, as it turned out, a day or two short of the time required for a veteran to have qualified for a medal for having served in the Second World War.

On a Monday morning very early in my incumbency I received confirmation from Q that the period of eligibility that Mr. McLeod, and probably others, was subjected to — one year, I think it was — had been arrived at arbitrarily and instituted into law by way of a regulation. The regulation was subject to review by the Governor in Council, a mythical reference to the Governor General that really means a minister can present a regulation to Cabinet to have it amended. In short, we felt Thompson could have accommodated this veteran if he wanted to.

To me, it was simply a matter of compassion, doing the right thing for a loyal and proud citizen of Canada in his golden years. With the passage of time it was possible to see the situation more clearly and recognize the magnitude of the contribution BCATP personnel made to the war effort. We didn't expect many veterans of WWII had been caught in a similar predicament, and fewer yet would still be alive. Regardless of how few or how many vets might have been affected by modifying the period of eligibility, such an act of compassion would not have changed the services and benefits that the Government of Canada was providing them. As a kind gesture from a grateful nation that might grant some peace to some veterans before they passed on from this world, I didn't think we would be setting a precedent that could have been exploited by other less deserving veterans.

I pitched the idea to Jacques Dubé, the Minister's chief of staff. The COS had the Minister's ear and understood his intent on most if not all issues, so I would not have to impose directly on the Minister's precious time. Jacques advised me that Minister Thompson had no intention of relaxing the period of service that had been decided upon for eligibility for the medal. I wanted to break the bad news to Mr. McLeod myself. Sadly, by the time we tried getting back to him, he had died. He went through his entire adult life feeling that his nation was not appreciative of the contribution he had made to the war effort. I was greatly saddened by his passing, and disappointed that the Office of the Minister had demonstrated such an unwillingness to be flexible on this issue. Such dispensation would have been cost-neutral and inconsequential to the system, but of massive significance to the individual veterans involved.

Before too long it seemed like everywhere I turned, people were lined up to unload on me their tales of woe about the Department and the VRAB. Of course there were the high profile cases of wounded Afghanistan veterans who captured the attention of mainstream Canadians: in no particular order, the likes of Master Corporal Jody Mitic, Master Corporal Paul Hughes, Captain Trevor Greene, Major Mark Campbell, and Corporal Billy Kerr. These folks were very much on the consciences of concerned Canadians because the terrible wounds they received in the line of duty in Afghanistan were a matter of public record. Their public notoriety is probably why, to my knowledge, none of these veterans approached our office with a complaint while I was the Ombudsman. VAC cares for people in whom the public takes an interest. I tracked their cases closely in the open media, but what wore on my soul were the dozens of desperate veterans who were, unfortunately, not on the public's radar screen.

I think that, for a long time, the magnitude of the harm and hardship that the families of disabled veterans have to contend with was being lost in the media's depiction of these tragic heroes, but it certainly was not lost on me. Tracy Kerr, the wife of Corporal (retired) Billy Kerr who is a triple amputee victim of Canada's military misadventure in Afghanistan, and her family participated in a short documentary posted on YouTube that gives us privileged insight into their family's nightmare. Entitled *A Soldier's Family*,[3] it describes the stress they endured during and after Corporal Billy's tour in Afghanistan. The terrible toll this kind of tragedy exacts on a family is burned into the soul of the viewer when Tracey's mother says: "Sometimes, I shouldn't say this, sometimes...why didn't he just pass away? We'd have been better off if he had just passed away."

In this short video viewers witness, firsthand, how the system fails to offer veterans who have become sick and disabled in the line of duty, and their families, a level of care and service that is commensurate with the sacrifices they make. I saw this kind of despair in families time and time again, and I have no doubt it happens much more often than I would have been privy to. Thanks go out to Tracy and Billy Kerr and their family for sharing their story with us. That they threw their hearts and souls out on their sleeves to document this piece of history is testament to their strength and courage.

The system will grudgingly provide whatever can be seen by the public to satisfy the obligations accepted by the people of Canada towards their veterans, but that is where it ends. Major Mark Campbell had worked for me in Afghanistan, and on a subsequent tour of duty lost both his legs to a command-detonated IED. As an officer, and a particularly tenacious one at that, he managed to hold the system accountable to provide him and his family with wheelchair accessible lodgings while he was still serving. However, others were not as lucky. Corporal Billy Kerr, for example, had to rely on charities and a local fundraiser by the City of Sudbury and surrounding area.

On another occasion, the spouse of a veteran who became a quadriplegic from an accident, in this case not in Afghanistan, confided in me about their fight for wheelchair accessibility. Apparently it was recommended by various subject-matter experts that, due to the nature of their family home, retrofitting was not practical. It was recommended that a new wheelchair accessible living area should be attached to the existing

---

3   Bfrburfordfilms, *A Soldier's Family*. YouTube video, posted October 25, 2012, https://www.youtube.com/watch?v=a8Jai_19N3U.

family home. The spouse told me that the Treasury Board ultimately rejected the application for this, citing that the additional square footage associated with such an annex would constitute a net increase in the veteran's standard of living, which was not permitted by the legislation.

What politicians say they are giving to veterans in need and what those veterans actually get are often two different things. The variance is the result of senior bureaucrats either responding to ministerial direction or taking it upon themselves to preserve the public purse. Some of the issues the bureaucracy will stick a claimant for are amazingly petty. One veteran suffered severe mobility problems and was wheelchair-bound, although he could walk very short distances with the aid of crutches. One time, while transferring from his chair to a bed he took a terrible fall. His head slammed into the floor with such force that his glasses flew off his head and broke. The Department refused to pay for the replacement glasses because he was pensioned for mobility not eyesight issues. Really? Had he enjoyed the full use of both his legs it is unlikely he would have broken his glasses in the first place.

That kind of deny bias and petty stinginess was evident everywhere, forcing vets to challenge the system several times just to obtain things such as simple hearing aids, or dental service to vets who grind their teeth due to PTSD. It didn't take much to convince VAC staffers of the proximate relationship of these symptoms to their service-based causes. Of course they could have stood their ground, but that most certainly goes against the liberal interpretation clause that has been used repeatedly in legislation for veterans, which I discuss later. These kinds of complaints were the mainstay of our office's early intervention analysts, and business for our EIAs was good.

And then there was the case of Harold Leduc. Harold served twenty-two years in the military, was diagnosed with PTSD, and is renowned as a knowledgeable and committed advocate for veterans. Founder and past national president for the Canadian Peacekeeping Veterans Association, Harold participated in various advisory capacities for Veterans Affairs and was subsequently employed on the Veterans Review and Appeals Board. He ran afoul of the Department when he alleged they had misrepresented advice that was proffered by subject-matter experts and feedback solicited from the veterans' community in the creation of the severely flawed New Veterans Charter. The Department also violated Harold's privacy by accessing his personal medical file many times for no apparent reason.

While employed on the Veterans Review and Appeals Board, Harold was harassed by other members of the Board, accusing him of being biased towards veterans. Members of the VRAB leaked private information about his post-traumatic stress disorder diagnosis, allegedly to discredit his work with the Board. In an unprecedented move, the RCMP conducted an investigation into the matter and the Human Rights Commission ultimately ordered the Board to pay Mr. Leduc $4,000, including legal costs, for the harassment he'd suffered. Leduc complained that the harassment did not cease thereafter...and then he was not renewed as a member of the Board.

For every high profile case that makes it into the news, there are dozens — if not hundreds, I can't be sure — of additional casualties that the families should not bear the sole responsibility to care for but the system ignores because the public has not taken notice. One such case that had a particular impact on me was that of Major (retired) Pat Patterson. This case serves to illustrate how out of touch and unprogressive the Department is.

Pat had impressed me when I was a young officer cadet in training and he was a captain at infantry school in Gagetown, New Brunswick. Captain Patterson was casual to the extreme — shaggy hair, dirty cap badge and boots, baggy combat clothing — but he knew his stuff and was very operationally focussed. Pat was a full generation ahead of me in the Regiment, so I kind of lost track of him. He had been seconded to the UN as a Military Observer and got hooked on that kind of work. His exploits were kind of legendary amongst those who knew him, consisting of several tours where he witnessed some of the most terrible tragedies of humankind.

As Veterans Ombudsman I finally caught up with Pat in Halifax. He was curled up in a foetal position on a bed in a long-term care facility, completely debilitated by dementia. I couldn't even recognize him. He looked old, well beyond his fifty-eight years, completely emaciated and feeble, eyes red and vacant. It was gut wrenchingly hard to witness when I approached the bed. I tried talking with him in a positive fashion, but he was unresponsive. Not knowing what else I could do, I started singing our three-part regimental march song, "Has Anyone Seen the Colonel/Long Way to Tipperary/Mademoiselle From Armentières." I can't remember which of the three resonated with him, but at one point a faint, faint, smile came to his face, an eyelid twitched, he clenched a fist slightly and let out what I perceived to be an ever so slight grunt. His wife, who had accompanied me on my visit, interpreted it for me. She told me Pat had said, "Lady Patricia." I must admit, the tears welled in my eyes.

The most tragic part of this story is that the responsibility to care for Pat Patterson all fell on his family. I probably would never have heard of this case, were it not for the engagement of a saintly doctor in the Halifax region who has dedicated her life to caring for veterans; Doctor Heather MacKinnon, retired navy lieutenant commander. Here I was, in a care facility with one of my early role models, Pat Patterson, a veteran diagnosed with severe PTSD who was a complete invalid as a relatively young man due to dementia, and VAC was nowhere to be seen.

As a layman ombudsman, I had heard speculation that severe PTSD could lead to early onset dementia, so I wondered how many similar cases might be languishing in institutions across our land. I asked the Department what they knew about early-onset dementia due to service in the CF, and you can well imagine what their response was. I decided to probe a little deeper to see if VAC was proactive on any issues that might affect the contemporary veterans, whom they seemed so intent on abandoning. I asked what they knew about another issue of great concern in the veterans' community: traumatic brain injury (TBI). They hadn't even heard of the condition. Sometime after I inquired, the Department sent me a paper about "mild TBIs" that was, in essence, dismissive of any long-term implications. The paper talked about concussions, not the trauma that is inflicted on the brains of the troops inside an armoured vehicle when a thousand pounds of high explosives is detonated right outside it. With all the subsequent controversy regarding head trauma in sports, which has garnered so much attention recently, I suspect that paper has experienced little enduring credibility.

The Department has also been negligent, in my opinion, for failing to embrace the utility of service animals in the treatment of stress casualties. Shortly after we stepped up our operational tempo, in January of 2010 I held a town hall meeting in Orleans. This was where I was introduced to service dogs, up close and personal. This meeting was particularly boisterous because veterans had come out *en masse* to berate me for the New Veterans Charter, for reasons that will become clear later in this book. Throughout the three or four-hour dialogue, I was aware that there were three people at the back of the room accompanied by as many German Shepherd dogs. After the open forum, this group approached me privately.

One of the dogs was accompanying a woman who told me she had been a medic in Rwanda. She said she'd spent most of the decade since the genocide locked up in her house, completely agoraphobic, on a regime of medications taken by the handful to treat the variety of maladies she was suffering from due to post traumatic stress disorder. She told me that her service dog had given her a new lease on life. Breaking down into tears, she sobbed that had it not been for her companion, she could never have left her home to come to my town hall meeting. Through her tears, she told me that thanks to the impact the dog had on her life, she was now taking only a couple of medications a day. To add to her grief, however, she informed me that VAC refused to have anything to do with providing or funding service dogs.

One of our investigators, Dominique Parisienne, had a deep personal interest in dogs and had taken it upon himself to open a file about service dogs. He had amassed a pile of evidence supporting the therapeutic benefits of these animals, and was eager to tell me about what he was learning at every opportunity. Dom related numerous ways that service dogs had helped their masters, such as alerting a veteran prior to the onset of potentially deadly seizures, intervening in situations that might otherwise have brought on intrusive flashbacks in a veteran, or interrupting a veteran, who was prone to becoming violent, at the smallest hint of agitation well before it flared into a full-fledged uncontrollable rage. There are hundreds more examples on YouTube, and that was enough evidence for me to take up the torch.

We approached the Department on that issue, and were told that there was no scientific evidence to suggest that dogs had any kind of legitimate therapeutic effect on PTSD casualties. I couldn't believe they could be so ignorant, so I countered that there was no scientific evidence because all the research in the private sector was in pharmaceuticals, which is where the big bucks are to be had. Despite this, there was so much anecdotal evidence of their efficacy that service dogs could not be ignored as a possible treatment. Based on a business case alone, I thought the Department might save so much money on prescription medications that service dogs would be a wise investment. I also wondered why VAC has a research directorate if not to find better ways of treating disabled veterans. They should be on the forefront of this kind of research and setting interim standards themselves, because service dogs are saving lives.

I thought that would have turned the tables, but the answer we received back from the Department was once again negative. They refused to reimburse the lady at all for the expenses she incurred in procuring a dog to help her. I was dumbfounded as to why or how that could be, and we were told that the person who trained that particular dog was not "certified." I could not understand what might possibly constitute credible certification if there were apparently no scientific grounds for the treatment nor national standards for trained service animals. The fact is, that dog was saving this lady's life, and service animals of all kinds — dogs, cats, horses, birds even — are saving the lives of thousands of veterans. This is an example of the kind of circuitous logic and obstructionism that veterans and their families encounter so often in their dealings with the government.

## Groups

Notwithstanding the litany of individual examples of malfeasance and malevolence towards veterans and their families that I witnessed firsthand, there were huge swaths of veterans who, as a group, the government has also treated with contempt. Louise and I had several meetings with aboriginal veterans groups, and I was shocked to learn how badly the Government of Canada has treated so many of our aboriginal brethren.

We were invited to a ceremony in Prince Albert that shall always stay with me. No alcohol was served at this event, and we all had a really good time nonetheless. I don't mean that in any derogatory way; it was truly inspiring to meet with people who were so committed to their culture that they would eradicate such a destructive blight from their lives. It was a life lesson to me that you can have a hell of a party when the only intoxicants are fun and friendship.

This event was so rich with their culture, with traditional drumming and dancing, and a central ceremony making presentations of handmade ornamental quilts to special guests. Now, my wife Trish is an avid quilter so I am somewhat *au fait* with the attributes of exceptional quilting, and the ones that were presented were truly extraordinary works of art. Sadly I was not a recipient of one, but I did enjoy some outstanding hospitality and friendship and gained a much better appreciation for our First Nations and the problems they face.

I can't count the number of times I was told by the veterans at that event how grateful they were that I was present. Visits by dignitaries and staff from Ottawa were usually brutally short and dispassionate. Not only were the government representatives often ignorant of aboriginal customs and traditions, any interest they displayed or overtures they made to learn seemed to many of the members of these communities to be insincere.

When my team and I set up later to hear the group's complaints in the first person, barely anybody came to meet with us formally. I suspect the organizers had scrambled to encourage some people to make us feel useful and welcome. It was explained to me later that their community — particularly their elders who had served in the World Wars and Korea, and had suffered from decades of unfair treatment — had become accustomed to being patronized or outright lied to. They felt it was a waste of time to voice their complaints to someone who had come from Ottawa to "help them."

I guess I should have realized it earlier in my career. The reputation of one Sergeant Tommy Prince is epic, and so is the story of how his life played out. Tommy was from Canada's First Nations, and a celebrated member of my regiment, the PPCLI. His skills and accomplishments as

*Rude Awakening*

a sniper in the Second World War and Korea were the things legends are made of. I was well aware of Tommy Prince the warrior, and of the hard times that fell upon him when he left the military, but I had viewed the tragedy of his life as yet another Patricia alumnus who fell victim to the evils of alcohol, like so many others have. I did not see him as a victim of the way the Government of Canada treated our warriors of aboriginal descent until, as Ombudsman, I learned the history of our First Nations veterans. Tommy's plight characterizes the way the system abandoned so many of our aboriginal veterans after they loyally served our country.

It was clear to me also that the problems our aboriginal stakeholders face are longstanding, extremely complex, and disturbingly unfair. Obviously, many of the problems our native Canadian stakeholders were confronted with were the responsibility of Indian and Northern Affairs Canada, but I had already confirmed that there was nothing in my mandate specifically prohibiting me from crossing departmental boundaries. Having accepted a little "mission creep," as we say in the army, in order to look after veterans of service in the RCMP, I locked on to the issues that our aboriginal stakeholders were seized of. At the same time, I recognized that the issues of our First Nations, Inuit, and Métis veterans would require extensive and sensitive study before we could weigh in with any credibility. Unfortunately, I was not able to kick-start this initiative before I left the Office.

One of the most blatant demonstrations of the government's contempt for our modern veterans was their practice of deducting the VAC Disability Pension from the veterans' Service Income Security Insurance Plan (SISIP) Long Term Disability (LTD) benefits. A report published by the DND Ombudsman in 2003 entitled "Unfair Deductions from SISIP Payments to Former CF Members," found the practice to be "fundamentally unfair." The government ignored these assertions, though, leaving the disabled and disadvantaged veterans no choice than to take their government — the very government for which they had served so selflessly and had suffered tragic and often traumatic, life-altering injuries and wounds — to court.

So, in March of 2007, Dennis Manuge and over 4,500 other disabled veterans initiated a class action lawsuit against the Government of

Canada. The claimants alleged that the claw back was unlawful, and was contrary to the Canadian Charter of Rights and Freedoms, a breach of fiduciary duties, unjust enrichment, a breach of public duty, and constituted bad faith on the part of the Government of Canada.

Although the outcome of the legal challenge was far from a foregone conclusion, the DND Ombudsman's report on the unfair treatment of our veterans was thorough and its recommendations well founded. As the Veterans Ombudsman, I was normally hesitant to endorse any initiatives of outside agencies, but shortly after I arrived at the Office I threw my support unreservedly behind that report. On May 1, 2012, the Federal Court of Canada ruled on the side of the claimants.

Thousands of veterans had suffered from the deceitful, callous, and parsimonious attitude of the federal government, and despite the positive outcome of the class-action suit, the financial damage caused to some veterans and their families was irreversible; some settlements fell short of the actual magnitude of the damage done, and others had been waiting too long for their final settlements to be of any help.

VAC does not hesitate to place veterans between "the rock" of their administrative demands and "the hard place" of civilian medical practitioners. CFB Cold Lake, a major base for the RCAF in northern Alberta, illustrates my case. Despite its rather remote location, or perhaps because of it, many veterans have retired there, particularly those who served in the air force — not surprisingly. At one of my town hall meetings I was told of the huge problems veterans in Cold Lake faced getting connected with a family doctor. Doctors weren't accepting veterans as patients because of the bureaucratic red tape and bullshit they had to deal with from VAC.

The Department also threw under the bus disabled military personnel from across the country, by demanding that when they submitted claims to VAC they had to get a CF physician to fill out the ream of VAC paperwork. In reaction, the CF implemented a policy that their doctors would *not* respond to demands VAC placed on disabled military personnel seeking veteran services and benefits. Understandably, satisfying VAC's bureaucratic imperatives would impinge on the CF's capacity to treat casualties and was a devious way for VAC to transfer some of their medical expenses to DND's medical budget. CF doctors were thus caught between a couple of rocks and several hard places of their own, wanting to do their best for their patients without disobeying a lawful command from their superiors. Often it is the case that the claimant loses out.

The government's irresponsible use of Agent Orange at Canadian Forces Base (CFB) Gagetown and their subsequent mistreatment of the victims of their malfeasance is nothing short of alarming. In 1956, the Department of National Defence, in conjunction with the US chemical warfare testing unit from Fort Detrick and Dow Chemical, began spraying toxic chemicals in the Gagetown training area. Agent Orange and Purple, containing TCDD dioxin, were used until 1967, after which only Agent White was used until 1984. The U.S. later determined that such chemicals were highly toxic and began to acknowledge that certain maladies their veterans were suffering from could be attributed to their exposure to those agents. Not so in Canada.

The Government of Canada has been typically evasive and deceitful on this life and death issue. They had the audacity, at one point, to claim that the agents had only been used in Gagetown for a total of three days in June 1966 and four days in June of 1967. The US Military, they claimed, had been invited to test only "two and one half barrels" (483 litres) of Agent Orange, Agent Purple, and other unregistered herbicides.

Corporal (retired) Kenneth Young and a small army of veterans and civilians, whose lives had been tragically disrupted by the ill effects of this mass poisoning, uncovered documented evidence to the contrary. Their alternate sources revealed conclusively that the magnitude of the damage was much, much more devastating than Canadians had been led to believe. Over three million litres were dispersed in the CFB Gagetown training area. It is estimated that 415,000 Canadians trained or were in the fields of CFB Gagetown during the toxic chemical years, as well as another 400,000 US National Guardsmen and 200,000 additional NATO forces.

On September 12, 2007, the Harper government announced an *ex-gratia* award of a seemingly arbitrary $20,000 to be paid to those who had an illness that could be related to the testing of US Military herbicides, Agents Orange and Purple, at CFB Gagetown. As is the Government of

Canada's practice with *ex-gratia* payments, they stipulated that the payments were neither an acknowledgement of the details of the claim nor an admission of liability. Understandably, they insisted that individuals must have had an illness related to exposure to Agent Orange, citing an early list of a dozen illnesses compiled by the US National Academy of Sciences' Institute of Medicine (IOM).

The US IOM has expanded that list several times since it was first published. The U.S. Department of Veteran Affairs eventually accepted the expanded lists, but VAC has refused to do likewise. And unlike the benevolence shown by our allies to their casualties, the Government of Canada further restricted eligibility for the *ex gratia* payments to a very narrow range of veterans; only those people who worked at, trained at, were posted to, or lived within five kilometres of CFB Gagetown, when Agent Orange and Agent Purple were tested, "in the summers of 1966 and 1967." Individuals must have been in the process of being diagnosed between June 1, 1966 and February 6, 2006 and, even more ridiculous, alive on the latter date when the Harper government assumed power.

The Government of Canada eventually relaxed some of these ridiculous time constraints, but not appreciably. What they have also failed to do is admit to Canadians the real scope of this disaster, offer fair compensation, or take the necessary measures to mitigate the ongoing health hazards to people in the area. A Base Gagetown and Area Fact Finding Project (BGAFFP) was formed, but it had no power to demand documentation or testimony from the government, DND, or the chemical industry. The BGAFFP clearly was prevented from identifying the real scope of the problem in Gagetown, although it did conduct soil tests and found dioxin levels as high as 17,300% above Canadian Council of Ministers of the Environment guidelines. Meanwhile, provincial healthcare systems continue to absorb the impact of this grossly negligent testing of hazardous chemicals in Gagetown.

In the opening months of my last year in office, I was visited by representatives of the ALS Society of Canada. They brought to my attention the sufferings of a young veteran afflicted by amyotrophic lateral sclerosis (ALS), commonly known as Lou Gehrig's Disease. ALS is a terminal sickness that tortures its victims with a long, agonizing death via a relatively rapid and progressive breakdown of neuromuscular function. Veterans seem to have a higher propensity for contracting ALS than the general population. The statistics are so compelling, in fact, that in the United States, veterans who fall victim to the disease are immediately and without question awarded full benefits. Not so here in Canada where the government had refused to acknowledge any relationship between early onset ALS and military service.

The ALS Society representatives described to me the case of an ex-soldier who was dying from ALS. His name was Brian Dyck. They told me that in the United States they determined that veterans, particularly those who served in the First Gulf War, had a statistically significant higher propensity to acquire early onset ALS. The exact cause had not been identified, but evidence of the association is unassailable. Brian Dyck was only forty years old when he was diagnosed with the disease, and he had indeed served in the First Gulf War. In addition to the terribly slow and painful death this young veteran was being subjected to, he was also forced to suffer the prejudicial and tight-fisted treatment of the Department.

This tragic case characterizes all that is wrong with the way Canada treats its veterans and their families. Brian first showed signs of ALS in 2009. As can be expected, he and his family were devastated by the diagnosis and sought some assistance from a support group. The ALS Society of Canada was well aware of the situation in the United States military, so they encouraged the Dycks to apply for benefits from VAC. Sadly though, the Society had already been down this path and was not optimistic about their chances of success. Sure enough, a negative response came back from the Department. In Canada, VAC argued, we do not use "Presumptive Rulings" the way that the Americans do, adding that there was no evidence linking Lou Gehrig's Disease and military service. The Society then decided to take this case to the Veterans Ombudsman.

When I first viewed their evidence I immediately recognized this as a classic example of where the Benefit of the Doubt was being unfairly interpreted to the detriment of veterans, which I discuss in much more detail later. Senior management in the Department told me the same thing they had told the Dycks and the ALS Society, that in Canada we do not use Presumptive Rulings and veterans must present a *prima facia* case to which the Department applies the Benefit of the Doubt. Not only did I find it insulting they would explain the Canadian system to me, it was wrong for them to suggest that claimants in the U.S. do not have to provide for a *prima facia* case to establish eligibility under a Presumptive Ruling. Also, their rejection of Presumptive Rulings is misleading.

What the government doesn't tell anybody is that they actually do use something similar to Presumptive Rulings, but they are far less formal than in the U.S. and VAC doesn't publicize them as such. The US DVA's use of a Presumptive Ruling for Agent Orange casualties is instructive. The reader will recall that VAC offered *ex gratis* payments of $20K to a narrow field of veterans, based on the list of maladies identified by the IOM as having a link to exposure to herbicides. That was the same list used by the US DVA for their initial Presumptive Ruling regarding Agent Orange. As the IOM expanded that list, the US DVA expanded eligibility accordingly under the Presumptive Ruling. VAC, on the other hand, refused to acknowledge the larger number of maladies.

The Secretary of the DVA at the time, General (retired) Eric K. Shinseki, testifying before the US Senate Committee on Veterans Affairs, described Presumptive Rulings and his role in creating presumptions under the Agent Orange Act:

> "The Agent Orange Act was a compromise between the desire for scientific certainty and the need to address the legitimate health concerns of veterans exposed to herbicides in the service. By establishing an evidentiary threshold lower than certainty and lower than actual causation, Congress required that presumptions be established when there is sound scientific evidence, though not conclusive, establishing a positive association between a disease and herbicide exposure."[4]

---

4 VA Disability Compensation: Presumptive Disability Decision-making: Hearing before the Committee on Veterans' Affairs United States Senate, One Hundred Eleventh Congress, Second Session, September 23, 2010.

An example of a practice here in Canada that is similar to Presumptive Rulings are used in the U.S. is how VAC treats veterans of the Korean War who come down with emphysema and chronic obstructive pulmonary disease, or COPD. The Australians determined there was a higher incidence of lung ailments such as these amongst veterans of the Korean War. So, as a result of this correlation, their government will virtually automatically rule in favour of Korean War veterans who make applications for services and benefits for such lung ailments. Based on the Australian experiences, the Government of Canada does too, although they do not refer to that as a Presumptive Ruling. VAC will refer to these as "policies," but they serve the same function as Presumptive Rulings.

When you peel away the layers of the government's official claim, it reveals more about the propensity of the Government of Canada to cheat veterans. In the United States, Presumptive Rulings, in a way, establish precedents — decisions that have been made already by the system — by codifying them into law to streamline the claim process that veterans must go through. What is different here in Canada is that VAC and VRAB not only have no intention of trying to make it easier for veterans to collect on what is rightfully theirs, they will actually go out of their way to make it more difficult for the veterans by concealing precedential decisions. In fact, VRAB is the only tribunal I could find in Canada that does not publish its decisions openly — clearly a deliberate act to disadvantage veterans. They have been rebuked for doing so, but they persist.

In the case of ALS, we arranged to meet with Brian and his wife Natali as soon as we could. This was a classic and compelling example of how completely dysfunctional the system is, so it was going to be an issue that I would go to the wall on. I told Brian and Natali I would take their case on personally, but by this time in my tour I was not at all confident that the OVO held any power at all to sway the status quo. I was therefore careful not to create any false expectations in them. I told them straight up that I might not get anywhere, but we were going to be in this together.

## Protecting Myself

As time wore on, the stress from my very public run-ins with the system and the terrible things I was learning about how we were cheating and mistreating our most seriously disabled veterans was taking its toll on me. I was falling into a routine of heavy drinking. While I knew my alcohol consumption irked some people, I never thought it was problematic. My dear wife Trish was well aware that I enjoyed the company of our veterans and often warned me, "the veterans need you as an ombudsman, not as another drinking buddy." As my relationship with government deteriorated, Louise pointed out that my drinking had gone too far. Even if it wasn't interfering with my work, allegations of alcohol misuse might offer my political master some ammunition he could use to discredit or fire me. The mission always comes first, so I quit drinking.

It was a pretty easy thing for me to do, actually — initially. I simply published an entry on my blog announcing my intention and then quit. Two factors prompted me to make a very public display of my intention to abstain from alcohol. First, I had only recently been inspired by reports about Master Corporal Jody Mitic, who as part of his rehabilitation after losing both legs below the knee in Afghanistan, ran a half-marathon on prosthetics. What an amazing man. Second, alcohol misuse is prevalent amongst people suffering from PTSD. So while quitting would be good for me, I also hoped to be an example to inspire other veterans to give up alcohol, the way Jodi inspired so many people to get on with their lives despite their physical disabilities.

I experienced a real eye opener soon after I quit drinking. My family began to loosen up and talk about my behaviour under the influence and how it affected them. They were worried enough about my PTSD, but the alcohol seemed to aggravate the symptoms. My dreams were wild, and unbeknownst to me I flailed in bed like a wild man. I was actually an angry ant under the influence — believe it or not, (apparently) angrier than I may have appeared to the public when I was sober. I never got physically abusive, but all the elements of emotional and mental abuse were certainly present even though my family has never said that was the case.

It wasn't long before I realized that becoming a non-drinker was the smartest thing I could have done. I will admit that I missed the camaraderie that can be had over a pint, and I will also admit that it is a constant battle to avoid temptation. I will go one step further to say that I have had moments of relapse, although my tolerance for alcohol has diminished such that I cannot consume much before feeling sick and becoming hung over the next morning. Two things remain constant. I value the sober state that I am in, and I know I would let a lot of people down, my family in particular, if I were to revert to my old ways. That ain't gonna happen.

CHAPTER 5:

# Homeless Veterans

Homeless veterans was an issue that I brought to the Canadian consciousness, and I think it would be safe for me to say it became the defining issue for me during my term as Veterans Ombudsman. That said, I cannot take credit for identifying the problem. Around the same time that I was appointed to be the Veterans Ombudsman, a major study in the United States reported that homelessness was hugely problematic amongst their veteran population. The very first time I was interviewed in my official capacity was with Nancy Wilson of CBC *NewsWorld*. Nancy asked me what the situation was with homeless veterans here in Canada but, of course, I was so new at the job I did not know if it was a problem. I promised I would find out.

Subsequently, I asked Louise if she would check with the Department. She had a hunch that they knew nothing about the subject. When she approached her contacts there, sure enough, that suspicion was confirmed. Without any investigation whatsoever they were quick to dismiss it as a non-issue, but I was not prepared to accept that response and took the issue on myself, calling it my "Leave Nobody Behind" campaign.

Standing up a campaign on homelessness caused some concern within our fledgling Office. We barely had any staff, and at that time many of them were employed on temporary contracts. Also, we were a long way from developing comprehensive operating procedures. My design, therefore, was to use "Leave Nobody Behind" as a rallying cry for visits that I would pay to homeless shelters while crisscrossing the country for my town hall meetings.

My first port of call after conceiving the campaign was a visit that Julie arranged for me to the Calgary Drop-in Centre. The director was very excited at the prospect of receiving assistance for the veterans who partook in the services of the centre so he rounded up some of the vets to meet with me. To my astonishment, on my first encounter with homeless veterans we met with at least a dozen. They represented just about every demographic except the First and Second World Wars and, hence, just about every age group.

The staff at the Calgary Drop-in Centre was amazing. They were eager to meet with me, and expressed their desire to meet with their professional counterparts in Veterans Affairs as soon as possible. They suggested to me ways that, within their own system, they could seal some cracks through which veterans might be slipping. They were very grateful for my visit and expressed their intent to raise the issue of veterans on their network with other homeless shelters in Canada.

The level of commitment I witnessed in the staff at the Drop-In Centre and the service that they provide their community is truly astonishing. I can't say enough about it. These are very pragmatic, solution-oriented people, and many of them were unpaid volunteers. When I was interviewed later, I indicated how impressed I had been with the attitude of the staff at the shelter, and how excited I was at the potential that existed for the government to partner with them to set-up pilot programs to help homeless veterans.

Through my search for homeless veterans I learned a great deal about what contributes to people becoming homeless: gambling addiction, drug and alcohol abuse, job loss and financial ruin, psychological problems. It appeared to me that those predicaments could themselves be a direct result of service in the military. Some people actually prefer to make a way for themselves on the street. It was also crystal clear to me that homelessness was indeed a problem in the veterans' community; one that the Department was neither aware of nor capable of dealing with.

Many veterans who become homeless never think to seek help from VAC, and the Department's ability to connect with veterans in need was and remains patently ineffective. VAC clings to their traditional methods of outreach that are not even adequate for veterans who are settled, so you can be sure that they don't even register in the lives of homeless people. I think the most common way that vets initiate contact with VAC is to walk into an office off the street. Many homeless veterans confided in me that it is particularly difficult for them to do, because they feel they are being judged for the situation they find themselves in. Despite the perceptions that many people might have regarding the homeless, they can be very proud and very private people.

A possible course of action for VAC, a simple first step at least, jumped out at me almost immediately once I started making the rounds to shelters. VAC had to establish a presence in the actual shelters, by distributing posters and handouts, establishing a professional relationship with the staff, and periodically making themselves available to the people living in the shelters. Sadly, in typical bureaucratic fashion, the Department opted to assign somebody at the head office to study the hell out of the issue rather than actually mobilize their troops in the front lines.

To the contrary, the people engaged in trying to eradicate homelessness in Canada are very proactive. Not long after I started making the rounds, they invited the Office of the Veterans Ombudsman to attend a meeting in Calgary of like-minded organizations called Project HOMELESS CONNECT. Our Office responded that we were grateful for the invitation, but we politely declined. While we were very interested in defining the scope of the problem with homeless veterans, it was not within our mandate to fix it. We would, though, encourage VAC to participate, and the Department agreed to do so.

On the home front, good ol' Q didn't waste any time gripping this issue. He identified an organization in the United Kingdom, which had been working with homeless veterans for years, and made contact with its CEO, Hugh Milroy. Hugh had established quite an effective network to find veterans living on the street, and a highly effective, action-oriented approach to getting them on their feet. He told Q that, in his experience, military personnel can be at risk of becoming homeless and destitute literally within days of leaving the service. The combination of the culture shock of leaving a highly regimented life in the military for the relatively unrestricted life on civie street, coupled with an operational stress injury or some other health or emotional problem — perhaps a dependency on drugs and/or alcohol, the loss of a job, or a marriage breakup — can cause a veteran to spiral out of control very quickly.

Associating culture shock to the act of leaving the military particularly resonated with me, and I am convinced that many civilians could have trouble relating to how daunting it really is. The military spends a huge amount of money and effort to inculcate young minds into the culture of the military, and even more time and effort into reinforcing regimented norms and behaviour throughout a service person's career. For dedicated military personnel, life becomes a battle drill. Many of the routine and administrative aspects of a person's life, such as getting paid, paying the rent or mortgage, and managing personal health and dental care, have been automated by the military system in order to maintain a high degree of readiness to deploy on operations around the world.

Shortly after Q and Hugh Milroy started corresponding, Hugh came across a Canadian in London who was "couch surfing" and claimed to be a veteran. In his fifties, this person was really in the hurt locker and, because he was a Canadian, the system in the UK was not going to provide him with the care he needed. This person's citizenship also limited Hugh as to what he could do for the guy. Q and Hugh conspired to combine efforts with whatever Canada's Department of Foreign Affairs and VAC could provide in order to bring this supposed veteran home. Once again, VAC wanted to proceed cautiously — read "slowly" — but this person required timely medical care. Q and a couple of conscientious public servants overcame some huge bureaucratic hurdles on this side of the Atlantic and managed to bring this gentleman home.

As it turned out, his claim to be a veteran was dubious if not outright spurious. It was not wasted effort for us, though, because we all learned some valuable and inexpensive lessons on what we would require to rescue veterans who fall on hard times. Rather than focus on the upside of this effort and how it contributed to the knowledge bank of helping veterans in crisis, the bureaucracy used it as justification to proceed more cautiously in the future. From my perspective we were trying to do what we perceived as the right thing to do. I was not worried about being called to account in this instance, and if we had been confronted with a similar situation I would have reacted the same way.

Another very special person the OVO was introduced to in our search for homeless veterans was Joe Sweeney. Joe was a Korean War veteran who fell on hard times following his tour with the Royal Canadian Regiment. He was what I came to recognize as a textbook case of a homeless veteran; one who had managed to pick himself up and sort out his life. He became a friend, confidante, and advisor on homeless veterans, and by reaching out to homeless vets in the Toronto area he was a virtual franchise outlet for the OVO. He became fully engaged in liaising with the shelters, one of which — the Mann Centre — he credited with helping him sort out his life.

In 2009 Joe worked with the Mann Centre and its director to arrange a very special Remembrance Day ceremony at the centre. Joe had managed to gain the support of the Queen's Own Rifles Regiment and choreographed a first class ceremony. There was a huge turnout, not only by some veterans who lived on the streets in the local area, but also by many private citizens. The occasion demonstrated that homelessness among veterans was indeed problematic in the Toronto area also.

I was privileged to have been invited as a VIP, in the company of people such as the Lieutenant Governor of Ontario at the time, The Honourable David C. Onley. His sincere empathy towards our homeless heroes was encouraging. While VAC was still struggling to control the damage they suffered from my repeated revelations, the public was definitely behind my campaign.

Later, Calgary City Policeman, Constable John Langford, who was also an ex-member of the Reserve Force with service in Bosnia during the war, got in touch with Q advising him that he had met several what we call "CF Veterans," vets who had not served in World War II or Korea, who were homeless. I was anxious to expand my knowledge base of this particular demographic of veterans, to ascertain what factors might have contributed to them ending up on the streets, so Q and I hopped on a plane to meet with them.

We arrived at the appointed time and place and met with Constable Langford and his shift supervisor. We grabbed some coffees and began comparing notes about homeless veterans. It wasn't long before it became apparent that we had been stood up by the veterans. Another lesson learned. Homeless people can have difficulty meeting obligations and they are frequently highly mobile, not staying in any one place for too long. Just when we had nearly abandoned hope, in walked someone whom Constable Langford recognized as one of our invitees. Strangely, he looked vaguely familiar to me, though at first I dismissed the possibility. But then this person arrived at our table and sure enough, said hello to me. As young men we had soldiered together in 3PPCLI.

I couldn't place the name but I remembered him as a young corporal or master corporal in Recce Platoon, a sub-unit where some of the more gung-ho and professional soldiers of an infantry battalion are employed. He told us the other vets probably wouldn't turn up, and admitted that he only came out because he was looking forward to catching up on old times. It was kind of bittersweet for me. He was part of an exciting time in my life, and he was clearly a highly intelligent and articulate young man. Sadly, and for some of the reasons I mentioned earlier, before he knew it he was living on the streets. He gave us some tremendous insights into life on the street and his perception of how soldiers might be prone to slipping into such a lifestyle.

Perhaps the biggest takeaway from this experience was the role that police could play in helping the Department track down veterans living on the street. A special bond develops between people who serve in the uniform — a bond that carries on even after people leave the forces. It extends laterally between soldiers and members of police and even fire services. We had come across another method of reaching out to homeless veterans. So even though we had been stood up by all but one of the people we had gone to Calgary to meet with, the trip was worthwhile.

Constable Langford continued his work with homeless veterans, and subsequently was honoured for it. It was an honour for me to meet yet another person who characterizes what it is to be Canadian.

From my very first day as Ombudsman, the Department was in a state of denial that there was a problem in Canada with regard to homeless veterans; at least, that was their official position in public. When we first scratched the surface of the homeless community, a senior bureaucrat from VAC asked Louise, with a nudge, a wink, and a smirk, if I had found any homeless veterans, because they hadn't. Louise could honestly answer yes, and was quick to add that people across the country were also continuing to come forward with information about homeless veterans. However, neither the Department nor the Minister seemed to be paying much attention.

Back when Louise was working in senior management at VAC she had been on the distribution list for a lot of routine departmental correspondence. By chance, when she began working in the OVO that practice had not been terminated. One such communication was called QP Notes, which the Department would prepare to ready the Minister for Question Period. With the rising awareness in Canada of the problem with veterans who had fallen into homelessness the Minister anticipated being bombarded with questions, so he had directed that a QP Note be prepared on the subject.

I didn't even know Louise was in receipt of such information, until that particular QP Note crossed Louise's desk. Its contents gave her cause for concern, so she sent it over to me. There was absolutely nothing prohibiting us from seeing Cabinet confidential documents and we were bound by the same security requirements that any employee of the Department is in the handling such information. In fact, I felt an obligation to the Minister to help him make informed decisions by making sure that the right messages were getting to him through the Department, so I thought it was entirely appropriate that we should be on distribution for these types of correspondence.

In this case, I thought it was highly serendipitous for the Minister that we were in the picture. This particular QP Note painted a very rosy picture regarding the Department's ability to look after the needs of homeless veterans. The Department pointed out that they had tremendous programs that are available to the homeless, and they listed them. That list included grounds keeping services and in-home care. Louise's concerns were well placed.

I advised the Minister's office and the Department that I considered the content of that QP Note to be "an exaggeration bordering on a lie." I added that if the Minister were to use the information contained therein to downplay the seriousness of the issue of homeless veterans, I would not be able to support the veracity of such claims. A public controversy could erupt.

I mentioned to Dubé, the Minister's chief of staff, that I would be quite happy to brief the Minister on what I was finding regarding homeless veterans, but he declined the offer. What he did do was ensure that the Office of the Veterans Ombudsman was taken off the distribution list for any correspondence between the Minister's office and the Department. I challenged him on the decision, arguing that this served as an excellent example of the service that we could provide the Minister to ensure he was armed with a balanced perspective of reality in the veterans' community. However, he would have none of it.

I was firmly convinced that the COS was wrong on this point, so it was time for me to exercise the prerogative to go to the Minister directly as his special advisor. The Minister granted me an audience, and I explained my position. He sided with his COS. I couldn't believe that he would leave any stone unturned in terms of optimizing his situational awareness as the frontman for veterans' rights, so I tried to plead the case. He wouldn't budge. It was clear that he had chosen sides. I wasn't fussed. To the contrary, in fact, I was going to double-down on effort to find veterans who were slipping through the cracks.

## Expanded Campaign

My original idea was that the "Leave Nobody Behind" campaign would relate solely to the issue of homeless veterans, but we soon discovered that one could not look at the problem in isolation. Homelessness mirrors a myriad of other human tragedies in the veterans' community that existed because VAC was failing to reach out to veterans, so I announced that "Leave Nobody Behind" would be expanded to embrace any veterans who were falling victim to the Department's complacency. It wasn't long before "Leave Nobody Behind" became the mantra of the OVO, guiding the thoughts and actions of our young professionals in the Early Intervention Directorate to help veterans who had been let down by the government they had served.

Then came that fateful event — locking horns with the Minister. It all started with one of my routine visits to long-term care facilities for veterans. This time it was Sunnybrook Hospital in Toronto. The long-term care facility at Sunnybrook is unique in that it is co-located with the Toronto district office for VAC. Visits to Sunnybrook were therefore very productive because I could kill two birds with one stone. On this particular occasion when I met with the district director I asked him point-blank the question of what, if anything, he was doing to address the issue of homeless veterans. Apologetically, he said they were doing nothing. I had visited Sunnybrook already at least once and I knew that this director, Stephen Little, was a hard worker and very dedicated to the welfare of veterans. His response was such that I felt obliged to offer him a little encouragement. I knew budgets were always very tight and it was very difficult to initiate any new projects without making cuts somewhere else.

My staff had planned for me to visit two shelters immediately after that visit to Sunnybrook: The Mann Centre and the Salvation Army. Like the other shelters I visited that had made such an impression on me, the staffs at these institutions were similarly deeply committed; their work was so difficult and they were doing such an important service for the community. Once again, there was no hint of VAC anywhere within their walls. Our visit to the Sally Ann was distinctly different from any prior shelter. This time there was a veteran housed in their shelter, this time the veteran himself had a request for us, and this time the staff were desperate for any assistance we could provide because this veteran needed extra care.

We visited the gentleman in the tiny room that the shelter provided him. The staff told Louise and me that he was extremely reticent to meet with us because he thought we were from VAC and we were coming to take away whatever benefits he was getting from them already. This kind of reaction to my meetings with homeless veterans was not uncommon. After the staff assured him that was not the case, he welcomed us into his tiny room. It probably measured 8' x 10' at the most. On one side of the room was a single bed, on the other side were all of his worldly possessions in small piles on the floor.

*Homeless Veterans*

He was in pretty rough shape. When I started asking him about his wartime experience, he became quite animated. He still had his record-of-service book, and his pride bubbled over when he talked about it. Sadly, over the years his medals had gone missing. He asked us hesitantly, and only after some coaxing by the staff, if we could get him some replacements. Whether it was pride, privacy, or fear of reprisal, we often encountered this kind of hesitation amongst the homeless veterans we encountered.

This was the first time any homeless veteran had ever asked us for anything, and Louise and I were only too eager to oblige. I am sure I speak for Louise also when I say that these kinds of encounters were particularly heartrending. This story had a happy ending in that VAC did become engaged in assisting the shelter staff with this gentleman's problems, and we were able to replace his medals for him. VAC made a practice of sending replacement medals to veterans in the mail, but this time Louise managed to intercept them. To make it even more satisfying, the Sally Ann invited me to a special medals presentation ceremony — the way it should be done. What an experience that was. There must have been thirty people present. Shelter workers, police officers from the area, firefighters, and patriotic citizens turned out to honour this proud veteran. To this day, I am moved by the memories of the event.

That was the happy side of the story, but there was an unfortunate aspect to it also. Shortly after my visit, a reporter who had been following my quest to get the Department to help homeless veterans asked me for a quick interview. When she asked me if I had seen any improvements in the treatment of veterans, my response was a categorical no. I may have been a little more passionate on this occasion because I had just encountered a veteran in such dire straits, but it was a statement of fact. I don't know if my passion came across in the newspaper article or if Minister Thompson just didn't like the truth, but in typical fashion for the government of the day, he went on the attack and tried to discredit me publicly.

Thompson told the press that that if I had indeed come across any homeless veterans I had failed as an ombudsman because I hadn't turned one single name over to the Department. He went on to say my actions were beyond the pale. I found the ignorance of the man laughable. Not only was he displaying his lack of understanding of the importance of confidentiality in the work of an ombudsman, he was implying that because people were homeless the Department had the right to intervene without a request from the veteran to do so. Perhaps he was duped by the propaganda provided to him earlier in the QP Note from the Department, saying that they actually had programs in place to combat homelessness, and he was frustrated because he wanted to offer the homeless veterans unsolicited in-home care and grounds keeping. I am actually smiling as I write this.

I had a feeling that a confrontation was inevitable because of the way they reacted to my observation regarding the QP Note, but I was disappointed nonetheless when it actually transpired. Conflict is seldom constructive, and this could have been avoided. But I am always up for a fight, and I was not about to take this unprofessional attack lying down. The Minister's outburst drew inordinate attention to the original article, and a media tsunami hit the Office. Before speaking with any reporters I took my media person at the time, Lee-Anne Peluk, in tow, along with a photographer who had been sent to us from the *Ottawa Citizen*. We paid a visit to the shelters in the Byward Market area that were within spitting distance of the Minister's office. The staff at every one we visited confirmed that veterans of all ages were frequent patrons of their establishments. Sadly, there weren't any readily available at the time for a photo op. That is, not until we got to the Sally Ann.

The staff at the Sally Ann had the same story for us about veterans who availed themselves of the services of the shelter, but they added that one of their more regular guests could probably be found at that time in the meal line-up. Sure enough, it was easy to pick the gentleman out of the line-up because he was sporting a beret with a poppy where a military cap badge would usually be mounted. A veteran who was probably in his eighties, he was seated at the time we met up. I introduced myself as the Veterans Ombudsman and he actually became hostile towards me. I thought he was going to rise up and take a swing at me, but I persisted. He wouldn't take my word that I wasn't from VAC, and he was scolding me for how long he had to fight for the benefits that were owed to him and warning me that I had better not try to take them away. I was getting nowhere with him, so I decided to take a different tack. I asked him about his wartime service, which he quickly seized on. He started telling me stories about his exploits in the Italian Campaign, and it wasn't long before I recognized his stories from my own regimental history. He was a Patricia!

The photographer asked us if we could take it outside where the light was better, and our veteran was now only too willing to oblige. Admittedly he was rather hard to understand, but he was very animated. We talked about all sorts of things for at least a half an hour. Lee-Anne had to break in because the gentleman was at risk of missing the meal. She volunteered to escort our veteran back to the meal line, which gave me a couple of moments to take stock of the experience. It was a very emotional moment. By this point in my term, the homeless veterans' situation in Canada had really gotten to me, but the regimental link I shared with this gentleman brought it all closer to home. What made it hurt even more was that Minister Thompson was so quick to wax on before any audience anywhere about how much compassion he had for veterans.

When Lee-Anne came back from the meal line she had tears in her eyes. She said that while she was walking with him the elderly veteran had said, "There, I hope that might help some of the guys who are having problems with DVA!"

As the drama regarding homelessness was unfolding, I unwittingly became a bit of a media darling. On the Friday, Julie Van Dusen contacted my office to request an interview on CBC's *The National*. You know you've really made waves if Julie Van Dusen wants to talk to you. We arranged for a meeting at 1500 hours that day. A little while later, Julie contacted the office to request a slight postponement. She had requested a meeting with Minister Thompson but he would only grant her an interview if it was done before mine. That was odd, but so what, I thought. I didn't have much time for the interview, because I had a subsequent interview with Tom Clark for his show *Power Play* in the front foyer of the House. My message to both of them was quite a strong one: How dare the Minister suggest in any way that I might be insensitive to the needs of veterans! I didn't care who he thought he was, but if he thought I was a shrinking violet he was in for a shock.

Early the next week I was summoned to appear in the Minister's office. Of course, and as expected, I was told to come alone — that is the way bullies like to play. Also, these guys are all about plausible deniability. When I was escorted into the Minister's office there were three people in the room: the Minister, his chief of staff Jacques Dubé, and one other person. The Minister was enraged, eyes glaring, all red in the face and bald head, in stark contrast to his grey hair. He was so abusive it shocked me, as I had never been treated by a superior in the CF in that manner, no matter how badly I had messed up. Just a bully. He regurgitated the garbage that he had spewed out to the press the previous week. Those hadn't been just sound bites that were taken out of context.

A politician once warned me never to say a good word about the Department because politicians would twist them against me sometime in my term as Ombudsman. I didn't pay that warning any heed because I wasn't going to play their stupid games. I would give credit where credit was due. The prediction came true, though, as Thompson had already done this childish play on words in his own defence when he was before a meeting of the Senate Committee.

Once, while commenting publicly about the gaping holes in the system and how the Government of Canada actually cheats many veterans out of what they rightfully deserve, I added in all honesty that we have many very good programs on the books for veterans and their families. On many occasions I also praised the great work that so many VAC staff do. Thompson was all over that like a giddy schoolgirl, accusing me of being confused and inconsistent; in one breath heaping praise on the Department and then in the next turning around and criticizing them. There are many good programs "on the books," but that doesn't suggest that senior bureaucrats allow them to be delivered to the veterans who need them, nor can you infer from that that there are not gaping holes and ineffective programs in the system.

In this particular meeting, Minister Thompson was raging on in huge generalities about all the great things the government does for veterans. Meanwhile his chief of staff was flipping through the press clippings and reading out statements I had made that he had highlighted, supporting his Minister's ravings. I countered that they knew as well as I did that while I had said those things, I didn't write the articles nor did I set the context of those quotes. Anybody who deals with the press has fallen victim to this kind of journalism, especially politicians. It is not lying, it is just a means of selling the news. It didn't detract from the truth of anything that I ever said.

Then Minister Thompson piped up with the allegation that some people were saying I was "a known liar." That was it. That was all the bullying I would take. I demanded to know who had said that. Of course, plausible deniability; Thompson didn't call me a liar himself, because then he could be accused of slander, except there were no witnesses in the room who would be inclined to testify in support of such an accusation if I made one. Neither would he reveal who the person or persons were that he claimed had called me a liar. I wouldn't let go of it. I told him that this meeting was over unless I was allowed to face my accusers. Thompson started waffling, trying to lead the confrontation away from his unfounded allegation.

Dubé kept his mouth shut but the third person in the room, who until this point had remained silent, piped up with a question. I didn't even hear what he said. Ignoring his question I immediately shot back, "Who are you?"

He replied, "I am Richard Roike," to which I countered caustically, "I don't care what your name is, what is your job? Why are you here?" I had been keeping my cool up to this point out of respect not for the Minister himself, because I had absolutely no time for the man himself, but for the office. The other two in the room, however, were on shaky ground. Roike told me he was the Minister's Director of Communications, which was ok with me so I asked him to repeat his question albeit in a curt fashion. I wouldn't say I managed to keep my cool, but I did manage to maintain my self-control.

Much later in my term I was interviewed by David Pugliese and related this story to him, saying how the Minister and his henchmen were so abusive that in any other circumstances I probably would have assaulted them for their bullying tactics. Pugliese went on to interview the by-then-retired Minister who said that was no reflection on him — it was a reflection on my character. Ouch! I guess I cannot hide from the fact that I will neither tolerate fools nor back down from bullies. Thompson, his ilk, and their minions rightfully deserve to be held accountable for treating people the way they do.

## Dirty Tricks

The week after the public showdown over homeless veterans between the Minister and me, Trish was leaving for work slightly before I was. It was garbage day, and I had put two black bags out the night before with our recycling bin. Just before I went out to the garage, our home phone rang. On the other end of the line was a very upset Trish on her cell phone. Trish never texts or talks on a cell phone while driving, so it must have been important to have made her pull over. Unfortunately, her cell phone battery died before I could get a clear message about what was upsetting her. I did hear enough before it cut out to know it had something to do with our garbage.

Because I had put it out the night before, I naturally assumed that she was upset that it hadn't been picked up. While I was pulling out of the driveway I never thought to look at our garbage; I looked up and down the street and saw that nobody's garbage or recycling had been picked up. Later that morning I phoned her on a land line to reassure her that the truck hadn't been by when I left for work, and that I had put our garbage out the night before. She was still shaken. She explained to me that she recognized that the garbage trucks had not been by yet, what she had been trying to say was that our garbage had gone missing.

Now, it is a common practice in most Ottawa neighbourhoods that when a household throws out something of potential value or use to someone else it will be scavenged the night before pickup. People have come to expect this, and will normally put out articles that might fit into this category a little earlier than normal. I got rid of a non-serviceable pool heater and an old exercise bicycle this way. Articles such as these are normally placed curb-side early, so that the scavengers can do their work before or shortly after dark, but this *never* happens with black garbage bags.

The week after we had our garbage stolen, Trish wanted me to delay putting our garbage out until the next morning. She didn't want to have it stolen again. Trish is such a kind and gentle person, so these kinds of episodes really worry her. I promised her I wouldn't, but I am not quite as intimidated by this kind of invasion of privacy. I purposely waited until well after dark when Trish was in bed for the night, and then I made my move. I filled the black bags once again and, without telling Trish so she wouldn't stress out, put them out to the curb.

The next morning Trish thought I hadn't put the bags of garbage out already, so she wasn't unnerved to see that the black bags were missing once again. I guess whatever somebody found or didn't find in my garbage the week before compelled them to come around for seconds. I have no evidence to link the "thefts" to the Minister's office, but this happening twice at the very time of a confrontation with the Minister was probably not a mere coincidence. Not since I had been with the Third Battalion PPCLI in Afghanistan on Operation APOLLO had I felt a threat against me personally. This was getting serious, and I couldn't afford to give my detractors any ammunition to attack me with.

CHAPTER 6:

# Internal Review

## Take 1

As much as I benefited from the experience by finding out what kind of people I was dealing with, my run-in with them was truly an unfortunate turn of events. Conflict has always been a way of life for me. I trained and competed in all kinds of martial arts: karate, judo, boxing, Muay Thai, wrestling. As a professional officer, my passion was not for getting promoted or being in charge, it was the orchestration of force and management of conflict. Despite my passion, I had learned that very little good ever comes of confrontation. Conflict is a necessary evil, a basic human trait, an inevitable eventuality of life, so the challenge is to make something good come out of it. This was no different, and it was the first time the OVO truly challenged the status quo. I expected there would be other occasions, so I sought to extract the lessons that could be learned so we could avoid such altercations in the future.

 I therefore initiated what I called an internal review. Recognizing that the Office was only minimally staffed, and any additional tasks I imposed on them took them away from their very important work on issues directly affecting veterans, I took it upon myself to compose the first draft of this document. In the review, I examined everything we did in the Office that pertained to homeless veterans, including the types and sources of information we had collected, and I made a few recommendations.

Four recommendations pertained to internal practices that the OVO should modify or introduce to avoid meltdowns of this nature in the future. Of course, we took them on. We also suggested two things that the Department and the Minister's office should do to enhance the way the OVO could contribute to the Minister's ability to improve the treatment of veterans and their families:

1. The Department should offer the Veterans Ombudsman complete and direct access to departmental information.

2. The Minister's office should use the OVO to verify that the Department was keeping the Minister accurately informed of issues in the veterans' community and how they were dealing with them.

Shortly after the showdown, I bumped into Dubé, whereupon I advised him of the internal review we were conducting. We were trying to be as balanced and objective as possible in the hope the experience might offer our Office some constructive lessons on how we could avoid rubbing the Minister's office the wrong way in the future. I told Dubé that once it was completed I would like to contact him to arrange a meeting with the Minister to discuss it. He was receptive to the offer. Shortly thereafter, on the afternoon of June 5, 2009 - and virtually out of the blue — my administrative assistant received a call from the Minister's office.

Louise was in Ottawa at the time and we just happened to be in a meeting with our in-house lawyer, Diane Guimet-Harris, discussing our internal review and the meeting I had requested with the Minister. The call was from the Minister's administrative assistant. What a coincidence that was. I told her that at that very moment we were discussing the internal review that I was doing for the Minister so I would put her on speakerphone. There wasn't much of a discussion, though. The assistant just told me that the Minister wanted to meet with me a couple of days hence. It was extremely short notice given that I was in the process of re-working my internal review paper and I was hoping to send over a draft for them to consider before we met. I therefore asked to postpone the meeting.

After consulting with someone in the background the administrative assistant came back to say abruptly that failure to appear in the Minister's office at the appointed time would be interpreted as insubordination and I would be referred to the Privy Council Office and the prime minister's office for dismissal. She then hung up in my ear, or rather in our faces, because Louise and Diane heard the whole thing. We sat there looking at each other dumbfounded. After we had picked up our jaws and collected our wits, Ms. Guimet-Harris called back to re-explain our position. Once again, Diane met with the same terse reply. She stumbled back into my office literally wide-eyed and looking confused, almost as if she had been wounded. She couldn't believe how she had been treated.

I immediately followed up with an email to the chief of staff, explaining our side of things objectively and concisely. All we wanted was some time for a pre-meeting with him as the COS before we met with the Minister. That was a manifestation of my military way of doing things, sorting out one's act with the COS, the commander's "right hand," so as not to waste the commander's time. I concluded with, "Bottom line, I will report when and where I am required." He replied that evening, agreeing to meet with me one-on-one beforehand. He added that subsequent to that meeting, my staff and I, no more than two in addition to me, would be meeting with the Minister at his convenience.

I was not about to allow the acts of intimidation that had been perpetrated by an administrative assistant on behalf of the Minister's office to go unchallenged. Even if the government objected to my informal definition of our independence — "decision-making without undue influence or constraints" — there was no way they could argue that acts of intimidation by the Minister's office did not compromise the independence of the Office of the Veterans Ombudsman. This was a dangerous precedent that I could not take lightly.

I had spent enough time in the public service to understand that bullying is a very common tactic of elected officials and senior bureaucrats. I had already heard of several cases during my very short term, even instances where the victims broke down into tears in front of the perpetrator and in spite of the mechanisms that were apparently in place to protect the rank and file. A redress mechanism had not been established in the mandate for our Office, so I was only too happy to test those mechanisms as well.

I looked up the legislation, Treasury Board regulations and policy directives, and felt I could argue that the very acts of intimidation intended to undermine our independence were prohibited as harassment in the workplace policies. I sent Dubé another rocket, using jargon cribbed directly from the guidelines. In an email to him dated June ninth, I said:

> I consider this type of [threatening] behaviour to be unwelcome and offensive. Indeed, the Treasury Board's Policy on Prevention and Resolution of Harassment in the Workplace explicitly constitutes "threats, intimidation, or retaliation against an employee, including one who has expressed concerns about perceived unethical or illegal workplace behaviours" as harassment. I trust that the necessary action will be taken to reinforce the values of integrity and trust that are the foundation of a sound organization.

I am told that when Dubé heard I wanted a harassment investigation carried out he was incredulous, although when we met later that month he was cordial enough. I mustered up all the courtesy I could in making it very clear to him that from my perspective this harassment complaint had nothing to do with me personally. I was quite happy dealing with bullies, but I would not tolerate them trying to intimidate me in my work as an ombudsman. Dubé replied that I could never make it stick. "You'll never win," he countered. "It will be our word against yours. Take some friendly advice: you don't want to do this."

The term "friendly advice" rolled off his tongue with the tone and demeanour of a mob boss, and it burned in my brain as if it had been a sniper's bullet. This confirmed the suspicions that had been haunting me. Thompson and Dubé were patently not interested in making this work. They had no intention of working with a Veterans Ombudsman in any way, shape, or form. Undeterred, I challenged that the word of the accused against the accuser is exactly what a harassment investigation is for, because a large part of harassment is the perception of the apparent victim. I wanted the Minister's office — Minister included

— to understand that treating the Veterans Ombudsman the way they did, not just me but whoever was going to succeed me as well, was hugely inappropriate.

Jacques was having no part of this. He tried to dismiss it by saying that the only way we could get to ground-truth would be to bring somebody in from the outside. I responded that I would have it no other way. I suggested that it would be highly appropriate to bring somebody in from the Privy Council Office, even though I knew by this time that the clerk had to have been complicit in, if not responsible for, setting up a sham ombudsman office. I even had a good idea that if PCO did investigate, the findings were already pre-determined to be against me; but I wanted to get this out in the open and let my stakeholders decide who might be culpable: the COS for trying to bully the Veterans Ombudsman, or me for fabricating a complaint. *Yippee-ki-yay!* I thought. *Bring it on!*

## Extorted Resolution

I left that office fully expecting that the wrath of Hell was about to be unleashed upon me. Harper and his henchmen in the PMO had already demonstrated time again how competent they are at character assassinations. I had already experienced a failed attempt of them trying to dredge up some dirt on me, and I *knew* I would not have any allies in government.

That character assassination was never to materialize. The next morning I received a phone call from the administrative assistant. She was very upset, crying heavily. She apologized profusely for being so rude to me on the phone the other day. She said it was her and her alone, nobody else in their office had put her up to it, and she was very sorry. I tried to get through to her that she didn't have to do this. She wouldn't step back from accepting full responsibility for her actions, so I gratefully accepted her apology. Public servants are truly lambs at the slaughter when it comes to their bosses and politicians.

*Those bastards!* I thought. *They're good!* I considered myself to be a disciple of the masters of manoeuvre like Sun Tzu and B.H. Liddell Hart, and my strategy for dealing with their assault on my character had been formulated accordingly. My defensive plan was quite simple. We would never stray from the moral high ground. This was strictly business, nothing personal. And while I am quite sure that those guys don't even know who Sun Tzu is, they were pretty adept manoeuvrists themselves. They had seized on the only course of action left open to them that would completely unhinge my battle plan. I had unwittingly allowed the initiative to slip into their hands.

## Internal Review: Take 2

When we finally got around to speaking about the Internal Review, Dubé reaffirmed the conclusion that I had drawn from his response to my allegation of inappropriate acts of intimidation. As diplomatically as our internal review had been drafted, he categorically rejected anything in it that impacted on the Department and his office. He discarded out of hand any suggestion that the OVO should be offered unfettered access to information. Then he had the audacity to admonish me for presuming that I had the authority to conduct a systemic review of the Department's work and how they advise the Minister. I tried to encourage him to view the OVO as a kind of reconnaissance platoon: the Minister's eyes and ears on the ground to enhance his situational awareness of not only the veterans' community but also how well the Department was responding to the needs of that community.

Dubé would not step away from his assertion that I was overstepping my authority, and that's how we left it. There was no doubt in my mind that they had no desire to give the OVO a meaningful role in improving the government's treatment of our veterans and their families. Moreover, it was clear to me that he had no intention of trying to mend any fences or build any bridges. He expected me to just back off.

## Making Nice With the Minister

After the pre-meeting with Dubé, I arrived at the meeting with the Minister as ordered, with my single witness in accordance with the direction. The Minister sat at the end of the conference table, gripping a small round rock in his hand that he had picked on the beach at Dieppe. He had the smile on his face that by that time I viewed as being so disingenuous I could hardly stomach it. I did though. He waxed on about his trip to Dieppe and how overwhelming it was to think of how our veterans landed on those beaches, yada, yada, yada. I tried desperately to conceal my lack of respect, or more accurately, the disdain I had for him. I was astounded that he could have the gumption to sit at the table professing his commitment to veterans as if nothing had happened.

He talked about how important it was that we work together — that it was all about the veterans. I had heard all this before, but now I was much better informed as to what his true intentions were and the way these guys did business. Despite this, I swallowed any animosity I had and was as professional and congenial as possible. After all, I had a job to do. For the same reason that I had initiated my own internal review, this was strictly business — nothing personal.

I saw Minister Thompson one more time before he resigned from his post. We were attending the City of Ottawa's Candlelight Vigil for Veterans, an event they hold annually during Remembrance Week. We just happened to bump into each other casually very shortly before the ceremony started. He was clearly uncomfortable and made some awkward attempts at small talk. "You all gung-ho, Colonel Stogran?" "You focused on the mission?" "You ready to go?" If the preceding confrontation hadn't occurred, it would have seemed the kind of inept small talk one would expect of a social misfit. Given our previous conflict, it could easily have been construed as taunting.

Either way, I was at a loss for words. I just smiled, extended my hand in a friendly gesture, said, "Yes sir!" and excused myself as quickly as the situation politely allowed.

CHAPTER 7:

# Parliamentary Committees

## Of the House...

I appeared before parliamentary committees too many times for me to count. I found these appearances, on one hand, to be a complete waste of time and effort because nothing ever changed as a consequence. The House Committee was particularly dysfunctional because of the lack of capacity and savvy of our elected representatives in managing government affairs — such is democracy. On the other hand, the work we did to prepare for them was a good opportunity for a "navigation check" to take stock of what we had accomplished and what more we should be doing.

Of course, political gamesmanship dominates the agendas of these committees, masked by a thin veil of genuine concern for our veterans and their families. I hasten to add though, that while the veil was indeed thin, I think for many MPs, deep down their concern for veterans was indeed genuine. I spoke privately with many politicians from both sides of the House and they all expressed their heartfelt sympathy for the plight of some of our veterans. On the government side, a few were more candid than others about the dilemma they faced between party solidarity and their consciences; they were just too timid to challenge the sick culture that infects our parliamentary processes.

And then there was Peter Stoffer, Veterans Affairs critic for the NDP. I differentiate between Peter and his party because his commitment to veterans is deeply rooted within him. The story of Peter's father's first encounter as a young boy in the Netherlands with the soldiers of the liberating Canadian Army has become a part of veteran folklore in Canada. Mr. Stoffer, the senior, was so impressed by the selflessness and respect that he witnessed in those Canadians that he immediately resolved to emigrate to their country as soon as he could. The NDP, on the other hand, with their politicking, posturing and promises and even though they have never formed a government, are every bit as guilty of the gamesmanship that has eroded our democracy as any of the other parties.

After my run-in with Minister Thompson over homelessness in the veterans' community my appearances before the House Committee became a whole lot less congenial. When I appeared before the Standing Committee on Veterans Affairs in April of 2010, Phil Coleman, Conservative MP from Brantford, asked me to help him, with his background in business, understand the needs-based approach. He posited that a needs-based approach would be different for almost every individual, suggesting that in his opinion there would obviously have to be some parameters and thresholds for awards in order to retain financial responsibility. He expressed concern for how difficult it would be to put measures in place to prevent veterans from bilking the system — my words here.

I really wanted to lecture this guy, from a business perspective, on how they should factor in the possibility of over-indulging disabled veterans into their business plan when they first consider sending our military into harm's way. Indeed, the complete lack of any correlation between Veterans Affairs and Canadian Forces operations in their business planning and budgets is a prime example of just how shallow the management practices of government are. Business background indeed! More importantly, Coleman's opening monologue started my "Spidey senses tingling" with the suspicion that he might be planting a hint that the Health Care Review was going to step away from the needs-based approach that was fundamental to the NVC. I had to act on my hunch rather than tear a strip off this guy.

I tried to challenge his insinuation that the needs-based approach needed to be controlled positively by the government and that he couldn't have it both ways. I alluded to the all-but-dead-in-the-water Health Care

Review and the terminology that Thompson had been throwing about. I suggested that for a needs-based system to work, the people that VAC has working on the front lines with veterans, the case workers, really have to become "case managers." They have to know the person with whom they are dealing well enough to know when the needs are legitimate, and to be able to say that if the veterans commit to the process of rehabilitation and reintegration and do their part, the system will look after them. That kind of case manager would also be in a position to identify unworthy clients, frauds or loafers. I knew it was a waste of ammunition, however, and that the Veterans Health Care Review would never see the light of day.

The Conservative members came armed with questions to — in typical Harper-government fashion — rebuke my claim of lack of inaction by Veterans Affairs Canada and even discredit me. Coleman, again, questioned my practice of offering advice and comments that he alleged were not based on "solid evidence and solid background." He suggested that my observations in homeless shelters and discussions with homeless veterans and staff at all levels in the Department and in homeless shelters were merely anecdotal information, "the kind we witness every day in our own communities, in our own circumstances, on a variety of issues, including perhaps some Veterans Affairs issues." He then asked if the advice I had provided had been "based on something more than anecdotal experiences?" I was incredulous. My recounting of my experiences may have been anecdotal in the way I presented them, but I was recounting eyewitness reports. I tried not to be too disrespectful to the member so I simply said:

> "I'm sorry, Mr. Chair, I wouldn't refer to them as anecdotal experiences. I would refer to them as my observations and discussion with individuals. In terms of rigour of evidence, you can't get much more rigorous than first person singular; talking to people on the ground and talking to homeless veterans. To me, anecdotal would be something you'd hear around the water cooler, and that's not the way I do business."

I didn't bother telling them that my personal observations and so-called anecdotal reports were being corroborated by government employees who were actually working the issues. Of course, due to their fear of retribution they would speak to me on the condition of retaining their anonymity, or they would "slip me a brown envelope" with insider information. I wouldn't have willingly violated that confidentiality, but what a sad statement about our government.

## And of the Senate...

I learned the hard way that Senate Committees are much more relaxed than House Committees. I kind of knew that already, but it didn't really register with me when I appeared there for the first time. I think from my military background I naturally took a more formal approach to any rendezvous with a senior-rank public official than I needed to. In the military I always strictly paid reverence to the rank differential, even when speaking with my friends and close colleagues who were promoted ahead of me. My reasoning was that this was good practice for if I ever found myself in a life and death situation and was given what I perceived to be a stupid order — by training myself to be deferential I would be less likely to tell the superior officer to go fuck him-or-herself.

Thus, when I first appeared before the Senate Sub-Committee my instincts kicked in on the side of formality. I didn't think anybody would mind. When it was Senator Nancy Ruth's turn, she admitted that this was her first time on this committee and asked me a harmless question. I replied to the Chair. One of the formalities that exist in the House Committees — but not in the Senate counterparts — is that all answers that a witness offers to the committee members are directed towards the chairperson, and Ruth ripped my face off and proceeded to slap me with the wet side. She damn well wanted me to answer her, not her commanding officer (as she put it). I wasn't fussed by how confrontational she was; I just apologized sincerely and carried on. I got through that little firefight, and when it came time for Senator Tommy Banks and Senator Joe Day to ask me questions, they tried to make me feel more at ease to compensate for any lasting effects of the verbal tongue lashing.

## Parliamentary Committees

For the most part, my early encounters with senators from both major political parties were amicable. After my run-in with Minister Thompson over the homeless veterans issue, my meetings with the Senate Committee became increasingly adversarial on the Conservative side of the table. I couldn't care less that they didn't agree with me; that was to be expected. What was discouraging was they weren't interested in finding out the truth. Just blind partisanship. Senator Pamela Wallin lost a great deal of credibility in my eyes. Wallin challenged me on my allegations that the Department had failed to do "anything." I emphasize "anything" here because she was not suggesting that I had merely exaggerated my claim regarding the Department's neglect. She was trying to suggest I was wrong or lying.

Wallin was particularly bush-league and ill informed. Her political hacks had clearly provided her with a private brief, but she wasn't very familiar with the subject matter so she flipped ferociously back and forth through it. On one occasion she even parroted the allegation that Mr. Coleman had made in the House Committee that I acted on "anecdotal" evidence. No doubt she was singing the words provided to her in the Harper songbook. Her dependency on her notes was so obvious that Senator Joseph Day asked the chairman if he had been left off the distribution of a briefing package, because protocol requires that committee members share briefs before meetings. Point taken by everyone.

My final appearance before the Senate Sub-Committee really demonstrated the sorry state of our democracy. It was on November 3, 2010, eight days before Remembrance Day, when Guy Parent would assume accountability to our stakeholders. Lieutenant General Dallaire was the Chair. In my opening statement I summarized the recommendations that I had made to MPs in the Standing Committee on what I felt should be done, as a matter of urgency, to break the culture of "deny, deceive, or defer" that possessed senior bureaucrats in VAC and the VRAB. Senator Wallin was at her finest, trying to discredit me with sound-bite rhetorical questioning: "Are you saying you just discovered these [NVC] issues in the last six months?" (The NVC had been implemented by the previous government five years earlier.)

If the conduct of Ms. Wallin was not just blind political partisanship, then she was displaying her total ignorance and ineptitude. I asserted that I had been very deliberate in my aggressive, unadulterated accusations of the Department and would like nothing more than to be proven wrong. I would have offered them the opportunity to convict me for defamation if they dared try, but I had no fear of that. I knew senior management was culpable. What a sad statement about our government. "If I may," I said, "I have been increasingly vocal and I would be more than happy to be compelled by subpoena to present evidence to whoever wants to see it." General Dallaire responded by saying that only happens in the US Senate, to which I answered, "I am saying I would like all this stuff to come out on the table."

Wallin went on to challenge my allegation of malfeasance on the part of government in their treatment of veterans with a completely unfounded and incorrect statement, saying, "You ascribe motive to them [the government], and I am wondering if there is any actual evidence of that?" I had been very careful not to "ascribe motive," as she put it. I had learned as a Military Observer with the United Nations in Bosnia the importance of reporting exactly what you see and not what you infer from what you see. I had always been careful not to suggest any reasons why the government was treating veterans the way they did. We all know why they would reduce benefits to veterans and then deny those that rightfully deserved them, but I never crossed that bridge. Wallin was not interested in discovering the truth; she was simply trying to discredit me.

She later commented on my pet peeve, the "benefit of the doubt," saying that I "explained that money should just be handed out to veterans and they should not have to apply for benefits or explain their circumstances." Once again, an outright fabrication. I had never suggested that veterans should be relieved of the responsibility to present a *prima facie* case to the government in support of their claims; I had only argued that the burden of proof imposed on veterans by VAC and the VRAB was grossly exaggerated beyond that which the legislation intended. She just kept at her contorted game of rhetoric. She even tried to undermine my complaint that the government was being secretive and obstructive by arguing that confidential informants were providing me with all the evidence I needed to do my job.

Then Senator Plett tried his hand at creating some contradictions in my testimony. He was so indignant and offensive that I decided I would revert to the convention that is used in the House Committee of addressing answers to the Chair. I thought that by speaking to General Dallaire I might be far less likely to launch a verbal rocket attack of my own at this rude parliamentarian. Plett immediately picked up on this, saying "Thank you for addressing the Chair when I asked the question, but I will continue with another question." I did not want to make this confrontation any more adversarial than it already was, so I gave way, a little. I used the first-person singular "Senator" to preface my comments rather than "Mr. Chairman," but I kept my verbal responses as objective as possible and fixed my eyes on the Chair, General Dallaire. In doing so I hoped that my body language would not reveal the complete contempt and lack of respect I had for these self-absorbed political parasites.

Then, Plett decided to further exploit veterans. He reflected on my statement that the Minister's announcement on October 15 - that "Canadian veterans diagnosed with ALS will no longer have to fight for their health and financial benefits" — was self-serving. Plett indignantly asked me what I thought was self-serving about that, which I was delighted to explain, looking straight at him.

I told him that what was self-serving about it was that someone would take the credit by feigning that they did something special, anything at all, to make the dying days of veterans suffering from ALS any easier when they simply should not have been denying them in the first place. What I wanted to say was that an apology would have been more appropriate, but I withheld the urge.

## Out With the Old

With an election over and the Harper government back in power, there was all sorts of speculation about a cabinet shuffle, particularly with our Minister. At the very least, we were half expecting to hear about Prime

Minister Harper giving Thompson a new mandate letter describing VAC priorities for the next term. We didn't hear much at all.

In July of 2009 it was announced that Jacques Dubé was leaving federal politics to become the City Manager of Moncton, New Brunswick. Louise and I figured this meant one of two things. Perhaps the prime minister was holding him responsible for the amateur way in which Thompson had treated the whole homeless veterans affair. Rumour had it that the PM had a direct line to all chiefs of staff, in order to keep his ministers in line. Alternatively, Dubé moving on could have been an indication that there was going to be a cabinet shake-up, at least with one position. Harper needed a lieutenant in the Maritimes, the Veterans Affairs portfolio should have been easy to handle, even for an intellectual and managerial lightweight like Thompson, and it was reported that Harper and Thompson were pretty tight. But perhaps when Thompson "turtled" in the face of the homelessness issue, screwing up everything he touched...well, friendship only goes so far. Dubé moving on earlier, in August, would allow the government some time for a smooth transition of power in the VAC portfolio.

It wasn't until January 2010 when the motive behind the move became apparent. One Saturday, seemingly out of the blue, Minister Thompson announced that he was leaving the portfolio; he would stay on as an MP but would not run in the next election. There were few token expressions of regret by his colleagues and very little backslapping done around the announcement, most of which was Thompson patting himself on the back. David Pugliese of the *Ottawa Citizen* quoted Thompson as saying, "I was fortunate to be raised in a family that believed in the values of honesty, hard work, and integrity." I hasten to challenge any suggestion that Thompson characterized the values of honesty and integrity. He knew exactly what he had done, or rather what he hadn't done, for the veterans and their families, many of them civilians living and working in and around the Gagetown area who were suffering from the apparent ill-effects of Agent Orange. I firmly believe that Thompsonhad let many of them down.

In an exclusive interview with the *Telegraph Journal* Thompson reflected:

"I'm one of the few members of Parliament who never had to take back a statement, who never had to apologize, and who never insulted individuals or groups in this country. I've always played by the rules that I believe elected politicians should play by, and I have been always very respectful of the political process."

Clearly he was taking a stab at his beloved party, the one he blindly supported at the expense of the veterans and their families. Thompson's delusion is either a compelling indictment of his character, or a telling example of the dissonance, the conflict between one's personal beliefs and value system and ones actions or conduct, that the culture of parliament inflicts on its members.

## Hail To The New Chief

Not long after Thompson resigned they announced his replacement, Jean-Pierre Blackburn. I was fully expecting that Blackburn would ignore me the same way Thompson had, but I was about to have that assumption dashed.

A day or two after Blackburn assumed the position I was having a meeting with my A-Team when there was a knock at the conference room door. It was my admin assistant at the time, telling me the Minister would like to speak with me ASAP. "I am eager to speak with him anytime!" was my reply, expecting that like the last minister I would schedule an appointment for later.

Linda replied, "He wants to speak to you now! He is waiting on the phone!"

"Oh!" I said as I grabbed my BlackBerry and sprinted to my office.

I wanted to kick things off on the right foot with this Minister, so I immediately commenced the conversation in French. The Minister tried a couple of sentences in English, but his mastery of the English language seemed much worse than mine of French, so we carried on pretty well in French. I had been warned by a friend of mine who has known Blackburn since high school that he is not the sharpest knife in the drawer and I should not trust him. My first impressions of Blackburn, however, were positive, and I had hoped my readiness to work in his first language might, in turn, have earned me his trust and confidence. The most remarkable thing to me was his apparent sense of urgency that I meet with him. Louise was on the next flight to Ottawa to accompany me on my introductory visit with the new Minister.

Going into the meeting I had heard a rumour that Blackburn had already directed VAC to give him a detailed representation of where the concentrations of veterans were in Quebec. I didn't care what his motivation was in doing so, although it was pretty apparent. Politics was clearly Blackburn's priority over policy, but I remained hopeful I could turn whatever embers of enthusiasm to help veterans and their families he might be bringing into the job into a furnace of flame. Once again, I tried to do the meeting entirely in French, although Louise had to come to my rescue a couple of times. Minister Blackburn appeared to be quite interested in what I had to say.

The first issue I presented to him was operational stress injuries (OSIs), which had been so topical in the news for such a long time. I went so far as to suggest to him that the OSI clinic at Ste. Anne's Hospital was, in my opinion, an indication of how pitiful the Department's commitment was to treating veterans with operational stress injuries. Ste. Anne's was a political hot potato at the time because the federal government was going to hand over the hospital — one of the last ones administered by VAC — to the province. I suggested that it wouldn't take too much to expand the clinic and turn it into a real centre of excellence that would serve not only veterans and their families but the interests of all Canadians suffering from mental health problems. I thought the Quebec connection would hit home with him, but it didn't appear to. He didn't even discuss the idea, so I wasn't sure if he thought it was a dumb idea or if my French wasn't serving me well enough.

I also pointed out to Blackburn that the system was completely broken, and how in my opinion the Department and the Veterans Review and Appeal Board had been cheating veterans for decades. That, however, was a work in progress. I also told him that I felt the New Veterans Charter was fundamentally flawed and urgently required a full review. I suggested that, in my opinion, the situation was scandalous, but because the NVC had been introduced into legislation by a previous Liberal government, if Blackburn on behalf of the Harper government asked the OVO to do a full investigation, the veterans would probably laud them as heroes.

In this meeting, I wanted to present a grave situation to Blackburn in the clearest of terms, so when I decided to make my presentation in French I made a point of confirming some of my intended vocabulary with Louise beforehand. By the end of the meeting, however, I wasn't certain the Minister had understood how grave the situation was for some veterans. Just to be sure, I followed up with a phone call to Blackburn's chief of staff. I had recognized during our meeting earlier that this gentleman was completely fluent in both official languages, and he had struck me as a pragmatist. On the phone I spoke to him in *my* first official language, just to make sure that I conveyed the seriousness of the situation as I perceived it. He assured me the Minister had understood, and that was the last we heard of it. That COS retired from federal politics soon thereafter, and Blackburn's buffoonery was set to begin.

In the early days, Blackburn had appeared to me to be a man of action. He had heard that the town hall meetings I had been conducting across the country were about to take me to CFB Valcartier in Quebec, so he asked if I would mind if he attended one. "Of course!" I said. I eagerly welcomed his presence but not his participation; even so, welcoming him to the meeting was not without some trepidation. Those meetings could get pretty feisty sometimes, with veterans pointing their finger and yelling blame at me for the ills of the Department. I was concerned that if the audience knew the Minister was present, the meeting could get very ugly very fast. Why blame me when they had The Boss there? I took my hat off to Blackburn, though, because he appeared at the appointed place and time. To the credit of everyone who participated in the meeting, the audience was extremely respectful but still forthright. Blackburn learned a little about what veterans were facing, and my staff and I could see he was surprised by what he heard.

My early impressions certainly did not support the criticism that had been levied against him when he first moved into the portfolio. First impressions are not always lasting impressions with me, however, and it was not long before I changed my mind about Blackburn. As I was increasing the intensity with which I was addressing some of the issues, I decided to make a formal observation to the new Minister regarding the bureaucracy's unfair interpretation of the "benefit of the doubt" as it is was described in all the legislation for veterans. Having reached an impasse with the Deputy Minister, Suzanne Tining, on this issue, I thought it was serious enough to merit an "escalation of force." So I sent Blackburn a letter outlining the issue. I had realized while Greg Thompson was still the Minister that the Deputy Minister was clearly running the show, and true to form Blackburn just parroted the same bullshit that Tining had already insulted my intelligence with. Blackburn merely regurgitated to me the Department's interpretation, which was precisely what I was challenging. In his response Blackburn didn't even make an attempt to refute my argument, or explain why I was wrong or how the standing interpretation did not disadvantage veterans as I alleged.

CHAPTER 8:

# Lousy Leadership

There is an ancient proverb, of Chinese origin I believe, to the effect that "a fish rots from the head down." During my life as a commander and combat leader I have come to recognize how true that axiom is. While it goes well beyond the scope of this book to examine it in any detail, suffice to say Canadians should understand that the episodes of callousness and misconduct they witness in their parliamentarians is firmly rooted in the culture of senior bureaucrats. Their propensity to abuse people trickles-down the senior echelons of government to poison the culture of the entire public service.

Throughout my term as Ombudsman, VAC was plagued with charges of breaching the privacy of veterans. The most notorious breaches were those committed against veterans' activist Sean Bruyea, which were so grave he received an out-of-court settlement of over $400K when our parliamentarians started to feel some heat. There were numerous other such offences of a more minor nature but equally unacceptable. When these revelations started to make the government feel uncomfortable, Canadians got an opportunity to see what bad leaders their political masters are.

Prime Minister Stephen Harper, in response to this rash of gross privacy violations that had happened under Minister Thomson's watch, placed the blame squarely on the Department's bureaucrats. He said, "The fact that some in the bureaucracy have been abusing these files and not following appropriate processes is completely unacceptable." Just the same, the rumour inside the government was the trail of evidence for the violation of Sean Bruyea's privacy led clearly to the office of the of Minister.

Jean-Pierre Blackburn was also openly critical of departmental employees for privacy violations that senior management and his predecessor had conspired to commit. That was where I had to draw the line as to my silence on this issue. In one of my blog entries I publicly admonished Blackburn for this disgusting demonstration of lousy leadership. How dare he blame the rank and file who stalwartly serve such a demented, dysfunctional institution.

Senior bureaucrats do not only promote such a culture of malice, they themselves have no empathy for their own troops. Most of my staff aspired to progress beyond the OVO, to continue their work in the Department or elsewhere in the public service. So, understandably, they were concerned that doing too good a job for me might cause them to be marginalized from the Department. Their concern was so pronounced that I discussed it personally with Deputy Minister Tining, though she discarded the notion out of hand.

Later, I also mentioned it in passing to a committee. Of course, when the Committee asked DM Tining about it, she again dismissed it as a legitimate concern. Nothing at all was done in the workplace to examine the claims of the staff, and no senior bureaucrat, the Deputy Minister in particular, made any effort to alleviate their anxieties. So my team continued to do their best work for me with that cloud hanging over their heads that, in so doing, they could be ruining their careers. That characterized for me how little empathy senior management in the public service has for their rank and file.

And then there were those privacy violations that were fired down the shit accelerator. It was well known in the Department which senior bureaucrats were directly involved in the violation, and it was also well known that no disciplinary action was taken against them. Instead, DM Tining used "group punishment" to make her problem go away. She mandated three days of privacy training for the entire Department and declared the matter closed. When the employees in the Department are treated like that, it is no wonder that veterans and their families might face staff members who are not as courteous or sympathetic as they would expect.

## Disingenuousness

Senior bureaucrats are guilty of malevolent conduct that taints the culture of the entire public service. They manufacture half-truths, deliberately skewing information that parliamentarians present to the people of Canada with the intention to mislead. I witnessed this in the first person sometime in the latter half of my term when I was introduced to a bogus study the Department had initiated, one that they misleadingly called an "Independent Assessment." This assessment was created on the premise that the demographics of the veterans' community were changing, conditions much like when the Cliff Chadderton and Justice Mervyn Woods were facing when they did their exhaustive study. Back then, veterans of the First World War were getting much older and the mortality rate was increasing considerably, but this time it was amongst veterans of World War II and the Korean War. Unlike the Woods Committee of the 1960s but typical of the deceitfulness of the government in the twenty-first century, this assessment was charade; it was hardly independent, and the outcome of the assessment had already been pre-determined.

At the time, there was a lot of rumour, innuendo, evidence, and spin on the street suggesting that the government was intent on reducing the size of Veterans Affairs Canada. VAC employees in Charlottetown were concerned that the head office would be hardest hit by the cuts. There was even rampant speculation that the head office would be moving away from Charlottetown — so much so that the new Minister, Blackburn and DM Tining made public assurances that it was not in the cards.

The cost of the contract for the not-so-Independent Assessment was set at below $25K so that it could be sole-sourced. In other words, the Department specified exactly who the contract would be awarded to. That was Keith Coulter, former Chief of Canadian Securities Establishment and Commissioner of Corrections Canada. Coulter was assisted by one other contractor and some senior bureaucrats from VAC. My meeting with Keith was courteous enough. In fact, he offered me some very useful insights into the system and some thoughts on how an ombudsman might function within it. Keith stuck to the story that he was doing a thorough and unbiased assessment of Veterans Affairs, but it was very, very apparent where he was going with it. He clearly differentiated between veterans of war service and retired members of the Canadian Forces, and he kept coming back to the fact that the number of veterans who had served in WWII was dwindling.

I took advantage of this occasion to educate Mr. Coulter. It wasn't so much the facts that he needed to hear, but a balanced interpretation of them. I made my point about the personal commitments and sacrifices of veterans and their families being the same, regardless of what generation they belonged to; modern day or war service. I made a point of emphasizing that if you included all the people who leave the CF as veterans-proper — some of whom were injured, wounded, or became sick while on duty — and considered the huge amount of discontent that was spewing from all sectors of the veterans' community, war service veterans included, concerning VAC's lousy service, one could reasonably infer that the Department was actually severely understaffed. I left it at that, and our Special Advisor Q gave them virtually everything we had that could be of use to them. They no doubt benefited from Q's seemingly bottomless pit of knowledge and experience.

Months went by while Coulter did the apparently independent and apparently objective assessment when, once again out of nowhere and all of a sudden, I was visited by the Independent Assessment Implementation Team. I thought this was a courtesy call and was eager to please; but somehow the intent appeared to be something more, quite frankly, than they were prepared to tell me. What I was hearing I didn't like, because it was leading me to believe that my earlier suspicions about the preconceived outcome of Coulter's assessment were correct. I tried to prod them about what Coulter's findings were, but they were tight lipped. I finally tired of the pleasantries and asked them, point blank, what they wanted the Office of the Veterans Ombudsman to do.

The question was so matter of fact I am sure it caught the implementation team leader off guard, because words seemed to be evading him. Finally he said that he was hoping to have the support of the Veterans

Ombudsman in implementing the Independent Assessment. I knew nothing yet of the status or content of said report, so it was premature for its implementation team to solicit my support. Also, if the content was going where I thought it was, they would have to present a pretty convincing argument if they hoped to ever get my support.

I thought that the veterans' community could challenge the results of Coulter's so-called Independent Assessment if it ever became public, and I believed that proffering my support to the Implementation Team could place me in a conflict of interest. More importantly, these guys must have thought this was my first rodeo, asking me to support blindly the implementation of recommendations that I knew nothing about. I simply told them that in my capacity as Ombudsman it was my practice not to endorse anything that I have no control over. I would await the reaction of my stakeholders before I did anything.

CHAPTER 9:
# Institutionalized Malfeasance

Veterans, by their very nature, are ripe targets for exploitation by a callous, parsimonious, and self-serving bureaucracy. I single out the bureaucracy, particularly senior bureaucrats, because the government's victimization of veterans has transcended the reign of successive Liberal and Conservative regimes. I hasten to add, I am not 'necessarily' suggesting a grand conspiracy exists; the victimization of veterans could simply be a manifestation of incompetence, intransigence, and/or the overall toxic environment that senior bureaucrats have created in the public service. Whether that or a warped set of priorities is the source of the problem, or all-of-the-above, would be hard to say definitively without a full, transparent public inquiry. The bottom line for me is, though, that senior bureaucrats have been the source of continuity.

In the latter decades of the twentieth century, attendance by Canadians at Remembrance Day ceremonies seemed to wane. While I have not seen any evidence that the government ever deliberately committed acts intended to diminish participation on Remembrance Day, it is clear the bureaucracy did the bare minimum expected of them, expending little or no effort to halt the trend or, indeed, stimulate increased attendance. Internally, the government treats commemoration as if it's just something else that they have to administer. As such, VAC has relegated the responsibility for commemoration to the branch that is also charged with policy-making and communications: in other words, the Department's policy wonks and spin-doctors. Were it not for the involvement of the Royal Canadian Legion, Remembrance Day probably would have been de-humanized and reduced in status from the commemoration of Canada's Wars, an act of healing for those involved, and a living reminder of the cost of war, to an event that simply marks the anniversary of an historical event.

The Government of Canada demonstrated just how little they understand about an act of remembrance versus historical anniversaries shortly after the Afghanistan War. No sooner had the Canadian Forces ceased operations when it was announced they would be patriating a monument from Kandahar that had been created in theatre by our troops to pay homage to our CF personnel killed in action. The government decided that the monument was to be accommodated by the CF "wherever they could find room for it."

At the same time the Government of Canada announced that a monument marking the 200th anniversary of the War of 1812 was going to be erected in a prestigious location on Parliament Hill, for which the artwork is expected to cost $780,000, and the final bill for landscaping and infrastructure could top $1 million. If it had been left solely to the government, they probably would have transferred Remembrance Day ceremonies to Canadian Heritage to be "administered" with other events in our history like the War of 1812.

Veterans Affairs Canada has become quite expert at exaggerating and exacerbating even the slightest differences between veterans, and have effectively enshrined a class system within the veterans' community. It is a very good example of a strategy, whether deliberate or unwitting, of "divide and conquer." As we have seen, Veterans of the Korean War were not always treated equally to those with war service in Europe, nor were the merchant navy, BCATP, POWs, and others. Each successive era of veterans, and many groups represented therein, have had to fight for due compensation. For decades the government has hammered away at the people of Canada with a subtle but compelling propaganda campaign of trivializing modern, post-Korean War veterans, Canada's peacekeepers.

Within the Canadian Forces, peacekeeping was a sideshow, a tiresome distraction from their real business of deterring Soviet aggression in Europe. While all eyes were fixated on our Cold War showpiece in Germany, the 4th Canadian Mechanized Brigade Group, the real action was taking place in all the hot wars that we were sending our peacekeepers to. Parliamentarians and senior management in the government, general and flag officers in the Canadian Forces included, deliberately concealed or downplayed the extraordinary professionalism of and grave personal sacrifices made by Canada's peacekeepers, particularly on occasions such as United Nations Operation in the Congo (ONUC), in 1960-64, the Turkish invasion of the island of Cyprus in 1974, and the battle of Medak Pocket in the Former Republic of Yugoslavia in 1993. Consequently, the people of Canada have been conditioned to believe that peacekeeping operations were bloodless offerings, and the wounding and killing of our peacekeepers were little more than unfortunate industrial accidents. Coincidentally, the government did not consider the sacrifices of the Cold Warriors to be any more significant than those made by of our peacekeepers.

During Canada's misadventure in Afghanistan, I used to gag whenever I heard dissenting, misinformed politicians lamenting the passing of the "good ole days" of peacekeeping. They would display the depth of their ignorance with public comments such as, "We shouldn't be sending our 'peacekeepers' overseas when there isn't any peace to keep." What they failed to understand and were negligent for not emphasizing with mainstream Canadians, was that we never sent our so-called peacekeepers overseas on operations unless there was a war. It seems that in the eyes of our government, it is not the act of making life-shattering personal sacrifices for Canada that matters; it's when the sacrifices were made.

Rather than detract from attention paid to our traditional veterans each eleventh of November, our peacekeepers, in a self-deprecating manner that is so typical of the majority of our veterans, lobbied the government for a piece of remembrance of their own. After years of hard work they established the peacekeeping monument called "Reconciliation" that is somewhat less spectacular than its big brother — the Cenotaph — and is located in a dignified, albeit less prestigious, setting at the centre of an intersection framed by St. Patrick and Murray Streets, Mackenzie Avenue and Sussex Drive, just north of the American Embassy and south of the National Gallery of Canada. Once a year, veterans of peacekeeping, their families, a few informed and empathetic Canadians, and only the odd

*Institutionalized Malfeasance*

politician, gather at their modest monument for a low-key ceremony. The date, August 9, was chosen because on that day in 1974 nine Canadians serving as peacekeepers with the United Nations Emergency Force were killed when the plane they were in, flying over Syria, was specifically targeted and shot down by anti-aircraft fire. On that day every year they remember the contributions and sacrifices that they and their comrades made to world peace and security, well out of the public eye relative to the heroes of the World Wars and Korea.

Similar ceremonies are conducted at select monuments across Canada, such as the Wall of Honour in Peacekeeper Park in Calgary. There, a healthy-sized gathering of loyal Canadians who know the truth about peacekeeping gather every year to remember and pay their respects. In my estimation, Calgary has been the scene of one of the larger events in the country on 9 August; sadly but understandably, the numbers of participants at Peacekeeping Day ceremonies are minuscule compared to the national sentiment that pours out for World War One, World War Two, and Korean War veterans on their big day. It is understandable, however, when you consider the way in which public perceptions have been manipulated for decades. Granting peacekeepers an obscure date to hold their ceremonies at less prominent locales effectively lowers their status in the eyes of the people of Canada relative to the "real veterans" on November 11.

Meanwhile, the government continues to come up with new ways to diminish the stature of "modern" veterans, to broaden the divide between them and the "real" veterans. The Government of Canada wanted to hold a state funeral to mourn the passing of Canada's last veteran of World War One, Mr. John Babcock. It could be argued that it was the right thing to do, so it was natural to interpret the Department's intentions as genuine. Indeed, it is nothing less than distasteful for Canadians to think otherwise.

The government had been so persistent in quietly trying to convince Mr. Babcock to accede to a state funeral that he made mention of it when I met with him. At that time, my naïveté as the Veterans Ombudsman had not yet been expunged but it still made me wonder why the government would be so dogged in their desire to honour Mr. Babcock with a state funeral, whether he wanted it or not. In retrospect and in light of the malevolence that I later witnessed in the senior echelons of government, I strongly suspect that the government was not pressing for it for the right reasons. I remain convinced that the government wanted to use Mr. Babcock's star power to emphasize the distinction between the passing era of our war service veterans and our less worthy modern veterans.

So instead of a state funeral, on Tuesday, November 11, 2008, they organized a "Passing of the Torch" ceremony, in which Mr. Babcock appeared on huge "rock star" screens on Parliament Hill holding a "Torch of Remembrance." The crowd that day, estimated to be some 25,000 strong, was greatly appreciative and erupted in a huge round of applause that one never would have expected at one of these solemn events. The bureaucrats got what they wanted; a huge spectacle that would capture the hearts and minds of Canadians, staged in a way that would reinforce their propaganda that Canada's veterans are in fact disappearing.

Mr. Babcock and the Second World War veterans were portrayed in civilian attire, while the veterans of peacekeeping sported the distinctive light-blue berets that characterized not having served in any "real" war. Canadian Forces veterans were represented by a young, physically fit member of the CF, in uniform. If the latter had to be a person in uniform, why wouldn't it have been one of those who had taken a bullet or a shard of shrapnel or lost a limb at the behest of our government? There are many severely wounded and exceedingly deserving service persons who might have better represented the true sacrifice of modern veterans.

When Mr. Babcock passed away, sadly, on February 18, 2009, Minister Blackburn quoted Prime Minister Harper as saying that the passing of Mr. Babcock marked the end of an era. On the contrary, for anybody who has served, Mr. Babcock actually represents the beginning of the legacy, a proud heritage of humble "service before self" that he and his comrades in arms — and, indeed, their families — established in World War One. Little did we know at the time that what the prime minister meant by his remarks was that it marked the end of the era of looking after our veterans.

## Culture of Denial

I entered the Office of the Veterans Ombudsman with an open mind regarding the bureaucracy, veterans' issues, and politicians — just about everything to do with the job and the situation I was stepping into. I had heard many of the urban myths that exist in the veterans' community, such as vets having to apply three times to get what they deserve. I originally dismissed such stories as proverbial "old wives' tales." Almost ironically, I would learn that it *was* often the wives of veterans who had the determination and the means to research the issues, consider the government's responses to their claims, and re-apply on behalf of their spouses in order to obtain the services and benefits they were entitled to. I would also learn that tale of three tries is not a myth.

After a while I noticed, anecdotally, what I thought might be a trend. Adjudicators seemed to deny claims on their first submission and approve them on their second submission 'low-balling' the respective awards. These would, more often than not, subsequently get increased on the third challenge to what might be considered a fair settlement; that is, if a veteran had the staying power to go through the process a third time. While I did not have enough time in office to prove my suspicions, the observations were compelling.

Some of the claims of modern veterans I witnessed that were denied by VAC and the VRAB clearly reflected a complete lack of empathy and understanding of the military. A classic example of this was a disability claim made by a trooper who, having retired, began suffering from terrible skeletal pain in his lower back and knees. The claim was denied because the veteran had never reported an accident involving those body parts that were causing him pain. Knowing that this person had spent almost his entire career doing the hard yards in the Airborne Regiment, jumping out of aircraft in the middle of the night, trudging on snowshoes pulling a toboggan, carrying a rucksack, and sleeping under a poncho liner on the ground, it is obviously reasonable to infer that service exigencies inflicted significant cumulative trauma on this trooper's body. The claim was subsequently approved on review, but it should not have been denied in the first place.

Those kinds of deficiencies abound, and, alarmingly, I found that many of the harsh criticisms that the Woods Report had made against the system in the 'sixties had resurfaced. Sadly, not only does the desire amongst government officials to do right by their veterans no longer exist today, but they often act, or fail to, in ways that cause our veterans great harm. In sum, the culture of denial resident in VAC and the VRAB severely limits the support that a grateful nation expects them to deliver to our veterans and their families.

## Tough Decisions

Some adjudicators within VAC confided in me privately that when they were confronted by tough issues that might test their understanding of departmental policies, they would simply deny the claim. Approved claims are subjected to a rigorous internal scrutiny, with major claims often being held up for months. One departmental adjudicator told me about a case that allegedly took eighteen months to see the light of day after it had been submitted to the head office. Several Board members told me similar tales. One person also told me that VRAB management occasionally overruled favourable decisions without consulting the presiding members or calling the claimants to reappear, and for no apparent procedural or evidential reasons. Unfortunately, I did not have enough time as Ombudsman to follow up formally on these kinds of complaints.

I also learned that the Department doesn't even examine departmental decisions that were subsequently reversed upon review or appeal by the Board. Such a feedback loop, I think, has obvious benefits for veterans and would have been very simple to implement and maintain. Quality assurance is a fundamental management practice, so I thought that it would have been a matter of due diligence.

I once suggested to Deputy Minister Tining that the sixty percent favourable rulings that the VRAB claims is actually a sixty percent failure for departmental adjudication. She replied that her understanding was that applicants are required to produce additional evidence before issues can go to review or appeal, so the Department could not be held accountable for incomplete claims submitted by veterans. I suggested to her that the Department's requirement to produce additional information was of their own doing. I pointed out that Service Canada actually contacts Employment Insurance applicants if information they receive is lacking in some way. Moreover, while such a requirement might be a simple way to weed out the frivolous claims, it also impedes applicants from redressing wrong decisions.

In my experience, the Veterans Review and Appeals Board, or VRAB, is a kangaroo court of the highest order. One does not have to dig too long or hard to determine that the depravity of that organization runs deep. Veterans who do not agree with the findings of their appeal with the VRAB are allowed to present their case to the Federal Court of Appeals. They must however, absorb the entire cost themselves, which I am told averages about $30,000. Veterans are often successful at these appeals, but VAC and the VRAB are not compelled to embrace contradictory rulings. On many occasions they don't. This kind of obstinacy is obviously a misplaced bias that runs contrary to ethos and intent clearly articulated in the Woods Committee Report.

In an effort to conform to quotas in their decision-making, Board members are notorious for rejecting or disregarding the credibility of supporting testimony and opinions given by witnesses, even in the form of medical opinions provided by professionals. The Woods Report states that this should not happen, especially in the case of the latter. I have seen cases where the VRAB has ignored certain evidence presented to them based on nothing more than a Board member's own lay opinion or hunch. There are even glaring examples where Board members have ruled that evidence was contradictory when it clearly was not, and where they have injected opinions or testimony of their own, which they then weigh as contradictory evidence.

Notwithstanding occasions where such evidence has been completely unfounded, it is patently wrong for Board members to challenge the applications of claimants as aggressively as one would expect the prosecution to attack evidence defending an accused. The Woods Report makes it very clear that these are not to be considered trials where there are two "sides" to a claim. The Board exists merely to assess the merits of a claim and apply the Benefit of the Doubt, which I shall discuss in a moment.

Most seriously, the VRAB blatantly violates many principles of natural justice in the way they do their business. One grossly unfair practice is the way they use the same people to chair appeals who hear initial reviews. While the VRAB insists that their members do not as a rule participate in the appeals of their own findings, they cannot be considered independent and/or unbiased. Anybody who has ever worked in the maze of cubicles and coffee pots that is the federal government knows how much business is shared over the dividers. It is inconceivable that there would not be instances when the appointed referees in a review and a subsequent appeal might exchange the odd bit of information regarding the case, along with the customary office pleasantries.

The Chair of the VRAB maintains a record of the decisions, favourable and not, of each Board member. I challenged him on the practice, suggesting he is exerting undue influence on the decisions made by Board members. Decisions should be based on the merits of each individual claim, not institutional quotas. Larlee shrugged it off as "quality control." I asked him what his definition of quality was, and how he sought to control it. Of course he would counsel the member whose decisions he does not agree with, but he would not admit as much. Despite being a practicing lawyer in his past life, I think John Larlee was unable to see the absurdity of this defence.

One of his Board members did, though: Harold Leduc. In October of 2012 Leduc went public with claims that he had been bullied for being too lenient on veterans. The Board took further measures to unfairly influence Leduc's decision-making by violating the privacy of his medical file to obtain information on personal medical conditions they could use to assassinate his character. There is absolutely no way that VRAB members are unfettered in their *prima facie* decision-making based on the merits of each application before them, whether they know or care to admit it.

The Board's most flagrant abuse of natural justice, in my view, was its failure to publish decisions. That practice denies other veterans who are similarly suffering from health conditions or enduring unfair treatment of the opportunity to use prior rulings as precedents to support their claims. The Chair admitted this failing to me personally, citing privacy and bilingualism as sticking points. They put a price tag of $5M on the translation of rulings and decided that it is too expensive. What is the point of spending any money whatsoever on a tribunal if their practices are so unabashedly unfair?

What the VRAB did is harbour fifteen "example cases" upon which they claim to base their decisions during the appeals process, but they refused to share these with the claimants or the Bureau of Pension Advocates (BPA). Technically these "example cases" amount to precedents, but whether or not it is fair to construe them as such is moot. The lack of transparency stands on its own as tacit proof of the unfairness of their system. Apparently today they will release select decisions, which they call "Noteworthy Decisions," that veterans may consider in their own claims, but there is no reason to believe that this is being done in a fair and non-prejudiced fashion.

Fundamental to the concept of natural justice is the perception of fairness, and these are just examples of the perceived unfairness of the system. They are not lost on the veterans' community, the service officers in the Royal Canadian Legion and ANAVETS, or the lawyers employed by the Bureau of Pension Advocates. They deal with them every day. The fact that the malevolence is so glaring is a scathing indictment of the system as a whole.

## Excessive Burden of Proof

My personal pet peeve, which I think characterizes the malevolent culture within VAC and the VRAB, is the exaggerated burden of proof that they insist our veterans must meet in making their claims. Legislation describes it as the "Benefit of the Doubt" (BOD). Specifically the BOD states that adjudicators shall draw every reasonable inference from the credible, un-contradicted evidence presented in a claim and the circumstances related to the case, and in the weighing of evidence resolve any doubt in favour of the applicant or appellant order to rule in their favour. I found in VAC and VRAB, disturbingly, that the formal interpretations of BOD they required their employees to apply when approving or denying claims represented a huge departure from the intent of the legislation. Chapter Eight of the Woods Report clearly conveys the intent that adjudicators who award benefits and services to people who have served our country so well — our veterans and their families — should err on the side of generosity rather than parsimony. Most importantly, the report clearly acknowledges that the BOD can lead to applications being approved even though the preponderance of evidence might suggest other causes of a claimed disability.

The report makes excellent representation of why this legislation was written the way it was, which was the impetus behind why I concluded that the Department's and the VRAB's interpretations of it were so, so wrong. Woods describes a system, the Canadian Forces, that is responsible for screening and selecting their recruits, training and equipping them, putting them into harm's way in the first place, treating them if they get wounded or injured or become sick, and for generating and maintaining the evidence that they will require to make disability claims. Woods' committee also acknowledged repeatedly that the system must always be expected to be less than perfect because the military must function in tumultuous and dangerous environments. Thus, the lesser burden of proof introduced by Justice Woods, the BOD, was intended to compensate for this imbalance.

Similar statutes exist provincially regarding workers injured on the job, but a study we had a private law firm conduct on our behalf in the OVO determined that the federal statute as it was designed for veterans is the most liberal. There is a very good reason for this. The federal government deliberately exposes, arguably, their most faithful citizens — Canadians who have accepted the condition of unlimited liability in the service of Canada — to great danger and potential harm in "workplaces" where they have little or (more often than not) no control whatsoever over health and safety standards. Provincial governments make laws compelling employers to make the workplace as safe as possible for their employees. Injured workers in the private sector may also be eligible for additional compensation when an injury is the result of negligence, while a CF service member who became sick, or was injured or wounded in the line of duty has no such entitlement.

When I examined the government's interpretations of BOD I was confounded why it would not include clear, concise definitions of what constitutes a "reasonable inference" and "doubt," which are fundamental to the BOD provision. I reflected on my experiences writing persuasive research papers in university and in the military, and *knew* that what I read in the Department's and the Board's interpretations did not describe in any way the nuances of "reasonable inferences" as opposed to "definite conclusions." Under BOD, one merely needs to demonstrate that his or her claim is plausible, which is beyond a mere possibility but well short of a certainty. Importantly, BOD legislation instructs adjudicators to draw broadly from not only the evidence presented by the claimants but all of the circumstances associated with their cases. This clearly does not simply offer adjudicators latitude, it compels them to accept — even seek out — hearsay, circumstantial, and indirect evidence that is not necessarily introduced by the applicant.

I encountered many VAC and VRAB rulings that, in my opinion, refused claims for lack of direct evidence. I observed some that, in my opinion, not only failed to make *all* reasonable inferences that flowed logically and reasonably from the evidence and the circumstances — remember my anecdote about the veteran of the Airborne with osteoarthritis in his lower back and knees — they made no proper inferences what-so-ever. Instead, decisions were solely those conclusions that necessarily and irrefutably fell from the evidence. Consequently, decisions often assessed the truthfulness of a claim, imposing a level of proof comparable to "beyond reasonable doubt" in criminal law or the "balance of probability" in civil torts. This practice is wrong, an assertion that is supported by the discussion in the Woods Report, and yet was commonplace in VAC and the VRAB.

That distinction is subtle, and therefore difficult for laypersons to comprehend or deduce for themselves. As I have witnessed firsthand, the distinction can be equally incomprehensible to lawyers whose education and experience have not engendered them with the propensity to think critically or who lack the capacity for original thought beyond what they were taught at law school. But I am not for a second suggesting that this is an acceptable excuse for the omission, because even the most cursory search on the Internet reveals all sorts of legitimate sources of legal definitions for "inference," even for a "reasonable inference rule."

Because the law directs adjudicators to *resolve any doubt in favour of applicants*, I also argued that the failure to describe in any of their formal interpretations exactly what sorts of things constituted their "doubt" represented another very serious omission. For ease of explanation, the difference between eyewitness testimony (direct evidence) and hearsay (circumstantial or indirect evidence) is defined by the degree of doubt that exists between them. It is "reasonable to infer," therefore, that resolving any doubt in favour of the applicant or appellant, means that any credible and relevant hearsay, circumstantial, or indirect evidence presented in a claim should be afforded equal weighting as eyewitness testimony or direct evidence. I observed instances where Board members not only failed to resolve doubt in favour of applicants as directed in the legislation, they actively sought evidence that would introduce doubt in order to rule against applicants.

Not surprisingly, none of the Board members or VAC adjudicators I met could accurately explain in their own words what a "reasonable inference" is or what constitutes doubt to be resolved in favour of applicants, from either an academic or legal perspective. Often they were not even able to paraphrase the formal interpretation of what they were supposed to adhere to in the normal course of their duties. Likewise, they were not able offer any credible arguments that challenged the correctness of my own interpretation.

VRAB states clearly on their website that veterans must prove their case based on the "Balance of Probabilities" (BOP). In my days with the OVO when I challenged the burden of proof that VRAB expected claimants to meet, the Chair, John Larlee, actually sent me a letter under his signature stating in black and white the same thing. BOP is the basis for decisions in civil court that are made in favour of a "preponderance of evidence." I have already pointed out how the Woods Committee report states outright that is inappropriate. If the creators of the legislation had intended the use of the BOP standard, they could have said so quite simply and unmistakably. Their intent was to direct adjudicators to approve claims if they were plausible, not necessarily "probable."

## Absence of Sincerity

In a speech given in Kitchener, Ontario, Harper announced the formation of the Office of the Veterans Ombudsman, adding that it was in accordance with their "strong commitment to openness and accountability." I have already admitted that as the Ombudsman I naïvely defended the mandate despite its apparent lack of teeth. I foolishly assumed that the gestures of admiration and respect that senior bureaucrats bestowed on our veterans and their pledges to support the Office of the Veterans Ombudsman were genuine. After all, I find it inconceivable that any Canadian would willingly and knowingly cheat someone who has made selfless and serious sacrifices for this country out of their just deserts.

That was then. I have since realized — too late, unfortunately — that senior bureaucrats will go to extraordinary lengths to disadvantage and take advantage of loyal Canadians.

## Dumbing Down the Mandate

The Order in Council that describes the mandate for the Office of the Veterans Ombudsman is a compelling example of how senior bureaucrats scuttled the ability of the Harper government to implement such an agenda, if they ever really intended to in the first place. I had been in office for a year or so when a brown envelope was slipped to me containing the documentation from the departmental project team that set up the OVO. I received initial drafts of directives, policies, and plans, some stamped SECRET, as well as a copy of the Treasury Board Submission. I had the whole enchilada.

Included in the documentation was the recommended mandate and authority for the Veterans Ombudsman. The departmental project team had suggested that a ministerial directive would be an appropriate means of delegating the requisite authorities to the Veterans Ombudsman, as it is in DND. In a document labelled SECRET they even submitted a draft of what the ministerial directive establishing the Office of the Veterans Ombudsman should say.

Once the paperwork was submitted to the senior management in early 2007, it didn't see the light of day until the announcement by the prime minister on April third. The bureaucracy had decided to issue authorities to the Ombudsman in the form of an Order in Council instead of a ministerial directive, as was recommended by the project team. That is innocent enough on the surface, and for all intents and purposes the Order in Council embraced most of the key recommendations that were contained in the Department's SECRET Establishment of the Veterans Bill of Rights and Ombudsman Implementation Plan dated March 2007. In fact, the OIC for the Veterans Ombudsman captures many of the duties, responsibilities, and prohibitions contained in the ministerial directive for the DND/CF Ombudsman almost verbatim, save for obvious differences between the two stakeholder groups and the environmental/operational complexities within DND and the CF.

One small but important detail was conveniently omitted. The DND ministerial directive clearly compels everyone in the DND and CF to support, assist, and cooperate with the CF Ombudsman "in accordance with the law." It also specifies in no uncertain terms that no employee or member of the CF may refuse or wilfully fail to assist the Ombudsman. Those imperatives, or any other obligation of the government to support the Office of the Veterans Ombudsman, were conveniently omitted from the OIC for the Veterans Ombudsman's authority. In other words, any assistance the senior bureaucrats provided to the OVO was nothing more than a professional courtesy. I found out the hard way that not only are senior bureaucrats not courteous professionals, they are downright disruptive.

On the photocopy I received of VAC's draft ministerial directive there is a clause that includes the phrase "in accordance with the law," where someone reviewing the document had penned "Which law? We are not legislated." The comment itself was wholly disturbing because there are laws governing access to information and information security to which the clause was referring. The comment hit me like a bag of rusty hammers because by this time I had seen too many incidents where senior bureaucrats were operating deceitfully and, I submit, with impunity above the laws of the land.

## Feigning Independence

It was commonly understood that the Veterans Ombudsman was independent, but nowhere could the actual definition of "independent" be found. Nowhere in my official mandate did it even say that I was independent. In defence of my status, I had to draw attention to the prime minister's official announcement of his intention to establish a Veterans Ombudsman in Kitchener on April 3, 2007. At that time, he described the Ombudsman as someone who would work separately from government: "operating at arm's length" to "raise awareness of the needs and concerns of veterans." The Deputy Minister used to throw that term at me; how she was protecting "the independence" of the office, but she, too, could not describe for me exactly what my independence entailed. Certainly she could define "independence" as a noun, but she had no idea what that meant in terms of the relationship between our two organizations.

I therefore described it for her, and the rest of government, any chance I got. I described my independence as my "ability to make timely and sound decisions based on all the relevant information and free from any untoward influence, constraints, or pressure; real or perceived," or words to that effect. With that definition in hand it would be much easier to identify occasions where our independence was being violated. I had hoped that, if nothing else, the Department would come back at me with the "official" definition. That never happened though because, as I learned, a lexicon that lacks specificity, logic, or practical applicability is a licence for scheming and plausible deniability.

## Constrained Logistics

One way the independence of the OVO could be compromised — insidious but certainly obvious in light of the definition I assigned to the term — was by the Department's inefficient delivery of so-called corporate services. Military planners worth their salt know that effective logistics are vital to the successful outcome of any campaign. Any civilian who knows anything about management would understand that this is true for projects of any kind.

The Department's lax and haphazard provision of support services was an extraordinary impediment to our ability to establish our operating capability. Our progress was such a disappointment to me that midway through my tour when I appeared before parliamentary committees I gave myself a failing grade. Despite the differences I mentioned earlier regarding our respective stakeholders, Andre Marin's hard work in setting up the Office of the CF/DND Ombudsman provided a template that should have been easily replicated. We were making things happen in the OVO, but in my opinion we were not progressing nearly quickly as an initiative of government should have. I would have expected that the OVO should have taken precedence over the internal initiatives of the Deputy Minister and the Department. While DM Tining assured me on several occasions that the OVO was the priority, in practice, the OVO frequently fell victim to waiting our turn in the queues for various support services.

## Improprieties With Information

Another way that the Department violated our independence — the most obvious one — was by controlling the information that we could access inside government. The first difference of opinion between the DM and me was over the interpretation of the verb "to review" as it is found in the Order in Council. Our mandate told us not only what we were expected to do, but it also had a list of things that we were not allowed "to review." On that list were such things as internal departmental legal advice, confidences of the Privy Council, decisions of courts of law and the Veterans Review and Appeals Board. Madame Tining interpreted "to review" as "to read," which was obviously incorrect.

The term "to review" is defined elsewhere in legislation affecting veterans as "to hear, to determine, and to deal with," which describes a much more empowered proposition than simply "reading" something. My rationale was that we would never challenge the decisions of a judge or seek to redress a judgement of the VRAB, but we could most certainly read them. The former, legal judgements, are public information and veterans would frequently give us copies to read of the latter, renderings of the VRAB. Louise, with her corporate memory *vis-à-vis* the early work that she had done on the project team in laying the groundwork for the OVO, agreed with my interpretation. She recalled that the verb "to review" had been selected for use in the project documentation because it was softer than "to investigate." Placing limits on what we were allowed "to review" was never intended to prevent the OVO from "reading" anything that we could obtain legally.

We hired the legal firm Heenan Blaikie, ably represented by Ivan G Whitehall, to do a legal analysis of the term. Ivan did an amazingly exhaustive and well-reasoned review of the term, and arrived at the same conclusion as we had at the OVO. To review was synonymous with "to investigate" and the mandate did not prohibit us from reading court and Board decisions, departmental solicitor-client privileges, or Cabinet confidences. The need to know of an ombudsman was easy to justify and OVO staff were legally bound to protect confidences of the Privy Council to the very same degree as any other departmental employees.

The Deputy Minister responded with a "Sharing of Information" policy memo that amounted to a lengthy and unmistakeable "too bad, so sad" and clearly conveyed her intent to control the messaging of the OVO. To me, withholding information from the OVO could conceivably prevent us from making balanced, well-informed decisions. In other words, withholding information would be as useful to the Department to control our messaging as deliberately providing us falsified or incorrect information. I therefore objected vehemently.

DM Tining proved to me time and again that her intent to "share information" was indeed going to be problematic. When the homelessness issue exploded I found out for an absolute fact, through my confidential contacts in select senior appointments throughout the Department, that they knew nothing at all about homeless veterans and most certainly had no plans to look into it when I inquired about the matter. When the people of Canada became outraged at the realization that their government was ignoring homeless veterans, the bureaucracy had to scramble to get something going to convey to the public that they were on top of the issue.

After a while, I was invited to meet with a VAC employee who had been assigned the task of doing a "strategic study" of homelessness in the veterans' community. I might add, this employee was eminently qualified academically to do so. I was actively engaged in gaining a better appreciation of homelessness in the veterans' community by visiting shelters across Canada, so I invited her to accompany me on one such visit to facilities in Halifax. I thought it was a very worthwhile experience for the both of us. However, I never heard about that study again...that is, until months later when we received a brown manila envelope at the office from an anonymous source.

In this envelope was a hard copy of the completed strategic study with stamps all over it depicting it as "secret." There had been a blatant attempt by the Department to withhold important information from the OVO. The Government of Canada defines information requiring special security measures as "designated" or "classified." The former pertains to sensitive information that, if disclosed, could harm interests other than the "national interest," which is considered the social, political, and economic stability of Canada. The latter, "classified" information, is information that if disclosed could harm the national interest, and a classification of "secret" signifies that compromise of the information could cause "serious injury" to the national interest. Really, a study on homelessness in the veterans' community could have caused serious harm to social, political or economic stability? Regardless, most of my senior managers were cleared secret and, again, surely the 'need-to-know' should have applied to the Veterans Ombudsman.

The Department just shrugged off that they were withholding information from us, countering that we had the study, didn't we? They also dismissed my suggestion that they had over-classified the document by labelling it "secret." They argued that some of the information in the report could end up in a Memorandum to Cabinet. If that was a legitimate argument, then the same classification could be attributed to every single piece of information that the government ever received. In my opinion, the disclosure of a study regarding homeless veterans not only could not have harmed the national interest, it might actually have served the public interest. Shame on senior bureaucrats for compromising their integrity by being drawn into petty politics.

The government is a master manipulator of facts, which they engage in routinely for matters of petty politics rather than national policy. Another example of informational obfuscation was their quiet abandonment of the "Veterans Health Care Review." If we believed Minister Thompson's rhetoric in his disingenuous and shameless promises, that review was destined to be a panacea for veterans disabled in the line of duty. He promised it would provide the government with a way to move from an entitlements-based system to one based on the needs of the veteran.

Thompson was still promulgating that misrepresentation a year after I was put in the job of Veterans Ombudsman. I was very much looking forward to said report because, in my opinion, a needs-based system was exactly what is required. Disabled veterans should be entitled to all the help their case managers think they need to provide for themselves and their families what they could reasonably have expected their career in the military would have offered had they not become disabled in the line of duty. I believe training and empowering case managers in system that is truly needs-based would provide more appropriate and timely services and benefits to veterans who are, themselves, truly committed to their rehabilitation, and identify malingerers for the system to deal with.

On March 5, 2008, then-Minister Thompson was appearing before the Senate Subcommittee on Veterans Affairs, when Senator Percy Downe knowingly asked about the Veterans Health Care Review. In a subsequent press release, Senator Downe quoted Thompson as stating, "The review is pretty well completed. It is going to provide us with a way forward," a response that, in examining the brief but terse commentary offered by Senator Downe during subsequent questioning, can be assessed as a boldfaced lie as much as a political half-truth. When the senator asked Thompson about the Health Care Review he had already learned that it had been quietly buried, having "all but disappeared from the Veterans Affairs website." When the good senator from Charlottetown, PEI filed a request for said report under the Access to Information scam, which

I will be saying much more about shortly, he was told it was "Protected Information." The quotation marks were in the senator's press release.

The point of this anecdote is that the bureaucrats handling the Health Care Review should have been compelled to release the document, or every part thereof that did not breach personal privacies or commercial confidences, or harm legitimate national interests. I strongly suspect that this report was buried not in the interest of the people of Canada or any portion thereof, but because it revealed that the New Veterans Charter, which I will also address more fully in the coming pages, would not be cost-neutral or the cash cow that the government had secretly hoped for. Consequently, the government retained the provisions of the NVC that disadvantage veterans financially and abandoned their intent to move away from entitlements to needs-based services as they had advertised, and the bureaucracy has continued with business-as-usual in denying and deferring those entitlements.

Not only is the government guilty of withholding information and propagating misinformation and possibly even disinformation, they will use a private citizen's personal information illegally. The government was caught red-handed breaking privacy laws to victimize veterans. Veterans' advocate Sean Bruyea's experience is one such case in point. In 2010, a request for Access to Information submitted by Bruyea revealed that the government had illegally accessed his personal records in VAC. Not only was his privacy grossly violated, but it was alleged that the government subsequently targeted Bruyea personally by modifying and cancelling some benefits. Senior executives apparently proclaimed their intent to "take the gloves off" in their dealing with this particular veteran. It seems they went so far as attempting to have him committed to a mental hospital.

The government would have us believe that the Privacy Commissioner exists to deal with such violations. That, however, is just part of the deception. While I was Ombudsman I discovered that my VAC file had been visited over four hundred times by people who had no business viewing it. At the time, and as I suspected, the majority of the violations were made by people who were merely curious about the new Ombudsman and since I was "part of the team," I dealt directly with the Director of

Security to correct any weaknesses or gaps in the Department's information security. However, in reaction to the gross malfeasance associated with Sean Bruyea's files, in October of 2010 I asked the Privacy Commissioner to carry out a formal investigation into my file's access.

I received a report in June of the following year, basically just confirming that my privacy had indeed been violated. About twenty of the more than four hundred times my file had been entered were inappropriate, and I was told that the respective agencies had taken the appropriate corrective actions.

I was hoping for more. I wanted to know why the people who had no reason to enter my file had done so. Had the government misused my private information for a more sinister purpose, like the fate that befell Sean Bruyea? I knew that they were not above playing dirty. When I put that to the investigator, Ms. Virginia Schwartz, it turned out their investigations are not mandated to ascertain why the information was accessed. She referred me to the Access to Information and Privacy (ATIP) program and told me that if obtained any evidence indicating that my private information may have been used to commit some other nefarious or illegal act against me, they would investigate that claim. Is it just me, or is it wrong to expect that an investigator would naturally determine the extent of harm that had been done?

Anybody who has tried filing an ATIP request knows that obtaining pertinent information can become a full-time endeavour. I had already made ATI requests to the Privy Council Office, the VRAB and VAC just before I left the OVO in October of 2010, at the same time that I had originally complained to the Privacy Commissioner. Each request was met with a call from their ATI coordinators, asking me to narrow the terms of my request. They reasoned that, as it stood, my request was so broad there were tens of thousands of documents that I would be faced with.

I agreed to limit my request to documents bearing my name whose subjects were not about veterans' issues or my stakeholders. In August of 2011 the VRAB had the audacity to present me with one single email written by a former chair in response to the announcement of my appointment to the position. In May of 2012 Privy Council also sent me a single document, almost completely redacted. By that time I had received nothing from the Department so I went back to their ATI Coordinator and told him that I wanted everything with my name on it. In July of 2014, I received a paltry 728 sterile documents. What happened to the thousands of documents I had been told existed?

I have yet to resubmit, thereby becoming a party to the circle of Canadians for whom ATIP requests are a full-time endeavour. I doubt I will. I have heard from dozens of veterans who, like Mr. Bruyea, had to turn the submission of ATIP requests into a bit of a cottage industry in order to obtain the evidentiary documents they were in search of. Right now it is just not worth my while.

## New Veterans Charter

Where the so-called Veterans' Bill of Rights and the mandate of the Office of the Veterans Ombudsman demonstrate the government's deviousness in manipulating public perceptions, the implementation of the so-called New Veterans Charter is the most egregious act of treachery any government has ever perpetrated against our veterans. The short title for the legislation, the "New Veterans Charter," is itself an example of the slick marketing that government uses to dupe their constituents, like the inaptly named "Veterans Bill of Rights."

The Veterans Charter — the real one, not the "new" one — was simply a name used to describe the programs emanating from a collection of statutes and regulations that were introduced during and since the Second World War. The "New" Veterans Charter merely added to or replaced some of the constituent parts of the original Veterans Charter. Many pieces of legislation and programs of the original Veterans Charter have remained in effect for modern veterans, although over the years regulations have been promulgated that have restricted them from some entitlements.

I am sure that history will remember the implementation of the New Veterans Charter (NVC) as a watershed event; not one of perpetuating Canada's legacy of looking after our veterans, but one of the Government of Canada having deliberately and progressively stepped away from its traditional obligation towards the veterans who had served our country, and their families. The NVC was not enacted by Harper's Conservatives; it was actually handed down by the preceding Liberal government of Paul Martin after years of studies and consideration. If one reverse engineers the events leading to this landmark piece of perfidious and parsimonious legislation, it is clear that it had to have been concocted by senior bureaucrats over successive governments, and delivered to the people of Canada by parliamentarians as a *fait accompli*.

Parliamentarians deceitfully heralded the expedited, unanimous passing of the NVC in the House as a demonstration of their unbridled non-partisan support towards our veterans. When the then-Minister of Veterans Affairs, Albina Guarnieri, announced the NVC in her speech of April 20, 2005, she called it "the most profound transformation of veterans benefits in half a century." And while the NVC does embrace some modern best practices, they can hardly be considered profoundly transformational. They are monumentally *evolutionary* in nature and, I would submit, an indictment on VAC for failing to keep up with modern methods in health care.

The majority of MPs who blindly joined the chorus in all likelihood probably had no idea how the NVC might affect the care of disabled veterans, but none of them can deny that they knew about the frugality of the bill. The only committee the bill did not evade the scrutiny of in the parliamentary process was Finance, which gave the NVC the green light only after they confirmed it would indeed save the government money. Guarnieri's speech tells us that she was well aware that veterans would not be pleased with the new legislation that affected their financial security. She urged, "I cannot stress this point enough, the pensions of current veterans and their survivors will not be impacted by these changes. They will continue to receive stable, monthly pension benefits."

The government of Paul Martin pushed the legislation through knowing that replacing disability pensions with lump-sum payments would meet with some consternation, but they also knew that the "profound transformation" Guarnieri boasted about was the amount of money the NVC was going to save the Feds. The political risk at the time would have been perceived as minimal, but nobody would have imagined that provisions of the NVC would be put to the test so publicly, so soon, and so thoroughly by the debacle in Afghanistan.

Parliamentarians acknowledged, in their rush to cash in on this legislation, that the expedited process to adopt the NVC might have allowed some flaws in the bill to slip through, so they agreed that the legislation would be subjected to "continual review." Presumably that meant they would amend the NVC as necessary to improve the stead of any disabled veterans who were disadvantaged by it. The credibility of the NVC began to unravel shortly after our return to Kandahar, and the bulk of the ire voiced against the legislation was focused on the lump-sum compensation that replaced the monthly pension for pain and suffering.

Shortly after I became the Ombudsman, VAC bureaucrats briefed me on the act. My instincts told me that veterans in receipt of lump-sum settlements were being disadvantaged compared to those who were previously awarded pensions for life. In defence of the lump sum, VAC staff argued that the potential for veterans to benefit from compound interest and the financial counselling that the NVC provided to veterans made the one-time payment far more lucrative than a pension for life. That briefing took place only a couple of months before the economic meltdown of 2008 when thousands of people lost their life savings.

By that time the NVC had been in effect for a couple of years and I pointed out to the VAC staff that, contrary to the promises, the NVC had never been formally reviewed let alone amended. When I suggested confidentially that it might be time for them to do so, they flatly refused to open the issue. I was brand new to the game, so I let that ride. Instead I asked if an actuarial study had been done in the creation of the new financial benefits. Departmental officials told me that they had one, and promised to provide me with a copy. It was months before they finally provided me with one, and to my surprise the Department's actuarial study had not compared the relative financial security of disabled veterans who were being cared for under the Charter versus the NVC, it merely confirmed for the government that they would probably be spending less money.

So within the OVO we embarked upon an actuarial study of our own, hiring a private sector firm with experience in the field. Their work demonstrated conclusively that the NVC was a significant step backwards for our veterans, especially those who were at the greatest risk from a financial security perspective. We provided the government with a copy of our report — quietly, of course, as I was in the early days of my role and still fully committed to working with the bureaucracy — but it again fell upon deaf ears. I had resolved myself to continue prodding the system to redress the financial security issues, but if that failed I fully intended to follow up with a more formal course of action. Queens University later did a similar, more exhaustive study that reinforced our findings, but the bureaucracy still did nothing.

Personally, I believe that it is wrong to give a seriously injured service person a fistful of money and send him or her away to invest it wisely for the future. The suggestion that a casualty would be in the frame of mind to care to invest wisely for the long term demonstrates a complete lack of appreciation for the states of mind of service persons who have had their way of life as they knew it traumatically terminated. Some people might possess the wherewithal to undertake informed and considered investments for their futures, but more likely the majority would instead be interested in self-medication, companionship, escape, and immediate gratification to alleviate the pain of their new reality.

Among other flaws with the NVC that we became aware of was the Earnings Loss Benefit (ELB) program. In short, the ELB is an income replacement program that ensures the income of disabled vets undergoing rehabilitation does not fall below seventy-five percent of their gross pre-release military salary. A glaring problem with the ELB was that it mirrored the Service Income Security Insurance Long Term Disability plan that had already been overwhelmingly rebuked as unfair and was the subject of a class-action suit. We brought this to the attention of the Department in a most constructive, low-key manner, but they were unswayed by this observation. They told me to my face that it "followed standard practices in the insurance industry." How was that a reason? Insurance companies are in the business to make money; government exists to care for its citizens — period. It was patently unfair.

Yet another significant flaw of the NVC was that it perpetuated a legacy of treating the members of our Reserve Force as being inferior to their counterparts in the Regular Force. Just as the bureaucracy imposed a class system that discriminated between veterans of the World Wars and the Korean War, wartime service in Europe versus wartime service at home, and traditional and modern veterans, the bureaucracy continues to treat members of the Reserve Force vastly differently from members of the Regular Force.

The complexities of the discrimination is beyond the scope of this publication to describe, but suffice to say the services and benefits available to Reservists are inferior to those of their Regular Force comrades in arms and they shouldn't be. The Reserves came to the rescue when the Government of Canada bit off more than they could chew in Southwest Asia. Reservists fought with distinction; their blood flowed as smoothly, their limbs took leave from their bodies as readily, and they died just as quickly as the members of the Regular Force. The Reserves are an integral part of Canada's defence forces, and their veterans are deserving of the same treatment as their regular counterparts.

## Military Culture and Culture Shock

The full name of this legislation, "The Canadian Forces Members and Veterans Re-establishment and Compensation Act" (CFMVRCA), is more appropriate than its short name, the "New Veterans Charter," because it more actually reflects the objective of the act. The intent is to get veterans established on civie street and pay them off so the government isn't bothered by them anymore. The government's creation of programs that are insurance company-friendly and can be outsourced to the private sector makes me suspect that there is a more sinister agenda at play here. I believe the endgame for senior bureaucrats is to reduce the financial liability represented by veterans who have become disabled in the service of Canada, and to draw-down the size of VAC if they cannot eliminate the Department completely.

In addition to the programmatic flaws with the CFMVRCA, a couple of which I have introduced, I submit that it suffers from a very serious flaw in the fundamental premise upon which their philosophy of "re-establishing" service personnel was based; its creators clearly presumed that the profession of arms is simply a job, and that leaving the military is just about getting another one. In a very superficial way, perhaps it is, but this is clearly an interpretation made by people who have never served their country in uniform. The average soldier with any time in will have changed jobs many times, learning and adapting to new relationships, terms of reference, skills, and desired outcomes. But the average military person only leaves the military once.

I personally changed jobs at least fifteen times in my military career, often accompanied by changes of locale, several times to different countries and cultures. That was easy-peasy because I was "A Soldier." Life and work were one and the same for me; they were simply battle drills. Speaking at the memorial service in Edmonton for the four victims of the Friendly Fire Incident in Afghanistan in 2002, my wife, Trish, described it so eloquently. She said, "Soldiering is not what my husband does; it is who he is." Trish and I had developed a domestic routine whereby my home life would not interfere with my military readiness and deployability. Conversely, when I was home I would simply conform to the family routine as a soldier following the orders of the residential sergeant major — Trish.

It is often said that it is easy for you to get out of the military but it can be hard to get the military out of you. What is missing from the equation is that a military force spends vast sums of money inculcating civilians into its culture, and virtually nothing to reprogram them for life back on civie street. Recruits, the majority of whom enter the military with very limited life experience under their belts, are virtually brainwashed into walking, talking, dressing, acting, and reacting in a specific and uniform manner. That behaviour is hammered into them daily for however long or short their careers may be. In the Canadian Forces I had the pleasure of working with some of the most dedicated, professional warriors who have ever set foot on a battlefield anywhere in the world. It is hard for me to imagine how any one of them was not military to the very core of his or her being.

Even people who may not serve long, in my opinion, are deeply affected from their time in the military; the only questions are how, and how much or how little. When they transition back to civilian life, their military upbringing may manifest itself as a reinforced sense of pride, confidence, discipline, honour, duty, patriotism, or fraternity. Alternatively, the residual effects of military service could be in the form of rejection of authority, disdain for seemingly liberal or permissive civilian attitudes, difficulty in conforming to or reading social cues, marginalization, or a host of other rebellious, contrarian, or otherwise unacceptable behaviours.

Leaving the CF is less about just finding a new job than it is akin to emigrating to a foreign land with a different culture. For me, it was a huge culture shock. I had left home at the age of seventeen, so I grew up in the military. When I became the Veterans Ombudsman I had to discover who the adult civilian Pat Stogran was. There is no doubt in my mind that this culture shock was not unique to my personal situation and for some people it is even more difficult to deal with than it was for me. Many, if not the vast majority, make the transition to the culture of civie street with little or no problem. Many veterans get assimilated back into the society from which they were recruited very handily, but even for them, their "regimental colours" are not far from the surface. This is especially apparent in the camaraderie that emerges when retired warriors congregate, when they encounter serving personnel, and even when they interact with uniformed members of other services such as the police.

Another important consideration that the policy wonks who created the CFMVRCA probably would not have realized is that the work of a soldier can be one of the most self-actualizing and satisfying things that a person might do. Merely passing recruit training is a huge accomplishment, the pride of which often stays with a person for a lifetime. So is the pride associated with having endured the rigours, challenges, and dangers of military training and operations. For many, no greater sense of purpose can be achieved in life than protecting innocent civilians from becoming targets or collateral damage in the terror and tragedy that is war.

I would submit that simply returning to the safety and predictability of garrison life can have severely debilitating psychological consequences for a soldier. Alternatively, the perception of having failed to accomplish a mission or protect non-combatants, as was the case during many so-called peacekeeping operations of the last century, can be just as soul-destroying. It follows that being marginalized by and thrown out of the military and then subjected to the mistreatment of Veteran Affairs Canada could have catastrophic consequences.

To put an edge on it, place yourself in the position of a member of the former Canadian Airborne Regiment in the mid-1990s. You deploy with the Regiment to the civil war in Somalia, enduring extreme hardship and facing unimaginable danger, and you serve your country with honour. When you return home, your beloved regiment that you served in with such pride is unceremoniously disbanded in disgrace. Nursing a painful disability you take your release from the CF. Life all of a sudden becomes very unfamiliar, and the only work you can find is a part-time job at Tim Hortons. Then, assuming you might even be aware that you might be entitled to support of some kind from VAC, to add heartache to misery you have to fight the bureaucracy every step of the way.

The debilitating effects of that culture shock — particularly as it manifests itself in our most seriously disabled veterans who require differentiated, personalized care — was clearly not fully factored into the CFMVRCA. I had the good fortune during one of our webinars to meet privately with Mr. Wolfgang Zimmerman. Wolfgang was the victim of a logging accident, and he overcame his misfortune to advocate for safety in the workplace and the rehabilitation of injured workers. As the executive director of the National Institute of Disability Management and Research, he was a key advisor in the formulation of the CFMVRCA. I pitched to him my theory of culture shock and the limitations I perceived of applying industrial accidents in the private sector as a model of how to transition disabled members of the Canadian Forces back to civie street. We didn't have long to examine my hypothesis, but he was intrigued by the apparent legitimacy of the argument. To Mr. Zimmerman, "military culture" had certainly been a consideration in the formulation of the CFMVRCA and within the subsequent CFMVRCA Advisory Group that he was also a member of, but the phenomenon of a "culture shock" *per se* had not been.

I am fairly certain that, based on my three years as Veterans Ombudsman, the CFMVRCA was supposed to set the conditions for the government to eliminate infrastructure committed to serving veterans and their families by outsourcing program delivery to the private sector. Theoretically, there are certain functions that the private sector should be delivering. For example, Right Management was contracted to implement and manage the job placement program of the CFMVRCA, an unambiguous niche-service that is well established in the private sector. Outsourcing makes sense in such cases. As far as outsourcing, or alternative source delivery, of government functions as a means of saving money, that is a controversial theory that the Government of Canada has already experimented with widely, achieving various degrees of success and failure.

Business cases to support or promote the practice of putting core public sector and military functions out to tender in the private sector I saw in the CF and when I served with the Australian Defence Force I thought were deceivingly biased if not outright spurious. Outsourcing may cost less up front, but I firmly believe you seldom get more for less. Often you don't even get the same for less — you just get less. Whether it is the loss of flexibility, quality assurance, commitment, empathy, or whatever, something has to go.

I think in the military context a little bit of degradation in certain services that are outsourced is acceptable because the effectiveness of the organization as a whole can compensate for the loss. In my experience, though, the military is astronomically more efficient and effective in the conduct of training and operations than the public service is at their primary function. In VAC's case, the circumstances they face with their more desperate clients are often so convoluted and complex that it would be difficult to imagine that a private company could fulfill the function. VAC's own service standards, when it comes to the more serious cases, are so woeful and the systemic problems so deeply ingrained that risking any degradation whatsoever due to third party delivery would be nothing short of reckless. Outsourcing is especially unacceptable when it is done so that the government can abrogate its traditional obligations to the people who served this country so well.

## The Social Covenant

I uphold that the New Veterans Charter was a deliberate attempt by the government to step away from any obligation, real or perceived, that the people and Government of Canada might have had towards those service personnel who have been disabled in the line of duty. In his 2004 discussion paper, *Honouring Canada's Commitment: 'Opportunity with Security' for Canadian Forces Veterans and Their Families in the 21st Century*, Dr. Peter Neary of Veterans Affairs Canada's Canadian Forces Advisory Council describes a social covenant between people in uniform and the country they serve that he suggests is implicit. Indeed, many people in the veterans' community have their own idea of what that covenant, sometimes referred to as a social contract, entails. Veterans Affairs, as part of their snake oil salesmanship of the CFMVRCA, has been quick to applaud this notional covenant while at the same time exploiting its ambiguity and vagueness.

As Veterans Ombudsman I argued that this social covenant is less abstract than it might appear. Traditionally, virtually all major pieces of legislation dealing with veterans' issues included a paragraph in the act that, I suggest, defines that covenant. The following extract from the War Allowance Act is an example:

> "The provisions of this Act shall be liberally construed and interpreted to the end that the recognized obligation of the people and Government of Canada to those who have served their country so well and to their dependents may be fulfilled."

In the latest legislation, the CFMVRCA, that social contract was conveniently omitted. Departmental officials told me this was done because the function is included in the Interpretation Act of 1985. What a crock! Sure, the Interpretation Act talks about the liberal interpretation of legislation, but nowhere does it describe the special obligation that the people and the Government of Canada have recognized towards veterans and their families. It doesn't take a lawyer to identify how malevolent that omission is. The liberal interpretation of legislation has been stipulated to fulfill what is formally described as a special obligation — a *de facto* obligation at the very least, if not a *de jure* because it is repeated in various pieces of legislation. By eliminating that clause, the federal government is, effectively, distancing itself from the suggestion that it has an obligation to care for people who have had their lives ruined answering its call, no doubt with the intention of unloading them entirely onto provincial healthcare systems.

CHAPTER 10:

# Going to the Wall

The government has repeatedly demonstrated they have no empathy for wounded veterans and their families. They hide behind rules of their own making, knowing full well they are cheating veterans, often the most desperately disabled and disadvantaged. The research they choose to act on is anything but progressive, all but ignoring the potential utility of eclectic means of dealing with and managing traumatic wounds and injuries — such as service dogs, yoga, music therapy — which other like-minded nations are embracing in the treatment of their own veterans.

In my time as Ombudsman, I felt the desperate anxieties and apprehensions of the wounded veterans and their families who were victims of such a depraved system. Some of the targets of the malevolence had served under my command. I personally knew many of those who have had limbs torn off of their bodies or who had lost their minds in the service of Canada, as well as others who have committed suicide. As I matured as Ombudsman, I was trying to force the system to view the issues in a more holistic fashion. I never let up on drawing attention to the post-conflict implications of Canada's military misadventures, and the critical role that Veterans Affairs plays in that lifecycle. As much as I may have been contributing to the awareness of senior bureaucrats of the issues in the veterans' community, I seemed to be having little impact on their commitment to remedy them.

## Called Up On The Carpet

In early 2009 I was summoned for an audience with Ms. Roberta Santi, the assistant deputy minister in the Privy Council Office responsible for senior appointments. I had a good six-weeks notice in advance of the meeting, enough time for my imagination to go wild wondering what it was about, although my conscience was clear. Louise assured me that our team was still holding the moral high ground, and to the best of her knowledge we hadn't run afoul of any public service rules or regulations. I was quite sure that we still had the trust and confidence of our stakeholders, so I began to get a pretty good idea what this was all about. I suspected that I was coming close to the end of my tenure.

I reported to ADM Santi's office as directed — alone. At the meeting she had her own note-taker, of course. Madame Santi acted cordially enough, but there was no friendliness in her demeanour. Usually when greeted by a public servant, I would receive comments, at the very least, about the good work we do for veterans and perhaps even a reference to my work in Afghanistan in my previous life. This meeting was strictly business, though, nothing at all personal.

She had with her a three-inch black binder, and in her opening comments she apologized for not seeing me sooner, as she normally met with everybody who is newly appointed to positions in government. I made the point that I doubted the meeting was required because I only had less than a year left in my term. That didn't deter her, though, and she started to take me, folio by folio, through the contents of that huge black binder. We ran into a sticking point very early on when she suggested to me that I worked for the Deputy Minister. I stopped her in her tracks and pointed out that if I reported to anybody, it was as special advisor to the Minister.

She disagreed, so I pointed out to her that it specified as much very clearly in the text of the Order in Council (OIC). Santi could not believe me, so she started flipping through the binder to find where the folio with the Office mandate was. It was soon apparent that her flipping was in vain — the OIC was not in the package. I was getting impatient, so I suggested to her that we just skip that point for the time being and carry on with her briefing. I offered to return at her convenience to brief her fully on the

Office of the Veterans Ombudsman but she declined, insisting that we get photocopies of the mandate before carrying on with our meeting.

Once that had been accomplished, when she cast her eyes on the relevant portion of the document she was obviously taken aback. She managed to make a good recovery by explaining to me in what I took as a condescending way that if I understood how our Westminster-style of government worked I would know, notwithstanding what it said in the text, that I work for the Deputy Minister. I pointed out to her that my training and experience in the Canadian Forces for over thirty years gave me a very up-close and personal understanding of the Westminster-style of government. Also, with a Master's Degree in Strategic Studies from the US Army War College, I could also describe for her the United States government, and explain the relative strengths and weaknesses between the two.

I summed up by referring her to the prime minister's announcement on April 3, 2007 about his intention to establish a Veterans Ombudsman. He made it very clear that the Ombudsman would work at quote — arm's-length — unquote from government. That suggested to me that if I did report to anybody at all in government, it would make more sense that it would be the Minister rather than the Deputy. I felt it was my job to make sure the Department was doing what they should be doing for the Minister, so that the electorate could justifiably hold him accountable for their problems.

Madame Santi was then very calculated in choosing her words when she said to me, in what I perceived as an attempt at an intimidating in-your-face tone, (albeit a sad excuse for one): "Yes Mr. Stogran, but you should be aware that there are various lengths to that arm." She breezed through the remainder of the binder — the larger portion that is — not paying it nearly the amount of attention that it warranted by the work that someone had put into preparing it. I am sure she thought she got her message across. On the face of it, she transmitted a warning for me to pull my head in, but it would not have the effect on me that she had hoped. I received her message as a challenge.

## Horns of a Dilemma

As we were heading into what was to become my last year in office, I decided to intensify my efforts to stimulate genuine efforts within the bureaucracy to make substantive and enduring improvements in the way they treat veterans. By that time I had already met with Deputy Minister Tining over the entitlement of war service veterans' widows to lawn and housekeeping assistance, and it was clear that the Department and the Board were circling the wagons and digging in. Some of the senior bureaucrats I was quite close to confided to me in the margins that their hands were tied, that the real culprits in all of this were the central agencies. By this they meant the Treasury Board Secretariat, the Privy Council Office (PCO), and the Department of Finance. They told me that gone were the days when the central agencies were committed to helping veterans. They suggested that there was a time when the Treasury Board was virtually a rubber stamp for submissions made by VAC to help veterans, but now anything to do with veterans went under hellish scrutiny.

All of a sudden everything was becoming clear to me: the soft mandate I had been given, the role of the PCO, the stalling tactics of a patronizing Deputy Minister, the ignorance of Ministers Thompson and Blackburn, and the biased and not-so-independent Independent Assessment of Keith Coulter's. With each passing day of my final year I was gaining an increasingly detailed and disturbing perception of how broken and morally bankrupt the system had really become. This deterioration in the treatment of veterans had transcended successive governments. The one common denominator in this continuous degradation in services and benefits and increasingly unfair treatment had been the senior bureaucrats, in central agencies, yes, but in my view those in the Department and the VRAB share the blame equally.

Based on this longstanding trend and my own experience in the way they had manipulated the introduction of an ombudsman for veterans, it was painfully obvious to me that senior bureaucrats are more interested in furthering their own careers by servicing the government's agenda at any cost — any cost to others, that is — rather than acting as a stable, balanced and objective "corporate memory" for implementation of the will of the people and the Government of Canada. It was clear they were all hoping I would busy myself with preparing and publishing reports that they could ignore and then I could just go away. Well, this was one ombudsman that wouldn't be ignored. I resolved to go on the offensive — all that was left to be determined was when and how.

I found myself, as per B.H. Liddell Hart's teachings on strategy, being on "the horns of a dilemma." On one hand I was hoping for a second term because I wanted to follow through on creating a system in the OVO that would endure after I left the Office. At the same time I sincerely wanted to work with the Department and the VRAB as long as possible to redress problems in a collegial fashion behind the scenes. If that was not going to happen, though, I was committed to exposing their malfeasance and mistreatment to the people of Canada. Blowing the lid off the pot would virtually guarantee that I would not be reinstated as Ombudsman; it would probably compromise my credibility as the Ombudsman, and perhaps even destroy any chance the OVO might have of making any progress with VAC and the VRAB.

My challenge, therefore, was to identify the "trigger" point: the latest I could wait to make the decision myself to go rogue, and what conditions would compel me to fall on my sword immediately. In the absence of such a kamikaze move, the writing was on the wall that I would leave the Office after three years of effort without having made much of an impact on the wellbeing of veterans and their families, and the reprehensible cheating of them would continue unnoticed and unimpeded. I couldn't wait too long, so I decided that I would make the end of September my final trigger to launch.

## Stepping Up The Tempo

Operationally in the OVO, from day one we had been advancing on a very broad front, so I decided that we would gradually narrow the focus of everybody's efforts as I neared the end of my term. I hoped to lay down some clear markers on files like Agent Orange, flaws in healthcare services, redundant and confusing administration, and the "deny, deceive, and defer culture" of the Department and the VRAB — especially their perverted interpretation of Benefit of the Doubt, which I felt was fundamental to that abhorrent culture. At the same time I wanted to maintain a reserve that would allow us to take on other targets of opportunity that we felt we could resolve in a timely manner — what we called "low-hanging fruit." It was still a pretty broad and aggressive agenda, but I considered it doable in the short time I might have had left.

By this time we had the Comm Ops team and the SOPs in place that could sustain a more ambitious and rigorous series of town hall meetings. Orchestrating the campaign still consumed a huge amount of the OVO's capacity but it was well worth the effort. The deeper insight we might gain was certainly beneficial, but I think the greatest benefit we gleaned from the extraordinary effort we expended to keep that show on the road was demonstrating to our stakeholders that they really did come first in the OVO. It also gave many disadvantaged veterans the satisfaction of being listened to; a feeling that is all too rare for many Canadians dealing with our government.

Not one single town hall meeting went by when I didn't assure my audience that I was as interested in hearing any complaints that our stakeholders had about the OVO, or even more-so, as I was about the bureaucracy. I wanted to make sure we were providing the best possible service to our stakeholders, and was prepared to account to our stakeholders for our flaws or failures. That was my way of ensuring that Canadians were getting the best bang for their buck out of the OVO.

## Internal Accountability

In the military, when command of a unit changes hands, a huge, independent stock-taking is undertaken of everything; from budget and infrastructure, to the conduct of operations and training. I thought this would be a healthy tradition to start within the OVO as well, and what better group to do such an audit than the Office of the Auditor General (OAG)? I had nothing to hide. I knew that we'd had some growing pains in the OVO, but that was to be expected. I had already created a shit storm during one of my appearances before a parliamentary committee by giving myself a failing grade for what I had achieved to that point. Still,

*Going to the Wall*

I believe that the only way you can truly improve is by being ruthlessly honest with yourself regarding the current state of affairs, and consistently hard on yourself to do better.

I contacted the OAG personally to break the ice. I was quite sure that it was not common for a government office to ask the Auditor General to tear them apart. As I expected, they were taken back by the request. There were also some problems to be overcome. In the first instance, the OVO came under the auspices of the DM of VAC. That would be a touchy issue for her. VAC had its own auditors who were supposed to assess programs internally. I had no doubt, however, that such assessments would be skewed to suit the fancy of the DM. In the final analysis, if I could make this happen it would be a real testament to the independence of the Office.

As I expected, the OAG did not undertake the audit. It had been a long shot in the first place. It was very short notice to get done before I left the Office, and the OAG had neither budgeted for it nor had personnel available to assign to the task. They had already been planning to audit VAC, and the government considered an audit of the OVO to be a departmental responsibility.

## Webinars

At the recommendation of Ricardo Angel, our IT guru, and as a result of his hard work we had another what-I-would-call "trail-breaking initiative" in Comm Ops — our use of on-line webinars. We conducted two sessions that were basically panel discussions conducted in real time over the Internet. In doing so, we were able to reach out to a very broad audience of stakeholders and enable anybody to participate. In this way I hoped that, as much as we would gain greater insight into the issues, we might also educate those people who were not aware of — or, as in the case of some vocal veteran "activists" — were misinformed about the issues.

Our first panel of experts included: Darraugh Mogan, representing VAC (by video conference call); Brigadier General (retired) Joe Sharpe, a well-known, well informed and well respected advocate for veterans;

Wolfgang Zimmerman, founder and chairperson for the National Institute of Disability Management and Research, and a key advisor to the people who created the notorious CFMVRCA; and His Excellency, Raulston Saul, an author, really smart guy, and proud Canadian.

We had an email feed that would allow people to pose questions of their own, but as I expected we had the same people engage with the same questions about the same issues. As much as that could have dragged us into the weeds or down rabbit holes of issues that were not broadly relevant — or in some cases not even legitimate complaints — our panel was hugely informative.

It was so successful, in fact, that I intended to commit to many more such events, although we only managed to conduct one more before I left. Our second panel was equally successful, and included: Dr. Muriel Westmorland from McMaster University, an advisor to VAC with thirty-five years of experience in occupational therapy practice, education, and research around the world; Brian Lee Crowley, author, public speaker, and managing director of the Macdonald-Laurier Institute, a national public-policy think tank based in Ottawa; and Major (retired) Bruce Henwood, the double-amputee veteran of the war in Croatia, noted advocate, and advisor to VAC.

Bruce's history is noteworthy. He and I were classmates at the Royal Military College in 1980 and some fifteen years later he succeeded me as the United Nations Military Observer operations officer in the UN Protection Force's Sector NORTH in Croatia. This was during Operation STORM in 1995, when the Croatian Army ethnically cleansed Croatia of over 250K ethnic Serbs. To hear Bruce recount the Croatian offensive absolutely curled my toes. I am not sure to this day I could have done what he did, transiting no-mans-land in his white UN SUV to negotiate a ceasefire, while Serbs and Croatians exchanged fire in a tank battle at unbelievably short range.

Bruce's personal intervention saved literally thousands of Serbs, defeated soldiers and terrified civilians, from unthinkable atrocities as the Croatian Army herded them like cattle to Bosnia Herzegovina. Bruce would lose his legs later when the patrol car he was driving hit an anti-tank mine near the village of Duga Resa, an area I knew very well. Had it not been for the first aid administered by his teammate, Bruce surely would have lost his life.

Bruce was subsequently awarded the Land Forces Commander's Commendation, in essence an "atta-boy slap on the back" formalized with a photocopied certificate and a tiny obscure pin for his uniform. His distinguished service in Croatia during Operation STORM was certainly worthy of a decoration or a formal Mention-in-Dispatch at the very, very least. This was "only peacekeeping" though, so the sacrifices are not worthy of the recognition of real warriors, or so the government would have us believe. But Bruce never lost his fighting spirit, and long before the mistreatment of our modern veterans became a national disgrace, he became a pioneering advocate for those who were disabled in the line of duty. His dedication, knowledge, and experience offered my panel a tremendous amount of depth.

Both webinars were overwhelmingly successful. They demonstrated clearly to me that Canada's intelligentsia, represented by our panel members, is firmly in support of veterans and their families. It seems only politicians and senior bureaucrats aren't. Our webinars also demonstrated how easy it would be for the Government of Canada to consult with Canadians, if they really wanted to.

## Paulette Confirms My Suspicions

One major accomplishment of our operations officer, Paulette McNally, was to produce our second annual report. Not only did she keep me honest, as I was one of the primary authors of that document, but she had a clear vision right from the get-go as to what its end-state should be, and how to distribute the work in order to get there. She cracked the whip to get all the deliverables from all the responsible authors and put together an outstanding report.

All along the way, our Director of Investigations & Research, Guy Parent, had huge problems. First of all, most of the accomplishments — particularly the major ones — that he claimed his directorate had delivered were actually the work of my special advisor, Q. Paulette was aware of this and had already included them elsewhere in the writing plan. Guy seemed incapable of accounting for the work his Investigations & Research team had done over the past year, even after following the detailed instructions Paulette gave him.

In the fashion of any outstanding company sergeant major, Paulette would have us seated in the conference room for her "Orders Group." She had red-penned the drafts we submitted to her earlier, and then issued orders for what she wanted to see from us in our next iterations. There was continual tweaking and some twists and turns occurred along the way, but progress was being made on all fronts. Invariably, the stuff Guy produced required a complete rewrite. We had a tight timeline to meet and Guy was behind, so he would have to leave the meetings immediately to do his revisions. Everybody was frustrated, including Guy. After a couple of repetitions of this scene, Guy blurted out, "You keep changing the goal posts on me." I was pissed off but tried to contain my angst, explaining to him that the goal posts were indeed moving for everyone as we harmonized the constituent parts, but he was the only person who couldn't keep up.

In the face of our considerably enhanced efficiency on the Comm Ops side after Paulette joined us and a mounting sense of urgency in the Office, it became increasingly apparent that Guy Parent was just not up to the job of director of Investigations & Research. I couldn't understand how he had worked his way up through the ranks in the Office of the DND/CF Ombudsman and came to me so highly recommended. By the time of our second annual report, his investigators had done some tremendous work individually, building our situational awareness on the issues confronting the veterans' community and skilfully mediating behind the scenes to resolve some cases of greater complexity. However, as a directorate, they were completely dysfunctional. "Funerals and Burials" was the only report that the investigators produced. The report for our second major investigation — "Red Tape" — was so bad it never came off the back burner I had relegated it to.

I counselled Guy on several occasions, but he was clearly in over his head. At one point it got back to me that he was complaining the investigators weren't getting any feedback from the head office. That was it. I arranged a private meeting with him when Louise could be present.

"Guy!" I said, "What you are calling 'the head office' is the office down the hall from yours, and my director of Investigations & Research is part of the OVO's head office! That's you. It's your responsibility as their director to provide our investigators that link to what you dismissively call the 'head office.' Coaching and mentoring our investigators is your job, and you do that by giving them feedback on their work." I shouldn't have had to counsel a director on something so basic.

I had been very patient with Guy, taking extra time to explain and re-explain things to him. I tried to coach him without drawing attention to my lack of confidence in him. Throughout my military career I had relied heavily on handbooks to assist me in my writing, so I asked Wilma to buy the OVO a bunch of them on logic and rules of writing — *Being Logical* by D.Q. McInerny and *The Elements of Style* by Strunk and White. We then shot-gunned them throughout the office so as not to undermine Guy or suggest that anybody's work in particular was not meeting the standard. Nothing worked and as we were getting into my third and potentially final year as Ombudsman it was clear to me that Guy wasn't up to the task. I had to do some house cleaning — and fast.

This being the public service, though, the Department's director general of HR advised me that it would be very difficult and time consuming to do anything about it. I didn't want to redirect any energy from addressing veterans' issues to dealing with Guy; nor did I want to complicate my life any further by trying to clean up the public service. I met with Guy and he agreed that he would work on a "special project" and we would work around him. That move allowed him to retain his dignity amongst the other people in the office.

Q then took over as our director of Investigations & Research and started following up on the issues that we had floated to the Department as Observation Papers. From the evidence they had amassed, Q and the investigators started manufacturing all sorts of ammunition for us to mount our all-out assault. Some of the investigators were confused by what they perceived as a change of priorities. Q was in a difficult position, being parachuted into the Ottawa office from Charlottetown as the director while his predecessor was still there. He did his best to help them understand what was going on without being critical of Guy.

None of the issues were all that new, only the sense of urgency was. In the end, nobody could deny that I had satisfied my obligation of 'due diligence' in coaching Guy and there was cause to replace him as director. Now, though, we had to make up for lost time.

## Meeting with the Chief of Defence Staff

For the majority of my term as Ombudsman I had deliberately distanced myself from the CF just to demonstrate to my team and other inquisitive parties that I had made a clean break and was working to a new set of rules. After a couple of years, however, I decided the time had come for the Office to reach out to the Canadian Forces, and I should pay a courtesy call to the Chief of Defence Staff, General Walter Natynczyk. I had a great deal of respect for Walt, whom I first met when I was a recruit at Royal Roads Military College in 1976 and he was in his second year. So many Military College types, when they were put in charge, behaved like they were guards at a POW camp, but I could see that Walt was a special kind of guy. He played the game the way it was supposed to be played and his looks really fit the part, but I could tell even when he was hazing me that he didn't take it all too seriously. When I asked for a meeting, Walt kindly agreed to receive me.

Of course, as the Chief of Defence Staff, his time was extremely precious, so I had to make this short and sweet. I was also hoping the CF's chain of command would help us promote our upcoming town hall meetings to the troops and allow us to use DND facilities when and where it might be more convenient for the troops and their families. I was also hoping to arrange to have a captain seconded to the OVO, an Afghanistan warrior who could relate to, and inspire, the young entry level professionals we had on the early intervention team. I would make this position a "shore billet" of sorts, ensuring that the young officer's professional development was continued and that he or she maintained operational readiness. In our meeting, Walt, the gentleman general, quickly agreed. Mission accomplished.

That was almost too easy. General Walt asked me to have my staff sort it out with his Chief of Military Personnel, or CMP, Major General Walter Semianiw. Then we got on with some catching up.

## Chief of Military Personnel

I reported the positive developments to Louise and asked her if she would make it happen with General Semianiw. Knowing Semianiw as I did, I knew it wasn't going to be that easy. I had known him professionally and personally almost my entire military career. I also knew his family fairly well. I don't hesitate to say that I never trusted him. He is amazingly adept at conveying a sincere, compassionate image, but he is ruthlessly ambitious and self-serving, and has left a trail of ruined careers in his wake.

I knew him well enough that long before I became the Ombudsman — long before I left the Forces, even — I resolved never to work with or for him. While I was still serving I briefly occupied the position of regimental colonel in the PPCLI, responsible for managing careers and key appointments within the regiment. Around that time, Major General Semianiw became the head of the PPCLI Regimental Guard, the senior regimental appointment for a serving member. Shortly thereafter I began receiving indications from a variety of sources that my succession plan for commanding officers was possibly being manipulated behind my back. I resigned immediately.

One of Semianiw's projects as CMP, which was introduced to the public with great fanfare, was the creation of the Joint Personnel Support Unit (JPSU). On the surface the JPSU looked like it would solve all the problems associated with disabled service personnel 'slipping through the cracks' when they returned to civie street. The problem was, it was formed out of the hide of the CF. In other words, there was no new money apportioned to the CF from Treasury Board that might have secured the longevity of this initiative. The so-called JPSU was merely a consolidation of the Service Personnel Holding Lists (SPHLs) that already existed in the CF across the country, and the plan very much depended on the drive and the initiative of the people employed in the JPSU to make it work. CF members were amalgamated with VAC staff who normally sat at a desk in a local district office and accommodated on CF bases. These became known as Integrated Personnel Support Centres (IPSC).

In my travels as Ombudsman I would visit the individual IPSCs that the JPSU managed. The people I met working in IPSCs were highly motivated, but again, the centres had a very ad hoc, temporary feel about them. To me the IPSCs represented the old cliché of rearranging the deck chairs on the Titanic, and I felt that their legacy would be a short one. They were clearly vulnerable to being starved of cash and resources when our Afghanistan casualties were no longer in the public eye.

The notoriety of the JPSU caught the attention of the media, which welcomed an initiative that would help our veterans. After a while, however, it seemed the reports we were receiving about the effectiveness of the IPSCs were not really accurate. One soldier told me that the troops would sarcastically refer to the IPSCs as the "Island of Misfit Toys" that you didn't want to be banished to.

With the simple announcement of the cessation of combat operations in Afghanistan and political promises of withdrawing completely sooner rather than later, many of those IPSCs began to suffer seriously, despite the best efforts of the dedicated but under-resourced staff. The situation became so grave that Sergeant Major Barry Westholm, who was employed in the JPSU, resigned very publicly out of disgust for the way it was being mismanaged. Yet another government facade that successfully distorted the understanding of mainstream Canadians of how their veterans are being treated. It came as no surprise to me, though. For me, Walter Semianiw's association with anything was a signal for me to be dubious, and that reticence proved not to be misplaced with this initiative.

It came as no surprise to me, then, that as soon as Louise engaged with Semianiw, he began to manipulate the situation. Initially he wouldn't deal with Louise, insisting that he speak with me personally. He knew full well how I felt about him and there is no doubt in my mind that he had no time for me either, and in my opinion this was an example of the kind of games I would have expected Semianiw to play. I was not going to allow him to meddle in the affairs of the OVO. Not only was Louise's substantive position as my director of strategic liaison established specifically to deal with other government departments and agencies, but at that time she was also acting as my deputy ombudsman. She was more than capable of representing the Office and had my full authority to do so. I felt that because Louise was not already tainted towards this person, like I was, she might have been able develop a constructive rapport with the CMP that would endure after I left the OVO. There was no way I would tolerate Semianiw meddling in how I ran the Office of Veterans Ombudsman, so I insisted that Louise go back to him.

Semianiw flatly refused to allow the OVO to conduct any town hall meetings for CF Members and their families on the bases. He explained that he intended to do the same thing in a joint initiative with Tining and VAC. The Veterans Ombudsman town halls, he erroneously claimed, would "just confuse the troops." That was a ridiculous suggestion. I could understand Louise's misapprehension at the validity of this deception, but I knew from my own experience in the CF that the troops were much more sophisticated than that. They know only too well what an ombudsman is, and I daresay they would not confuse me for Semianiw and Tining. To be clear, by that point in my incumbency, there were most certainly few people in Canada who would have confused me and the Office of the Veterans Ombudsman with any aspect of the federal bureaucracy. I let Louise continue trying to work with Semianiw, who eventually conceded only to allow us to participate in their town halls. Louise didn't have to ask me to know that this compromise was a complete non-starter.

We went to great lengths with all of our initiatives and operations to make a very clear and unassailable delineation between our activities and those of any other organizations, especially VAC. At our town hall meetings we inevitably ended up responding to questions that should have been posed to a representative of VAC, VRAB, the Minister and/or occasionally the CF. This was such a frequent occurrence we could see the utility in having representatives from those organizations as members of our cast, but rejected the idea because we wanted to be seen to be independent. Instead, we strongly encouraged representatives of those organizations to attend as members of the audience and join in the Q&A any way that they were comfortable with. If there were no VAC representatives to field questions, our team did have the knowledge to answer many of the questions, and we did so, but we always, always emphasized that we were not speaking in any capacity on behalf of the bureaucracy or the government. Nor were our responses in any way an endorsement or expression of support for the actions of the responsible branch of government.

I was incensed at Semianiw's ongoing obstructionism and tried going back to the Chief of Defence Staff, General Natynczyk, but couldn't get past his chief of staff, a colonel. He indignantly referred me back to the Chief of Military Personnel with the tone and demeanour that a colonel might speak to another colonel, not the Government of Canada's representative for the fair treatment of veterans, nor, I daresay, a private citizen. I let it go. In the meantime Semianiw, in his devious way, suggested to Louise that the two of them just take a step back and let their bosses sort it out.

Their "bosses" weren't going to be engaged, however. It wasn't important enough to me to waste all this extra energy or risk degrading the independence of our Office, reducing the stature of the Veterans Ombudsman, or undermining our credibility in the eyes of our stakeholders. Obstructionism notwithstanding, our dance card was filling up with informal requests directly from Canadian Forces bases and institutions to have us come and speak with their members and their families, both on bases and in the communities immediately adjacent to them, and in some cases both.

## Chief of Land Staff

I was disappointed that I might not be able to reap the benefits of the positive influence that a young war-fighter officer would have had on the young aspiring professionals in the OVO, but I had another trick up my sleeve. By chance I encountered Lieutenant General Leslie Andrew, whom I had known since we were captains and who was at the time the Chief of the Land Staff, when we were laying wreaths at the annual National Aboriginal Veterans Monument in Ottawa to mark National Aboriginal Day. We had a short chat during which he asked me in a seemingly empathetic tone if there was anything "the army" could do for me. I immediately threw down the marker, a young captain who was a veteran of Afghanistan to act as a liaison officer. Without hesitation he replied "Done!" quote — unquote.

I was pleased, but it was short-lived. A month or so passed, and after hearing nothing back I contacted an old friend of mine from college days, Major General Ian Poulter. I did not want to appear impatient given General Leslie's gracious and decisive gesture of support, but knowing Ian personally and given that his job was on top of everything happening in the army, I hoped to find out the status of the secondment without attracting any attention. Ian apologized, saying that Leslie had decreed that he would only provide the liaison officer if NDHQ would give the army credit for the position against the joint billets that the individual services — army, navy and air force — must fill throughout the CF. Those billets and credits are controlled by Chief of Military Personnel Semianiw, on behalf of the CDS, Natynczyk, so needless to say, it wasn't going to happen.

In sum, the general and flag officers in the CF have done little to curb the victimization of the troops by the Government of Canada. Semianiw was subsequently seconded as a three star general to serve in Veterans Affairs, and he attained his use-by date when Minister O'Toole pulled General (retired) Natynczyk into the Department as Deputy Minister. I assert there is a reason why McKay called Walt the "gentleman general," and it is not just because Walt was popular with the troops — although he was. I am eager to see if, as Deputy Minister of Veterans Affairs, Natynczyk is finally going to assume any personal risk and take a stand for the vets — finally.

## Blueprint for the Fair Treatment of Veterans

We received requests for interviews and appearances from across the country and my A-Team in Comm Ops and I tried to accommodate them all. I was exhausted and really sick of saying the same thing over and over again, but I had to do it. We tried to keep my final act of defiance separate from the regular functioning of the Office under the leadership of Louise and Colleen. On top of it all, I was trying to finish a draft of what I called the "Blueprint for the Fair Treatment of Veterans." I had come up with an idea to create an end-of-tour report, a consolidation of the history and philosophy behind the way veterans have been treated in Canada together with my observations and the lessons I'd learned during my work in the veterans' community.

This project became the centrepiece for my town hall meetings in my final year, where I would share some of my lessons learned as Ombudsman with as many citizens as possible, in order to solicit their criticisms, complaints, ideas, and opinions for consideration in the development of this document. I also intended to solicit comments and ideas from parliamentarians, subject-matter experts in disciplines related to the care of veterans, and other "beautiful minds" in Canada. We decided on the term "blueprint" so as to imply that the document would be subject to modifications, refinements, and interpretations, and to avoid confusion with departmental policies and parliamentary white papers.

I had had a crack at a first draft, consolidating what I had learned in the job about the history, traditions, and realities of caring for our veterans, and Q factored in the nuggets that we had picked up from our stakeholders at our many town hall meetings. I wanted the end product to be short. I called it a comic book version of the Woods Committee report that people could easily read and relate to. I wanted the philosophy that we articulated in this document to be as historically consistent and broadly reviewed as it could be in its conception, so that its message would be as thorough, relevant, and timeless as any pamphlet-like document of this nature could ever be. We sent drafts out to academics, parliamentarians, pundits, and advocates — as many people as possible — to solicit their comments and ideas.

I had thought, perhaps naïvely yet again, that if I could develop some broad generic principles from the work of the Woods Committee, subject-matter experts, select advocates and advocacy groups, and my own lessons learned from Canadians of every walk of life, this blueprint might become a seminal reference in its own right for officials when they redressed the NVC, as they most surely would have to.

There were huge mounds of data and opinions that had to be digested and sorted into some coherent form, so we had a contractor assigned to work with me on the task. I was very excited at the progress we were making and the eagerness with which so many notable and knowledgeable people were contributing their thoughts, comments, and constructive criticisms. I knew I might have bitten off more than we could collectively chew in the closing months of my term, so I was bound and determined to "chew like hell." But alas, it proved to be a bridge too far. I would not able to finish the document and get it on the street before I left the Office.

## Throwing Down the Gauntlet

As a military officer I had already spent a long time in the bureaucratic jungle of National Defence Headquarters — enough to know that these institutions cannot turn on a dime. After two years in the Ombudsman role, trying hard to work within the system, by early 2010 I decided the time had come for me to take advantage of the good will that the senior bureaucrats had been extended to me and start moving some issues. I needed a simple one to present to DM Tining — one that I thought the bureaucracy could address quite easily, if they felt like it. Little did I know that issue would end up as the gauntlet I threw down to start the war.

The issue I chose was the inconsistent treatment of the widows of WWII veterans with the Veterans Independence Program. If a veteran had applied while he was alive for both grounds keeping and in-house services, the widow was allowed to keep both services upon her husband's passing. If a deceased veteran had not applied for either, the widow was allowed to apply for both. But if the departed Veteran had only applied for one but not the other, the widow had to make do.

There were many cases where veterans had opted only for grounds keeping and not housekeeping, because they fully expected their wives to look after the home. Let's face it — that was the way many men in the day thought. What that meant to the wives, unfortunately, was that there were two classes of WWII widows — who could very well be living beside each other — one of whom was in receipt of full benefits and the other who was being discriminated against by the government based on the outdated beliefs of a bygone era.

When I met with DM Tining I described the situation in detail. I had long since realized that she personally knew very little about actual issues such as this and how they impacted the veterans' community. I emphasized that some widows were being severely distressed by this blatantly unfair treatment. They even created an advocacy group called "Widows on the Warpath." I deliberately used hyperbole to push my point home, suggesting that the government was knowingly bullying helpless widows, just like the dastardly banker in the old Western movies who foreclosed on their mortgages. Again I used some strong language in an attempt to prompt some action or, at least, challenge the DM to counter with some factual evidence defending the discriminatory way they were treating some widows.

Nothing of the sort. Instead, the Deputy Minister acknowledged the inconsistent treatment, arguing that it was in accordance with the regulations and she couldn't possibly go to Treasury Board to ask for more money for veterans. I was gobsmacked. It was bureaucrats who for the most part created those very regulations that needed to be changed. I challenged DM Tining, "If you aren't prepared to push this case forward, then who is looking after the veterans' interests?" She shrugged and advised me that I could go to the Minister if I wanted. Oh, that went without saying, thank you, but I knew that would be a useless exercise. I had long since learned that the Minister only did what the DM told him to, and of course what the prime minister told him also.

At that moment, the fog of war lifted. All the promises of working together in the best interest of the veterans evaporated with the fog. I saw the true colours of the people at the top of the organizations I was working with. I was all right with this, though, because at last the battle lines were clearly drawn. It was going to be me against the machine. Then and there, I made the decision that I was going to go rogue; all that was left to be determined was when and how.

## When Declaring War — Timing is Everything

I kind of figured that I might be facing my last annual report as ombudsman, so I wanted to enshrine in it all that I had learned about the veterans' community, its demographics, the challenges it faced, and my outlook on what I thought the issues were that the OVO would have to address. At the same time the document had to contain sufficient operations and management information to satisfy the bureaucratic imperatives of the report, but I insisted that as much as humanly possible we would avoid speaking "managementese" or presenting any bureaucratic pretext. I wanted it written in plain English to present "the truth how I perceived it" — no holds barred. I went so far as to include a paragraph on my approach to ombudsmanry and "speaking the truth as I see it," and never missed an opportunity to invite my detractors or people who did not agree with that perception to offer me evidence to the contrary.

Indeed, our Office was very open to dissenting or contradictory points of view; in fact, we proactively sought them out. The processes we were developing *vis-à-vis* our relationship with the Department and the Board, our "Observation Papers," and the public disclosure of any and all evidence that would not compromise security, privacy, or the administration of justice were intended to facilitate this. Anybody and everybody knew where we stood on our understanding of issues and those who thought they had something to contribute could engage proactively in our pursuit of ground truth.

The DM took it upon herself to release to me only the information *she* felt I needed, and in doing so she absolved me of any responsibility for unfair, biased, or incorrect observations that we might have made in the absence of any evidence, open or confidential, to the contrary. Same with John Larlee, Chair of the VRAB. That should have been their undoing when the shit hit the fan, but instead the Government of Canada just circled the wagons.

It had become painfully obvious to me by this point in my tenure that senior bureaucrats and the central agencies were responsible for what amounted to the deliberate cheating of disabled veterans. Not only was the fallout of such contemptible conduct plainly apparent in the streets of the veterans' community, but many lower-level VAC staff would complain to me, in strictest confidence, of course — that they could not do their jobs because they were slaves (my terminology) to dogma being inflicted upon them by the callous and parsimonious culture that consumed the upper echelons of the public service.

In the meantime, it wasn't too late for me to fold into the text of our annual report this allegation that the central agencies and senior bureaucrats were responsible for the shameful treatment of veterans. It was a bird in the hand for me, the one sure chance for me to record for posterity the reprehensible conduct I observed by senior bureaucrats in undermining the treatment of our veterans.

The main message in my report to our stakeholders became one of exposing this corruption. In my opening "Message from the Ombudsman" for this paper — what became my last annual report as Veterans Ombudsman — I wrote:

> "Canada continues to send its sons and daughters — our most valuable national treasures — into conflict zones around the globe. This in the context of an increasingly dangerous world where international terrorists and transnational criminals have the capacity to threaten sovereign states. NATO's involvement in Afghanistan illustrates this threat. The outcome of NATO's involvement in Afghanistan might be as important an event to the future security environment as was the formation of NATO in 1949.
>
> "At the same time, Canada has undertaken to modernize the legislation that underpins the treatment of Veterans of these missions and their families: The New Veterans Charter. (NVC). This legislation will affect generations of Veterans. In addition, federal agencies are experiencing a generational power shift. The new generation at the controls seems not to have the same understanding or empathy for Veterans and their issues as former public servants.
>
> "This is causing confusion and consternation within the Veterans Community. While Members of Parliament

*Going to the Wall*

and Senators continue to strongly support Veterans and their families, there appears to be a considerable lack of understanding within central agencies of exactly what it means to implement the Government of Canada's mandate in relation to Veterans."

In keeping with our remit to allow anybody whom we mentioned in our reports the opportunity to comment on their own behalf, I sent a copy of our late drafts to the clerk of the Privy Council and the secretary of the Treasury Board. This was in addition to also sending it to the Minister's chief of staff, the Deputy Minister, and the Chair of the VRAB. I was most interested in how the clerk and secretary would respond.

The secretary of the Treasury Board blew us off completely, not even offering us an acknowledgement of receipt. The clerk sent me a customary letter of acknowledgement and expressed appreciation for being offered the opportunity for comment. That was it, but it was too easy for my liking. I suspected that this was going to bite me in the ass.

## The Trigger

Well, the government ended up making it easy for me to get off one of the horns of my dilemma about how far to push before falling on my sword. They made the decision for me. I was sitting in my office at the end of one day, at about 1700 hours, thinking I was alone, when one of our investigators, Dom Parisienne, arrived at my door. He said he had just received a call from the Department of Veteran Affairs at 66 Slater Street, confirming that someone would be present in the OVO to sign for a very important letter for the Ombudsman. I told him he could tell them to send the courier to me personally.

I pretty well knew what the letter said before I opened it. It started off by telling me what a great job I had done for the veterans, blah, blah, blah. I read a little further and the purpose of the letter became apparent. My services were no longer required beyond November 10, 2010. The timing of the arrival of this letter, August 10, could not have been more perfect, although I did have mixed feelings. I was disappointed that my work for veterans would be coming to an end. On the other hand, I was greatly relieved to know this early that there was no reason I had to hold back any longer from exposing to Canadians the terrible way that our government treats the people who have made major life sacrifices for our country.

What was interesting was that at the time I received this letter, the Minister and Deputy Minister were away in Apeldoorn in the Netherlands, basking in the glory of our veterans from a previous generation. The letter had actually been prepared by departmental staff and signed by the Minister's signing machine in his absence. Was it any coincidence that this letter would follow so closely on the heels of the letter from the clerk of the Privy Council regarding my second annual report? I wondered briefly, but a conspiracy theory was not the matter at hand. The matter was that the government had transferred the initiative back to me and I was going to seize it. I immediately alerted my senior teammates to this turn of events, and began scheming as to how I could make the most of this opportunity.

## Mixed Messages

I fully expected the government to be exceptionally cunning in the way they would "eliminate" me. They made Machiavelli look like a girl scout leader. A clever stratagem they had used before to rid themselves of other senior public servants who were critical of the government was to just quietly let their terms expire and have the organization absorb the losses as long as it was politically advantageous to have them do so. In my case I think the clerk just wanted to be rid of me, and clerks of the Privy Council, in the shadows of our elected officials, wield such ruthless power with impunity that they are not accustomed to being subtle when dealing with "internal problems."

Minister Blackburn was clearly not in control of the situation. In the aftermath of the announcement, he stumbled around trying to explain the government's rationale for letting me go. David Pugliese at the *Ottawa Citizen* quoted Blackburn trying to insulate himself from the controversy by saying, "Mr. Stogran was not fired. We think, after three years, a new person will give new suggestions." Blackburn went on to defend "their decision" to release me from the job by saying that the government felt three years was enough time for one person to serve in positions such as ombudsman. My chosen successor, however, contradicted the Minister completely. He was hired for five years. If Blackburn and the Department really had been in the market for a "new person" with "new ideas," they probably would not have taken a chance by replacing me with one of my directors... unless there was something in it for them.

## Conditions for the Attack

By this point in time, I had already pulled together my own A-Team. Louise was up and running as my deputy ombudsman with Colleen Solterman as her wingman in the role of director of strategic liaison and executive support. They were ably assisted respectively by Paulette McNally and Christopher Gillis, another highly competent and driven idealist from the Department. Michel Guay and the early intervention gang were continuing to break down barriers and resolve issues. Charlie had taken over the investigators, and while there was some confusion and angst percolating that we had to iron out together, it seemed they were all pulling in the same direction.

My Comm Ops team was rapidly finding their feet, not just to stand but to run. Shana Allen came to us from the Dairy Board, and Lucille Hodgins had bags of experience doing media relations as a political staffer. Wilma Hanscombe, Tammy Lidstone, and Sandra Martin were handling all of the logistics and administration in the Office, and there was tons of it.

## The Message

I met with my A-Team the very next day after receiving the letter of non-renewal. There were mixed emotions. I heard at least one gasp of relief in the room. We kicked around a bunch of ideas. I finally settled on a two-pronged approach. I was going to have a press conference and announce my disgust with the callous, disingenuous, and parsimonious way the government treats our veterans. It would be my intention to cease holding town hall meetings for our stakeholders only; instead, I was going to communicate with as many Canadians as I could to expose the degree of depravity that existed within VAC and the VRAB.

A righteous challenge can galvanize groups and bring out the best in good people, and it did so this time. I wanted to keep Louise and Colleen focused on the prize. I was going to fight this counter-offensive supported by elements of our Comm Ops team, while Louise salvaged what she could of a harmonious and effective relationship with the Department and the Board. Concurrently, our front-line operators continued to resolve any issues they could in my wake. As we developed the plan of attack for the press conference, Shana, Lucille, and I made sure that this wasn't going to be about me and my non-renewal. This event was all about the veterans who were being cheated and treated so poorly.

I was hoping to bring representatives from all the various demographics in the veterans' community to Ottawa to participate. We knew that we had some stalwart advocates who would jump at the chance to make a public display of their discontent. I was also hoping to get some of the wounded young soldiers from the war in Afghanistan to join us. I knew I could count on Bruce Henwood and Paul Franklin, another dynamic spokesperson for wounded veterans who had lost both of his legs in Afghanistan. Bruce and Paul were both retired. That didn't satisfy the requirement, though, because I was hoping for some "colour" — green CF tunics. I had a line on Mark Campbell and Jody Mitic, both of whom were still serving and extremely well spoken, but I was hoping for some new faces also.

## H Hour[5]

The Friday morning before my press conference I made a call to my old friend and colleague, Walt Natynczyk. I had not spoken to Walt since the Semianiw incident, and then only briefly to step away from the meddling of his Chief of Military Personnel. This was going to be my last

---

5   Military terminology for the time at which lead elements of an operation cross the "Start Line" or "Line of Departure," when the operation is considered officially launched. It is the time upon which all planning and preparatory actions and time-critical subsequent actions are based.

opportunity to really do something for the veterans, so I thought I would give it a whirl.

I had to leave a voicemail, but Walt was good enough to call me on my cell as I was closing my garage door first thing in the morning the day before the conference. I asked him if he would help me out, and I assured him that the troops would be well briefed not to talk about legislation, the government, or the CF policies regarding their injuries. All I really wanted were people who could explain that coming home wounded, particularly as an amputee or a serious psychological casualty, was not as easy as filling out the paperwork for VAC, wisely investing your lump sum payoff, and carrying on with life. You virtually have to learn life over again.

Walt wasn't quite forthcoming. Once I explained the event to him he suggested that I go to Bruce Henwood. He started telling me everything I already knew about Bruce, the champion of veterans' rights. I interrupted and tried to impress upon Walt that a rare opportunity to do something that will really help veterans was presenting itself to us and how important it was that "we" did this right. As if he hadn't heard a thing I was saying, Walt went on to suggest Paul Franklin as well, and started detailing the impressive list of things Paul had done for veterans.

Walt is a very, very nice guy: the "gentleman general," as Peter MacKay put it in announcing Walt's appointment to Chief of Defence Staff. He was too nice of a guy to come right out and tell me to "pound salt," but it had become abundantly clear to me that he didn't want to help the veterans in the way I had envisioned. Since I didn't have time to play around, I finally came right out and challenged him on it. "So Walt, I think I hear that you are not going to help me publicize how poorly the government is treating our young soldiers and the families of our young soldiers who are wounded and killed in action."

He replied, "Sorry Pat, I just can't."

As I got in the car and drove to work, a lot of things were going through my mind, but not *What is wrong with Walt?* To the contrary, in fact, I was asking myself, *What is wrong with me?* I tried to see this whole situation from Walt's perspective. There was absolutely no doubt that I was on an inevitable collision course, and I was quite sure I was going to end up on the receiving end of this crash. Walt had at one time struck me as a warrior, so what was I missing here? When does a normal person stand up for something? Was I taking the easy way out by being a non-conformist?

In the end, I decided that I couldn't live with myself if I chose to conform to a hypocritical system that abuses people who have made sacrifices for it. After all, I had been an agent in promoting that system to the troops under my command, so I had to take some responsibility for the system letting them down. "Naw, it's not me," I decided, "It's their problem!" I was headed on a collision course, so I recognized that I had better pick up speed.

I was very disappointed not only with Walt, but with the lack of support of any kind from anybody who had ever worn the maple leaves of a general or flag officer in the Canadian Forces. In the build up to this event I had not heard private words of encouragement from any retired brass who had been publicly feigning support for veterans: not Admiral Larry Murray, General Rick Hillier, or Lieutenant General Charles Belzile, to name just a few of the more conspicuous personalities.

## Foot in Mouth

The Minister and his staff could not have been more helpful in setting the conditions for this showdown. By complete happenstance the Minister made a series of proclamations that demonstrated the Department's disdain for veterans and intent to abandon them. Blackburn came up with the brilliant idea that, instead of getting one big payment, soldiers would be offered the option to have their money spread out over months and years. For example, a payment of $200,000 could be spread out over five annual payments of $40,000 each. Huh? Any veteran who chose this option would just give away the advantages advertised earlier of accrued interest over the timeframe for the payout. I doubted that any veteran would ever be stupid enough to ask for "deferred losses" even if they were suffering from major psychological and emotional injuries.

Then the Department announced they had done a survey on behalf of the Minister to determine the level of discontent that existed within the veterans' community towards the new lump sum payouts for wounded veterans. By this time I had seen too many examples of surveys and consultations that the Department had set up to 'rubber stamp' their actions. Blackburn trumpeted across the country that sixty-nine percent of respondents were happy with the lump sum payouts. "Our survey indicates that the lump sum award is the preferred option for sixty-nine percent of those veterans who have received this benefit," he said in a statement. "This shows us that the changes that were made in 2006 were the right thing to do." The survey also found that eighty-five percent said their lump sum payment was well used and seventy-one percent said they had invested some portion of the cash. One didn't have to peel that onion very far to find out, even without the details of how the survey was conducted, that there was more than met the eye with these results.

For starters, the question that was asked was not even relevant to the arguments over whether a veteran is better served by the CFMVRCA lump sum payments or by the monthly payments previously provided under the superseded Pension Act. The question that had been asked was whether veterans would prefer a lump sum payment as a single payment, or as payments over time *with the same dollar amount*. Basically, it was a take-it-or-leave-it solution to the grievances of service personnel and veterans regarding the lump sum. The Minister also glossed over the fact that respondents suffering from mental health conditions were less likely to indicate a preference for single payments or to report that their lump sum they had received for their disabilities had been well-used.

And then for the *pièce de résistance*. In the month leading up to my hastily organized press conference, John Ibbitson and Kate Allen reported in *The Globe and Mail* that Canada's veterans were "ebbing away" – 1,700 veterans from World War Two and the Korean War were passing away each month — and government officials were asking how much the Department of Veterans Affairs should be cut back as a result. Earlier, Keith Coulter had submitted the confidential report on his "independent" assessment to Blackburn on the future role and responsibilities of the Department. Blackburn confirmed the suspicions that Coulter had aroused in me earlier in the year; that his mandate was to justify the government's intention to reduce the size of the Department.

"We know that we will need fewer employees in the future," Blackburn was quoted as saying, adding that no decision had been made on whether layoffs would be needed or if the workforce could be trimmed through attrition or relocation. As I was about to launch my press conference alleging that the government was intent upon abandoning our veterans, Blackburn inadvertently helped our cause by announcing their intention to further degrade their ability to look after those who served our country so well.

## The Assembly Area

On the day of our fateful press conference, August 17, 2010, Minister Blackburn was conveniently back in his constituency in his lesser capacity as minister of state (Agriculture). He was announcing that Canadian maple syrup producers would be benefitting from up to $4.3 million in funding to create new opportunities for this "pure, quality product." Meanwhile, back in Ottawa, anxiety was high. The assembly area was our office in the fifteenth floor of Constitution Square on Albert Street in Ottawa. That morning as I was making my way down the concourse towards the west tower where our office was situated, my personal cell phone rang. I looked at the call display, and it was Major General Lewis Mackenzie. For once my morale took an upward turn. The rest of them may have been notoriously quiet, but not good ol' General Lew, who in the very title of his latest book published in 2008, admitted that *Soldiers Made Me Look Good*. Here he was calling me on the very day of our tiny rebellion to voice his support for the veterans.

General Mackenzie started with the normal small talk, told me what a great thing I was doing and that he couldn't believe that a government would treat disabled veterans so badly, and then he got to the point of his call. Corporal Jody Mitic and another soldier wounded in Afghanistan, Corporal Andrew Knisley, were going to race an Acura TL in the Targa Newfoundland high-performance car rally. Supported by Honda Canada, with their drive the pair hoped to raise $150,000 for the Soldier On fund, a Canadian Forces trust that assists injured soldiers in returning to full and active lives. General Lew said that Honda was worried about the

*Going to the Wall*

attention they might attract from Jody's participation in my press conference and were threatening to pull their sponsorship. He asked me if I could keep Jody out of the picture. My morale plummeted, but I assured the general I would talk to Jody.

I arrived at the office to find we had a great turnout of vets who were eager to make representation on behalf of their hurting comrades. We had wounded troopers representing a variety of corps and regiments who were still serving; both CF and RCMP veterans, family members, friends, and concerned citizens. I immediately pulled Jody aside and advised him of my conversation. Jody is very much a mission-team-self oriented warrior, and his instinctive reaction was to do the right thing for the cause. I impressed upon him that he was also doing something groundbreaking for veterans by driving in that race, and a warrior cannot lose sight of the war in the heat of battle. Jody acquiesced, but very grudgingly.

I had intended to have a special meeting with the CF personnel immediately following my welcoming address to all of our eager participants, just to make sure they understood what they were allowed to say to the media. I wanted these troops to present themselves to the public as the consummate professionals they were, and I didn't want them to get in trouble with their chain of command. Just before that happened, Master Corporal Jody Mitic, a leader and role model in the eyes of all the troops who had been seriously wounded in Afghanistan, told me in private that he had just received an order from the Chief of Defence Staff's office prohibiting the military personnel from participating.

To their credit, several of the young troopers were still determined to reveal to Canadians how tough life is for a family that has a parent or sibling who comes home from military operations with physical or psychological injuries. I deeply appreciated such selfless determination, but I wouldn't allow them to jeopardize themselves in disobeying such a clear and direct order. I figured we could get the message across without them, but the help of some senior officers at any time would have really boosted the impact we might make. Getting everybody from our office tower at Kent and Albert over to the press gallery was, at the risk of using an old and tired cliché, a lot like herding cats. We did get there, though, and had a chance to conduct a quick reconnaissance of the auditorium, and to give confirmatory orders in the press gallery conference room.

Unfortunately, we discovered that the stage would not seat as many people as we anticipated, so I had to make a command decision as to who would represent the veterans. That caused a lot of grief for some people who had come a long way hoping to attract some attention to their cause. I was at the point where some people were just going to have to grin and bear it. This was not about the individual issues; it was to illustrate for Canadians the depths of depravity that exist within a system that was touting itself as looking after our veterans. The final cut included myself with four veterans:

- Kenneth Young, the tireless advocate on behalf of victims of Agent Orange and a sufferer himself;

- Brian Dyck, dying from ALS and a victim of the Department's and the Board's perverted interpretation and application of the Benefit of the Doubt legislation;

- Dennis Manuge, the injured party and lead claimant in a class-action suit against the government's Service Income Security Plan (SISIP) Long Term Disability plan for Canadian Forces personnel; and

- Ron Cundell, a veteran who had been fighting VAC for years and was extremely well versed on the wide variety of stupid practices within the Department that frustrate veterans and deter them from getting what they have earned through personal sacrifice.

Just before we walked onto the stage, I pulled Brian Dyck aside for a private little talk. From my perspective, Brian's speech was going to be the keynote. I wanted to draw special attention to his personal plight with particular emphasis on the tragedy his family had to bear witness to. I asked him if he would mind if I was quite blunt in the way I introduced him. This was our last desperate opportunity to obtain any care for his family after he passed. Warrior that he was, he didn't have a problem with it and did not hesitate to give me the green light. In fact, more than a green light, he gave me *carte blanche*.

## Going Rogue

### AUGUST 17, 2010 PRESS CONFERENCE

At 2:00 p.m. precisely, I was seated with four other Canadian Forces veterans at a table on the stage of the National Press Theatre. The auditorium, which holds about fifty people, was packed. I had been told to expect a good turnout from the press and I was hopeful, but honestly, I hadn't been optimistic. I thought that the media attention I had attracted to this point in time had been very narrow. On the contrary, though, the audience was very broad, in fact, attracting many of the who's who in the press gallery on Parliament Hill. This full turnout was fortuitous, as the wider coverage might serve to enhance the impact that this kamikaze run of mine, as Canada's first Veterans Ombudsman, might have. Little did I know that we were about to send the country into a tailspin.

After my opening comments and introducing our speakers, I handed the microphone over to Kenneth Young. I had first met Ken at one of my town hall meetings in Victoria, BC. He had travelled all the way from Nanaimo to educate me on the issue of Agent Orange. A retired army corporal, his knowledge of the Agent Orange issue was nothing short of astounding. He was self-taught and regarded internationally as a subject-matter expert. He was also personally suffering the ill effects of the government's reckless use of that chemical mixture at Canadian Forces Base Gagetown in New Brunswick. At the conference, Ken told the Canadian public about the horrendous harm that the government had inflicted on so many military personnel and civilians living in the area.

Brian Dyck was next to speak. Brian's condition had deteriorated terribly since I had last seen him only a few weeks prior; on this day, it was all he could do to muster up the strength to appear at the press conference. In introducing Brian, I gave the audience a short history of the disease and my relationship with the Dyck family, adding that I wanted all Canadians to suffer along with them. I pointedly told the entire nation that I wanted them to witness Brian die his slow and painful death while

VAC and the VRAB "jerked him and his family around." These were strong messages that seemed to grab the attention of the audience, and they listened attentively to what Brian had to say.

After telling his story, Brian ended his speech with the words "If you don't want to stand behind our troops, you are welcome to stand in front of them." Admittedly this saying is a bit of a cliché, used for years as an expression meant to garner support for troops, but when Brian said it I almost stood up and cheered. A couple of insensitive journalists had the gall to draw attention to this in their articles posted after the conference — to what end, I have never understood. Regardless, Brian the Warrior once again demonstrated his readiness to take a bullet for the team by throwing it out there as a rallying cry. Of everything that happened at the press conference that day, that sound bite seemed to resonate most powerfully with Canadians afterwards.

Dennis Manuge, an injured party and the lead claimant in a class-action suit against the government's SISIP LTD insurance plan for Canadian Forces personnel. While serving at CFB Petawawa, Dennis had broken his back. Although granted a monthly disability pension, his benefits were clawed back from his pension income once he was medically discharged from the army a year later. He described the tribulations of the lawsuit that he had launched on behalf of our veterans to fight this, which the Supreme Court of Canada eventually ruled in favour of. Finally, Ron Cundell, a veteran who had been fighting Veterans Affairs for years, gave a lucid description of the wide variety of seemingly senseless practices within the Department that frustrate veterans and deter them from receiving the benefits that they have earned through their personal sacrifice.

In the interest of time I stuck to my prepared script, but as I listened to the tales told by my spokespersons I became enraged, as many, if not all Canadians who witnessed our exposé did too. It wasn't too long before I couldn't take it any longer and just had to make some extemporaneous comments. I drew attention to a picture of me after my return from Afghanistan that the Conservative Reform Alliance Party, or CRAP (predecessor to the present-day Conservative Party), had used on one of their propaganda brochures without my permission. I told the audience that at the time I had objected to being used for political propaganda, but as a professional soldier, I'd kept my mouth shut. But this time I wasn't a soldier and I wasn't going to be used as a patsy again by these people.

While I was on a roll, I referred to a meeting I'd had with a senior member of the Liberal Party whose day job just happened to be a senior analyst with Treasury Board. Shortly after my triumphant tour in Afghanistan, some people in the Liberal Party had tried to lure me into politics. At a Liberal Party reception I met this person and was particularly impressed with his insightful and analytical outlook on life and politics. I was so impressed, I invited him to lunch to further discuss my potential in politics. At lunch, my guest from the Liberal Party surprised me. The first thing he said was that in his opinion, politics wasn't for me, or vice versa.

I was shocked, but he didn't have much difficulty convincing me. He told me that politicians would rather have soldiers die on operations than come back with disabilities, because once you erect a gravestone for someone who was KIA (killed in action), most of the controversy is laid to rest at the same time. Disabled veterans, on the other hand, are a liability that government would like to rid themselves of. He suggested that I wasn't the kind of person who could abandon my principles for party politics like that, so I likely would never be successful as a politician.

He didn't have to say anything else to convince me that I wasn't cut out for politics. I shared this account to round out the stories told at the press conference that day, just to say that my experience as Veterans Ombudsman confirmed what he had said about politicians and their readiness to abandon wounded veterans.

On the stage at the National Press Theatre the five of us made our pitch for the forty-five minutes we were allotted, which seemed to pass in a flash. We successfully made steps towards revealing to Canadians how terribly the Government of Canada treats our veterans. That day we also raised the ire of the people of Canada and instigated a wave of heated activism within the veterans' community that rightfully continues to this day.

## NAÏVETÉ

This press conference had been a long time coming. I had assumed the appointment as Canada's first Veterans Ombudsman in 2007. Criticisms had been swirling about that the new mandate lacked teeth, but I challenged them. In retrospect, I cannot believe how naïve I had been. I had argued that the robustness of the mandate was not an issue because, I foolishly believed, everybody wanted to help veterans. Indeed, everyone from the Minister on down promised to do everything they could to help me improve the plight of our veterans who may have been disadvantaged by the system.

The Deputy Minister of Veterans Affairs, Suzanne Tining, and her senior bureaucrats, insisted that the Order in Council authorized me to be a "squeaky wheel" to which they could "apply the grease" in order to get important changes through the system. Minister Greg Thompson never missed an opportunity to remind me how I, as Ombudsman, didn't need to worry about the mandate because at the end of the day I could take my concerns to the people of Canada and nobody in government would want to risk being accused of disadvantaging veterans. I foolishly believed them and resolved myself to working with the bureaucracy as much as possible to address and redress the issues.

## CHARACTER ASSASSINATION

By the time of the press conference, the Harper government had already established their notoriety for their all-out personal assaults on anybody who dared challenge them. It was interesting that their assassination of my character never materialized. I guess they really couldn't, because there was plenty of open-source evidence supporting my allegations and Canadians stepped up to defend their veterans. Also, many of my former superiors and subordinates that I had soldiered closely with in the CF lined up to praise my honest and frank approach to doing business.

Notwithstanding that I was disappointed that none of the immensely popular retired generals offered any support to those hurting veterans who had served them loyally, it wasn't long before Canada's top soldier, General Walt, the Chief of Defence Staff, had to shit or get off the pot. During a press conference on another issue, a journalist challenged him on the stance I was taking. Walt didn't have many alternatives, replying that the concerns raised by the Veterans Ombudsman are "absolutely correct issues" and the controversial CFMVRCA "doesn't work for everyone."

But then there was Don Martin, at the time a journalist with the *National Post*. I thought his column might be the advance guard for the counterattack of character assassination that I had expected from the Conservatives. Martin called the press conference a "slightly queasy military tactic," as if he knew anything about the military. He had the audacity to refer to the veterans as "props for Stogran's personal war" and suggested that the only newsworthy development was that I was not getting my contract renewed.

He had fired the first salvo of personal attacks against me. In his article he quoted a senior source saying that I was legendary within the ranks for being "excessively antagonistic." Martin said his senior source said I was "all vinegar, no honey." Apparently I was known to blitz senior bureaucrats with vitriolic emails when, as Martin put it, I perceived that my positions were being ignored, delayed, or rejected. As a result, they did not feel inclined to do me any favours by expediting my files.

In my opinion, spinning the story to be about me trying to save my job, and perhaps even his insulting of veterans, was a blatant act of political partisanship by Martin intended to gain the favour of the Harper government — full stop. One day he might even be able to follow the footsteps of Mike Duffy and Pamela Wallin into the Senate. Shortly after publishing this article, Martin followed Mike Duffy to CTV as a political pundit on Power Play, where in the concourse of the Centre Block he could rub shoulders with the blue bloods of Canada's political elite. Coincidence? Whatever! What was more pertinent and absolutely inexcusable, which Martin did not seize on, was that even if I did ruffle some feathers with some vitriolic emails, how abhorrent is it that the senior bureaucrats who gave counsel to Martin would think that they were getting even with me by allowing the veterans to continue suffering?

Being honest and frank are attributes that must be lost on those "senior sources" who Martin suggested had condemned my demeanour. Some of those senior sources could very well have been wearing a green baggy suit in the CF, because the majority of my colleagues who managed to get a star on their shoulders were nothing more than senior bureaucrats in uniform. That was why we failed in Kandahar, and sadly, why none of those uniformed bureaucrats stepped up to support the troops they had sent over to Kandahar to be butchered by the Taliban as fodder for their own ambitions.

## Stress Reduction

The days and weeks that followed the press conference were hellish. For the remainder of the week I was either running across town to be or on the phone with someone being interviewed. I would have liked to have thrown in the towel right after the press conference and walk away from the whole thing, but I knew I would have to fuel the fury of sympathetic Canadians if anything productive was going to come of my tiny act of defiance. Also, I thought conducting such a mutinous press conference without allowing the government enough time before my term expired to make a big deal of firing me seemed to me to demonstrate a lack of courage.

By the end of the week I was a wreck. Saturday morning I sat in our family room with Trish, having our customary cup of coffee, and completely burnt out. I didn't want to talk; I didn't want to do anything. We just sat in silence sipping our coffees. Then through the front door burst my daughter Molly. "I got called into work, can you look after Tango for the day?" she asked, with her pup bounding through the door in front of her and running rampant around the house. Tango was a rescue dog who had to be coached and coddled out of some kind of traumatic past, but was still at that time a long way from being the joyous pet that she is today. I seem to have a way with dogs that I couldn't transfer to my relationship with bureaucrats, so I was the dog-sitter-by-default in our family. "No problem!" I said. But privately I thought, "Oh great, this is going to be nightmarish!"

Tango seemed to sense my duress, though, and immediately calmed down. She was nowhere near the relaxed and attentive dog that she would develop into later, but she was nonetheless considerate of the mood that

I was in and behaved accordingly. We had a wonderful day together. I must have taken her for at least half a dozen walks to the park. Sadly, our Labrador retriever, Rocky, had passed away a year earlier and Trish and I had decided that we would not adopt another family pet. Tango had had such a profoundly positive impact on my demeanour by the end of the day, though, that after Molly took her home I sheepishly asked Trish if we could get another pup.

Apollo was born only a couple of weeks before I left the OVO and came into our lives six weeks thereafter. He and I have been inseparable ever since. On our way home from the breeder on the 22$^{nd}$ of December, we arrived at the Trenton interchange on Highway 401 precisely when Corporal Steve Martin was embarking on his final trek, the painful procession down the Highway of Heroes. Trish, Apollo, and I stopped to pay our respects as the cavalcade made its way onto the highway, a moving and eerily fitting invocation ceremony for our new family member who would help me deal with the aftermath of my rude awakening as the Veterans Ombudsman.

## Strategic Council

Prior to the press conference we had scheduled the first meeting of our strategic council and, purely by coincidence, the meeting happened to follow in the wake of the upheaval and ass-covering we stirred up. Once again, this council was composed of the heads of VAC's stakeholder group as a means of being inclusive without compromising the independence of the OVO. It was also coincidental that the Minister later announced a meeting of one of his advisory groups that was comprised of many of the participants in this strategic council, which was to be held a couple of days thereafter. I had considered postponing my meeting so it would not appear that I was trying to subvert the Minister, but I figured *Screw it, I'll do it.* I had very little time left in my mandate, and I was well beyond trying to accommodate anybody's sensitivities.

I tried to urge some of the key players within the advocacy groups to take advantage of the turbulence — if not outright crisis-state of government — in order to force substantive and enduring changes. They were certainly free to do what they wished, but I hoped they would avoid feeding the government with ideas for some scraps that they could throw out to placate the veterans. I was surprised — no, *floored* — by the response. I was actually accused of carrying on like I was taking all the credit for improving the treatment of veterans. There were some hard feelings because some of them felt they had been doing good work for the veterans before I came along.

I tried to be as diplomatic as possible, but I reminded them of the role they'd played in the CFMVRCA being rushed through Parliament, knowing fully well that it was flawed, and that the government had promised it would be a living document and continuously reviewed and improved, but after almost five years had done nothing. I also let it slip that they too had done nothing. I emphasized that many veterans were being severely disadvantaged by the flawed legislation and that several exhaustive reviews had been done that presented the government with reams of recommendations on what needed to be done to fix it. I made it very clear to the representatives at the table that the so-called "stake-holder groups" had failed to call them on it. I summed up with, "How is that working for you?"

I also took advantage of the occasion to brief the council on the events leading to the press conference, and how I had divorced myself from OVO operations and ceased my town hall meetings with veterans, in order to connect with Canadians and let them know how their veterans were being let down by the government. My most important message to them was my suggestion that the time had come to stand firm and insist that the Minister effect some enduring and substantive change. I left it at that.

## Subsequent Meetings with Government

As much as Don Martin might have suggested that I was just grandstanding, I was committed to initiating substantive and enduring change above all else. Martin never reported on the secret meetings I had with a very senior member of Stephen Harper's personal staff. He probably wouldn't have known about that. Martin would only have reported what "they" wanted him to report, and they wouldn't have wanted him to know that the PM had sidelined his Minister by having his personal advisor meet with me personally and in private on two occasions.

Harper's emissary first expressed his concern about how the press and the opposition would exploit the fact of the meetings taking place if word of them got out. I am a man of honour, so I would not breach this confidentiality even if I thought it might put me in a better position to force the government's hand. I knew that the people in politics have no such honour and would have had a field day if these meetings had been leaked, but I stuck to my principles.

The first meeting was much less than constructive. I arrived at the Langevin building and was escorted to a conference room on the first floor. I carried with me a photocopy of a propaganda brochure from Stephen Harper's defunct Reform or CRAP (Conservative Reform Alliance Party) days that had a photograph of then-Lieutenant Colonel Stogran fresh out of Afghanistan prominently displayed on the front fold without my permission. I was fit to be tied, and I had not come to negotiate.

At that first meeting I was so angry that we accomplished nothing, so I swallowed some humble pie and asked for another. He courteously agreed. This time I was escorted into a conference room adorned with black and white photographs of Prime Minister Harper playing piano. I assumed they had been taken when Harper played the Beatles's "With a Little Help From My Friends" at the National Arts Centre, a characteristically insipid performance by the prime minister, vainly attempting to replicate Bill Clinton's endearing saxophone performances. That was just what I needed at this point, something to stoke me up.

Harper's emissary came with only one thing in mind. After the opening pleasantries, he flipped open his note pad and asked what they could do in the short term for the veterans. I saw this as him fishing for scraps, scraps that they could then feed to the veterans to get everyone off their back. I had already made it very clear what needed fixing: the insurance-company culture that was denying veterans what they not only deserved but that they were entitled to under legislation. There were already all sorts of recommendations from advisory groups that they themselves had convened; all they had to do was follow through. I was adamant that the arbitrariness and deceit of the system had to change. We concluded the meeting without having achieved anything, except that the emissary made it very clear to me that they experienced as many frustrations with senior bureaucrats as it appeared that I did. That revelation haunted me for months after I left the OVO.

I again expressed my sincere appreciation for his indulgence for having agreed to meet with me a second time after my last angry meeting with him.

## ALS Revisited

After a couple of months of controversy following my press conference, the government took measures to ensure that veterans suffering from ALS would no longer be the victims of such an abject system. On Friday, October 15, 2010, almost two months to the day after Brian Dyck challenged Canadians to either stand behind our troops or in front of them, and precisely two days after his funeral, Minister Blackburn announced that ALS victims would receive, as he called it, "increased benefits."

Blackburn went on to describe home care support, services, adapted wheelchairs, medical resources, and housekeeping services, all of which were the extant benefits that any veteran who had incurred a disabling wound, injury, or sickness in the line of duty was already entitled to. Neither legislative nor regulatory changes were required, and any policy changes were cosmetic in nature. All that was required under the existing law was an attitudinal shift. While I am happy that some good came as a result of my tiny rebellion, sadly the "deny, deceive, and defer" attitude of the government persisted. This notwithstanding, as much as I look back on my three years as Veterans Ombudsman with contempt, I am grateful that I may have improved the treatment of our veterans suffering from ALS, and of their families.

Before I left office, I had to award one more Veterans Ombudsman's Commendation. I awarded it to Natali and Sophie Dyck, as the recipients of a posthumous award to Brian. May you forever rest in peace, my brother; you lived up to the mission-team-self ethos to your last breath.

You dragged the public into your home to share your dying moments with your family, which was the catalyst for improving the conditions for many, many people in your situation. I will strive for excellence in your memory, Brian.

## Phoenixes

As traumatic as my revelation was that the senior bureaucrats conspire to disadvantage veterans, a lot of good has come from my rogue act. First of all, many more veterans have been drawn to the fight for fair treatment. Vets who were previously complacent about their place in society began joining associations and, indeed, creating them. More importantly, Canadians from all walks of life rose up to support their veterans in the face of such unfair treatment. Radio talk show hosts across the country could not get enough first person commentary on the plight of Canada's veterans, and when I appeared as a guest I never ceased to be amazed at the anger of callers. The problems veterans were facing were regular features on the front pages of newspapers, and Canadians were donating generously to all the charities that were springing up, to do for veterans what the Government of Canada should have been doing.

The Department quickly invited many of these new upstart organizations as members of full status in the Department's "stakeholder groups," to sit at the table alongside the age-old institutions like the Royal Canadian Legion, the Army, Navy, Air Force Veterans Association (ANAVETS), and Cliff Chadderton's National Council of Veterans Association. Bolstering the status of what would otherwise be relatively obscure veterans groups, and pumping up the egos of their founders and directors in such a manner, was a masterful strategy on the part of the government and is an outstanding demonstration of VAC's omnipresent strategy of divide and conquer. This seemingly benign and empathetic gesture conveys to the Canadian public the image of a department that is inclusive and receptive, but in reality it severely disrupts the capacity for the veterans' community to speak with a single voice. The end result is making it easier for the Government of Canada to impose their agenda.

While the veterans were becoming increasingly confrontational with the government, several very constructive initiatives were also beginning to appear. I first heard of the Veterans Transition Program (VTP), a group-based therapeutic program developed by the Department of Educational and Counselling Psychology and Special Education at the University of British Columbia, while I was the Ombudsman, but I was never able to arrange my path to cross with theirs while I was in office. The VTP had developed an outstanding reputation for its effectiveness in helping veterans of all eras who had been traumatized by active combat, to transition back to civilian life.

Founded by Dr. Marvin Westwood and Dr. David Kuhl at the University of British Columbia, they relied to a large extent on the generous financial support of the Royal Canadian Legion BC/Yukon Command. The VTP have made some progress in convincing VAC of their efficacy, but unfortunately the apparent partnership did little to increase the VTP's presence in the veterans' community. The public service's penchant for showmanship over effectiveness has meant that the program staff continues to struggle to reach out to the injured and wounded veterans who would really benefit from the VTP.

In 2015 I happened to visit my case manager at Veterans Affairs in Ottawa. As we reviewed my case history, I realized that there was no record of me having participated in a session of the VTP, so I thought I would feign an unsolicited request to take part in it. My case manager, as helpful as she was trying to be, had never heard of the program. This was a shameful indictment of the bureaucracy's inability or unwillingness to get the word out.

Another potential phoenix that rose out of the ashes of my term as Veterans Ombudsman is particularly exciting. The Equitas Society out of Vancouver launched a class-action suit against the Government of Canada alleging that the CFMVRCA actually discriminates against modern-day veterans. The national Canadian law firm of Miller Thomson LLP has agreed to represent, *pro bono*, disabled Canadian Forces members affected by the CFMVRCA in the lawsuit asserting that, in essence, it should be their constitutional right to be provided disability benefits that are at least comparable to those of other Canadian employees.

The Equitas lawsuit was the brainchild of Jim Scott, an ex-police officer and father of three. Jim became involved in this lawsuit when he saw how badly the government was treating one of his sons, who was wounded in action in Afghanistan in 2010. As Jim met more sick, injured, and wounded soldiers returning from the Afghan conflict, he was aghast to learn of their disproportionately low settlements under the CFMVRCA, relative to the program it replaced and others in the private sector. Thereafter Jim successfully approached the national law firm Miller Thomson who agreed to represent disabled Canadian soldiers across Canada to seek a fair and equitable review of their benefits through the courts. Jim formed the Equitas Disabled Soldiers Funding Society under the Society Act in British Columbia on September 19, 2011. It raises the funds necessary to cover disbursement costs such as travel expenses for claimants and witnesses, medical reports, and court costs.

The fact that a private citizen such as Jim Scott was able to convince a major, reputable national law firm such as Miller Thomson that there are grounds to take on such a monumental case *pro bono* is damning in and of itself. The suit has, as of this writing, been certified by the BC Supreme Court, although the Department of Justice has filed an appeal and has demonstrated its intent to dig in and fight the veterans to the end. I doubt that will occur, however, because I have a strong feeling the government will not want the courts to potentially expose the magnitude of their contempt and malevolence vis-á-vis the way they treat disabled and disadvantaged veterans.

## Exposing Their True Colours

In 2013 the Equitas Society presented their class-action suit to the BC Supreme Court for certification. In response, as the defendants in the case, the Department of Justice lawyers basically rejected any notion that the Government of Canada had any legal or moral responsibility to care for veterans beyond the social services that are extended to all Canadians. While the parliamentarians were busy in Ottawa arguing deceitfully that they were fulfilling a sacred trust that existed between the government and Canada's veterans, senior bureaucrats were dismissing as myth the slightest suggestion of any such social covenant, explicit or implicit. This event alone demonstrates the huge disconnect that lies between what the government tells us and what they truly believe.

CHAPTER 11:

# The March Continues

The government's march towards shedding their responsibility to care for our veterans has continued unabated, notwithstanding the best efforts of the many people who rallied to my call for change. The very hiring of my successor, Guy Parent, is a blatant example of how the Government of Canada will brazenly and deliberately do whatever it takes to obstruct any intrusion into their private empire. Deputy Minister Tining knew that I had determined Guy was not up to the challenge of improving the treatment of distressed veterans. Senior bureaucrats knew full well that Guy Parent would be quite happy to swirl his hands around in the finger-paints of public incompetence and deception for another few years, and that is exactly the kind of person the government wanted in an ombudsman.

Parent demonstrated to the government his reticence to take a principled stand from the moment they screened him to become my successor. When Parent first confided to me that he had been selected as my replacement, he lamented at how arduous the psychological assessment was, and wondered if I found it as such. I hadn't been subjected to such a screening. Clearly my frustration with the system and decision to go rogue had caused the government consternation so, knowing full well that I had been diagnosed with PTSD, they decided to make sure my successor did not suffer from the same disability. Guy knew as well as I did that a common complaint from our stakeholders suffering from PTSD is that potential employers discriminate against them. I would have objected to the screening. Not Guy, though. Guy should have known better than to allow the government to use prejudicial hiring practices, especially when it comes to screening employment applicants for Operational Stress Injuries.

The *Canadian Human Rights Act* (CHRA) charges employers with a duty to accommodate employees suffering from physical or mental conditions, so long as it does not impose undue hardship on the employer regarding health, safety, and cost. The CF is not only exempt from such a duty, to the contrary, under "universality of service"[6] the military is allowed to release members who are not physically fit, employable, or deployable for general operational duties. A federal public service policy provides for the priority hiring of Canadian Forces and RCMP members who are released with service-related injuries/illnesses, presumably a quid pro quo from a grateful government for the exemplary loyalty demonstrated by these veterans, as well as a means of resolving the dichotomy that exists between the provisions of the Canadian Human Rights Act and Universality of Service.

As much as the Government of Canada might like to crow that they are equal opportunity employers, such is certainly not the case when it comes to Canadians who answered the Government of Canada's call and became disabled as a consequence of their act of patriotism. In the years from 2007 to 2012 the number of RCMP and CF members who had been released for service-related medical reasons and were eligible for transfer to the public service averaged around 488 veterans annually, with a low of 307 veterans in fiscal year 2012/2013. The average number who transferred successfully each year was only about 174, or 35%, except in fiscal year '12/13 when the public service reported hiring a measly thirty-one[7] veterans (ten percent). It is absolutely inexcusable that the Government of Canada, with a workforce in the public service that amounts to over 262,000 employees, cannot accommodate a couple of hundred more veterans who were disabled in the line of duty every year.

---

6   http://www.forces.gc.ca/en/about-policies-standards-defence-admin-orders-directives-5000/5023-0.page

7   http://www.psc-cfp.gc.ca/arp-rpa/2013/appendice2-annexe2-eng.htm#table41

In November 2013, the Government of Canada enacted legislation that would afford disabled CF members the highest priority for hiring in the public service, and Monsieur Parent heartily applauded the government's gesture[8], with some extant concerns. That year, with a carry-over of 179 cases from the previous fiscal year and another 105 new medical releases, there were a total of 284 disabled veterans who were eligible for transfer to the public service. Of that 284 disabled veterans, the public service hired a pathetic forty-three, only fifteen percent made the cut.

As I followed the events in the veterans' community after I left the OVO it became very clear to me how wise the DND Ombudsman, Yves Côté, had been back in the day when he advised me to avoid giving the veterans the impression that I was "collaborating" with the government. Monsieur Parent has repeatedly embarrassed the Office by acting more like a cheerleader than an ombudsman. He is quick to endorse the announcements from the Government of Canada before they have run their course in the veterans' community, as he did with the priority hiring of veterans legislation. I believe this puts him in a position of a conflict of interest if-and-when those announcements do not achieve that advertised intention or fail to meet the needs of disabled and disadvantaged veterans. The OVO also spends an inordinate amount of effort, I believe, doing work the Department should be doing to communicate with veterans, with such things as Guy's inveterate "myth busting" efforts on his blog.

I don't deny that as ombudsman I may have failed to live up to the expectations of the government, but as an experienced ombudsman nonetheless, Monsieur Parent seems a little too eager for my liking to appear in happy-snaps with the Minister, in particular accompanying later-disgraced Minister Fantino on a junket to Italy. I am quick to commend the OVO for the one-off complaints that they continue to resolve on behalf of individual veterans, but six million dollars is too much to spend to generate a complaints section within VAC and augment their communications effort. Every little bit helps, yes, but as Guy Parent completes his first term as Ombudsman he has failed to effect

---

8   http://ombudsman-veterans.gc.ca/eng/blog/post/214

any substantial and enduring change to the deeply systemic failures of the Government of Canada in their mistreatment of our veterans. The degree to which Parent has improved the quality of life for our most severely disabled and desperate veterans is hardly worth the $40+ million dollars the taxpayers have invested in the OVO since its inception.

## Deceitful Transformation

With any kind of oversight having been effectively neutralized, the conditions were set for the senior bureaucrats to follow through with their plan to dismantle the Department. Suzanne Tining left the public service on July 16, 2012, and was replaced by Madame Mary Chaput who had been well groomed to do the dirty work. Prior to becoming the Deputy Minister she had served as Tining's Associate Deputy Minister of the Department since October 12, 2010, during which time she championed VAC's five-year so-called "transformation plan." True to form, Chaput embarked on an aggressive campaign to reduce the capability of the Department to care for our veterans. At the end of the day the so-called "transformation" is supposed to cut $226M from VAC's budgets, which in my well informed but admittedly superficial estimation would be *easy* to achieve by eliminating bureaucracy. By that I don't mean shifting the same garbage around into different bags, I mean eliminating layers of oversight and supervision, and empowering front-line care managers. That, however, was not Chaput's plan.

The responsibility of the Government of Canada for the care of disabled Veterans goes beyond the financial compensation and the provision of services. The government also has an obligation to identify new and emerging maladies that result from their military misadventures and recklessness. Notwithstanding their negligence in dealing with routine issues, we have already seen how incompetent and/or disinterested VAC is at dealing with any unexpected health problems associated with military service. I described how little the Department knew about homelessness, early onset ALS, the mid-to-long-term implications of traumatic brain injuries, or the possibility of early onset dementia due to severe PTSD, one can expect that there are other issues that hitherto have not entered our consciousness. For instance, there's the possibility that mefloquine poisoning in the CF has ruined the lives of many veterans of debacles such as Somalia, Rwanda, and Afghanistan because they were administered the drug in copious quantities. Also, marijuana may possess some neuro-protective properties that might be useful for victims of severe PTSD and TBIs. We can be certain that, if-and-when the government hands its obligations to veterans over to the private sector to manage, new issues will seldom, if ever, see the light of day.

My confidential sources inside government tell me that the Department has already begun transferring functions to the private sector, which has caused degradation in the level of service provided to our veterans. One employee characterizes the DM, Chaput, as "a headhunter whose only mission is to get rid of people and save money." Under a banner of "cutting red tape" the Department set out to make administrative decision-making even more centralized, outsource administration and service delivery to the private sector, close district offices and piggyback their functions on Service Canada outlets, and increase their use of IT.

Virtually any reduction of the bureaucratic run-around that frustrates veterans was merely coincidental, as the measures taken were clearly intended to reduce the involvement of government administrators and service providers. The veterans who are in most need of help from the government will continue to be disadvantaged and frustrated. As of this writing, the pre-authorization of all dental claims has apparently already become the responsibility of three dentists who work for a private insurance company, and all claims for all benefits — drug, dental, physiotherapy, and psych services — will be further centralized under private control.

Insiders have told me that the march to eliminate the liability posed by veterans will continue unabated with the transfer of responsibility to administer all treatment benefits to organizations such as Blue Cross by the end of the 2014/2015 fiscal year. While the timeline is the subject of speculation, I am sure this is the intent, and the turmoil of an impending election and potential change of government will provide the perfect distraction to allow these changes to be made without public scrutiny.

David Pugliese of the *Ottawa Citizen* reported that VAC has eliminated over 900 out of 4,000 full-time employees since 2009, and transferred the work over to the private insurance company, Medavie Blue Cross.[9] Some of those jobs were culled even after the government appointed the former CDS, General Walt Natynczyk, as Deputy Minster of VAC, to repair their image and presumably clean up their act. VAC closed nine district offices, suggesting that the Department's enhanced web presence, Service Canada outlets, and about twenty Operational Stress Clinics would fill the void. Nothing could be further from the truth when it comes to our most severely disabled, disadvantaged, and desperate veterans, particularly those suffering from traumatic stress injuries. These casualties need the personal touch of experts to intervene proactively and professionally and steer them in the right direction.

Empathetic human interaction is one very important component to mitigate the harm done to veterans due to traumatic stress endured during their military careers. A computer terminal in a Service Canada outlet or an iPad app is simply not a suitable alternative. Another source told me that the last three client surveys conducted by the Department found that email and the Internet were the *least* favoured methods of dealing with the department. Apparently, undisclosed departmental surveys revealed that even so-called "new veterans" preferred to talk to knowledgeable VAC employees face to face, and none of the veterans groups were in favour of the increased emphasis on call centres and online services. That has not deterred the Department.

The Dominion President of the Royal Canadian Legion, Gordon Moore, finally broke with tradition and spoke out against the gross mistreatment of veterans by the federal government. In a letter dated November 8, 2012, he expressed "grave concern" with Ms. Chaput's so-called "transformation." Moore made specific reference to the closure of district offices and the possible termination of the long-term care survey or project, and suggested the Department may be overstating how much information technology tools might improve service delivery. Indeed.

---

9   http://ottawacitizen.com/news/politics/more-cuts-at-veterans-affairs-as-some-services-privatized

Closing of offices and reducing the capacity to deal in person with veterans is good for business — government business, that is. It saves them money in overhead, makes it easier for bureaucrats to do their work, and there are fewer vets around to make claims. Some veterans are disinclined to deal with the restricted access to the Department and others are killing themselves. At this point I could launch into a discussion of all of the stats and arguments for and against the suggestion that suicides are problematic in the CF and veterans' community, but it is not worth the effort. Since my rude awakening as the Veterans Ombudsman I know the data for these kinds of issues are subject to being distorted and manipulated by the Government of Canada. Suffice to say, therefore, that given the gravity of the consequence of failing to act appropriately, if even a single suicide can be directly attributed to the work we have our service personnel do, then we must err on the side of caution and do everything we can to prevent them.

> "In the oppressive late-afternoon heat of April 23rd at the sprawling air base outside Kandahar, Major Michelle Mendes made the dusty walk to her living quarters. Inside a sparse room, the 30-year-old sat down on her bed with service pistol in hand, and shot herself in the head."[10]

Back in 2005, then-Captain Michelle Mendes worked for me in the Joint Operations Group. Athletic, motivated, highly intelligent, vivacious, Michelle certainly seemed as if she was destined for great heights in the military. Regardless of how thin you slice the rhetoric, the bottom line in this case is that service in the military contributed to this young lady taking her own life. The only speculation remains how the actions or inaction of the CF and VAC might be exacerbating the problem of suicides, and how the problem might be mitigated.

If nothing else, we must not be doing anything that could aggravate the situation and risk the chance of driving anybody to take his or her

---

10 http://www.theglobeandmail.com/news/national/did-we-push-her-too-much/article4277429/

own life. The implementation of the New Veterans Charter did just that in the case of at least one veteran. Shortly before committing suicide one soldier who had suffered a serious back injury in Afghanistan confided to a comrade his concern about "being discharged from the army and not having financial security."

## Damage Control

In the closing days of his ill-fated tour as Minister of VAC, Julian Fantino — ex-top cop in Toronto, demonstrated the lack of respect he and the government he represented have for the veterans. On one occasion Fantino ignored and subsequently insulted veteran Ronald Clarke and a group of veterans who had accompanied him to Ottawa specifically to meet with the Minister. On another occasion, Fantino ran away from Jennifer Mignault, a frustrated wife and primary caregiver of a veteran suffering from PTSD, who had confronted him in front of television cameras to complain about the lack of support she and other family caregivers were getting from the government.

Before Prime Minister Harper fired him from the portfolio, Fantino tried desperately to feign empathy and engagement. He signalled his intention to address the shortcomings of the CFMVRCA, suggesting that he would take some months to carefully consider recent reports from the Veterans Ombudsman and Standing Committee on Veterans Affairs. What a load of bunk. The Department had been in possession of literally hundreds of recommendations already that they quietly just filed away.

In 2005 VAC approached my old friend Bruce Henwood to sit on an advisory committee aptly called the Special Needs Advisory Group (SNAG), and he soon became the Chair. SNAG was one of four advisory groups VAC had convened at the time; the others dealt with mental health, gerontology and one specifically convened as the New Veterans Charter Advisory Group. SNAG itself identified very serious gaps within the NVC as it pertains to benefits and services for spouses and children of seriously disabled veterans and survivors of service-related deaths, which are resident in the superseded Pension Act. In December 2010, VAC abruptly shut SNAG down, but not before the Advisory Group presented the government with 185 recommendations to improve the NVC.

Flash-forward to 2014: In June, the Government of Canada initiated a Parliamentary Review of the NVC culminating in release of *The New Veterans Charter: Moving Forward Report* by the Standing Committee on Veterans Affairs. Bruce, as the Chair of SNAG, was not called to testify, and the committee disregarded SNAG's fifth and final report, *"Unforeseen Consequences of The New Veterans Charter: A Financial Step Backwards for Seriously Disabled Veterans and their Families."* However, an actuarial study I had contracted with a civilian accounting firm when I was the Ombudsman and a similar study conducted subsequently by students at Queens University already demonstrated conclusively that over the course of their lives seriously disabled veterans are severely disadvantaged financially by the CFMVRCA compared to those administered to under the Pension Act, which it superseded. Regardless, parliamentarians danced around the issue of a fair and straightforward way of narrowing that gap in compensation. Fantino was in possession of more than enough recommendations to act on long before they had Guy Parent's report to mull over for half a year. If the committee can be trusted at all, they determined that of the hundreds of recommendations that the various advisory groups had submitted to government there were at least fifty-seven that remain unfulfilled.

The one thing that parliamentarians seem to do to take the heat off is to promise more money. I have continually asserted that the programs are not as serious a problem as the deceitfully parsimonious senior bureaucrats who are charged with implementing and managing them. Regardless, a parade of shit-deflecting ministers continued making all sorts of promises to dump money into the hopper, knowing full well that such money does not necessarily make it through the bureaucracy and into the hands of the veterans who need help.

The first announcement about proposed changes came in mid-September following my press conference. Minister Blackburn promised $2 billion in increased benefits, to include $1,000 more per month for "severely wounded" and guaranteed a minimum $40,000 yearly income for the severely wounded during rehabilitation, or for life if they are unable to return to work. But wait, there were more empty promises of cash infusions to follow when Stephen Blaney became Minister, and they started coming fast and furiously from Erin O'Toole, who succeeded Julian Fantino as Minister. In an attempt to settle the ire of Canadians the government made huge ovations to promise the following:

- $52.5 million over five years in additional support to establish a Legacy of Care for seriously injured Canadian Forces personnel and their families.

- A $200-million funding announcement for mental health facilities that was to be spread over fifty years, although the government initially boasted that it would be over a six-year period.

- Retirement Income Security Benefit; a monthly income support payment beginning at age sixty-five for moderately to severely disabled veterans.

- Family Caregiver Relief Benefit; a tax-free, annual grant of $7,238 for veterans' informal caregivers, often the spouse or other devoted family members.

- Critical Injury Benefit, a $70,000 tax-free payment for the most severely injured or ill Canadian Forces members and veterans.

- Broadened eligibility criteria and a supplement for the Permanent Impairment Allowance (PIA) that together are supposed to provide approximately $600 to $2,800 a month in life-long monthly financial support to Veterans who have a permanent, service-related injury or illness.

- Enhanced benefits for injured part-time Reserve Force members and veterans, commensurate with full-time Reserve Force and Regular Force veterans.

Ignoring, for the moment, the change of government that occurred since then, details of how these promises may have morphed, overlapped, were superseded, or expired mattered not, because there remained one huge obstacle to these programs ever helping their intended recipients: senior bureaucrats. One fun part of the puppet show of government is political prestidigitation, whereby parliamentarians keep our minds occupied by telling us about all the money they will pour into VAC's piggy bank while senior bureaucrat are secretly handing the money back to the Government of Canada. Since 2006, while Erin O'Toole and his predecessors were keeping us occupied with their fast talk, unbeknownst to the Canadian public the Department funnelled over a billion dollars of program funding promised to veterans back to the Central Registry.

In defence of the Harper government, Treasury Board President Tony Clement argued that billions in federal funding left unspent each year is a sign of good financial management. How can such grossly inaccurate budget forecasts ever be considered "good financial management?" Minister O'Toole made a lame-assed excuse that the lapsed money was not lost to the Department, and that Canadians just don't understand the Estimates process. I understand the Estimates process, Mr. O'Toole, enough to know that money that lapses in a given fiscal year and is not specifically approved to be rolled over in the next fiscal year is gone. That money that should have been spent on helping veterans is gone.

## The Road Ahead

When I served in Bosnia during the Serb offensive against the enclave of Gorazde I saw ordinary people, the occupants of the city reinforced by refugees who had fled the onslaught, taking a stand to defend themselves. As a Canadian I was in a strange situation; I found myself in mortal danger alongside the defenders, but strangely detached from their life-and-death struggle. People, para-military civilians armed with hunting rifles and a few military weapons, were fighting desperately to protect their farms and families. I remember thinking at the time that if I was wounded or killed, my family would be well cared for. These people, however, had it all on the line — just like Canada did in the World Wars. For these brave Bosnians fighting the armies of Serbia and the Bosnian Serbs, there were no thoughts of veterans' benefits or post-conflict rehabilitative care. For them, it was only about survival. It strikes me that probably would have been the case for the average citizens who left the farms, forests, and factories here in Canada to fight Hitler's genocidal tyranny.

No doubt very few of those Canadians who answered the call for World War One and Two had any intention of making a career of the military. Like the guardians of Gorazde, the vast majority of Canada's military in the World Wars simply wanted — wrong, they **had to** protect the way of life they hoped to return to after the defeat of the Nazis. For a country engulfed in war, the only aspiration is that victory will lead to the restoration of normalcy. In Canada we did better than that, though, we went out of our way to recognize and remember the valour of our veterans, and we also went to extraordinary lengths to compensate and care for them for their sacrifices.

Today, unlike during the World Wars, only a tiny minority of our citizenry place themselves in mortal danger to uphold our values and protect the Canadian way of life. They and their families suffer the same fears, anxieties, apprehension, and sorrow that our entire nation endured in the World Wars, so it would be reasonable to infer that if they were injured, wounded, or became sick in the conduct of their duties, the modern veterans should be treated much the same as their ancestors, the traditional veterans. But they are not.

Of those Canadians who accept the condition of unlimited liability in the service of Canada's military today, the vast majority have chosen to do so as a career. At the very least our service personnel need to know that if they become disabled in the conduct of their duties that within their capabilities they will still be able to provide for themselves and their families what they reasonably would have expected of a full and successful career in the Canadian Forces. That is, I believe, where we let so many of our most desperate and disadvantaged veterans down. Not only do veterans have to fight for anything they can get out of the system, but VAC is still failing in so many ways to address adequately the needs of veterans who are having severe difficulties reintegrating into the private sector.

Admittedly, some things have changed since I had my tantrum on 17 August 2010, most of which occurred in the run-up to the 2015 federal election. I have to be suspect of those changes, because I have seen too much intransigence, malevolence, and incompetence in the Government of Canada to expect otherwise. In my estimation, the Government of Canada has left a long line of breadcrumbs that suggests their intentions are somewhat less than genuine.

In an interview with Legion Magazine, Minister O'Toole emphasized that veterans and their families "have to know that our system is fair, quick, and focused at giving them the benefit of the doubt or making it easier to get to yes." He acknowledged that the government had a ways to go to make the system "work a little bit better," and hastened to emphasize yet again that the benefit of the doubt is at the core of what they're doing to improve.[11] In typical fashion, however, while the Minister was saying one thing to the public, the bureaucracy was busy behinds the scenes doing something else. On their website the VRAB still advertised that applicants must "prove, on a balance of probabilities, the facts required to establish entitlement to a pension or award." Readers will know, that is the burden of proof that must be met in our civil courts, and as I have already discussed, if the legislation intended that, it would have said that.

As a parting gasp of desperation before the election in October 2015, Minister O'Toole heralded recent amendments to the New Veterans Charter introduced by Bill C-58, particularly the preamble that describes the purpose of the NVC. Readers will recall that such a social covenant, sacred obligation, or whatever we are calling it now, was deliberately omitted from the New Veterans Charter. O'Toole would have had us believe that Sir Robert Borden, his "favorite Prime Minister," never used the term 'sacred obligation,' implying that the pre-amble his government was introducing to the NVC was their attempt to codify Borden's intent and would lead to the "liberal application going forward." The original preamble that simply acknowledges the special obligation that the people and the Government of Canada owe to their veterans and tells lawmakers that said obligation should be "interpreted liberally" never prevented senior bureaucrats from being perversely restrictive in their application of the laws comprising the Veterans Charter. Why should we expect anything different going forward?

---

[11] https://legionmagazine.com/en/2015/07/q-a-with-minister-otoole/#sthash.Hfq9zWgJ.dpuf

To the contrary, there were strong indications that, under Minister O'Toole's stewardship, the government was going to buck tradition even more by abandoning any intent to err on the side of generosity. Under the guise of fulfilling "the recognized obligation of the people and Government of Canada to those who have served their country so well and to their dependents," which constitutes the traditional preamble in its entirety, the government engaged in the skulduggery of word play that, I believe, reveals their underlying intent. In the New Veterans Charter the government has replaced that traditional preamble with the unwieldy:

> The purpose of this Act is to recognize and fulfil the obligation of the people and Government of Canada to show just and due appreciation to members and veterans for their service to Canada. This obligation includes providing services, assistance and compensation to members and veterans who have been injured or have died as a result of military service and extends to their spouses or common-law partners or survivors and orphans. This Act shall be liberally interpreted so that the recognized obligation may be fulfilled.

I tend to share the concerns voiced by BGen Joe Sharpe in the *Legion Magazine* article, that the terminology leaves the intent of this preamble open to interpretation. He says, "'Just and due appreciation' does not match with the soldier's unlimited liability. I see the use of limiting language as a legal precaution — much more suitable to a contract than a covenant." The government also used such precise phraseology in other proposed legislation, such as "a severe and traumatic injury or acute disease," "the result of a sudden and single incident," and "immediately caused a severe impairment and interference in quality of life," which are used to specify eligibility for the Critical Disability Benefit. That doesn't leave much latitude for the bureaucracy to interpret them liberally, let alone to be "liberal in their application."

O'Toole's repeated reference[12] to pre-existing conditions upon recruitment and a seemingly more proximate and causal interpretation of what disabilities can reasonably be considered to have arisen from military service is alarming. This is in direct opposition to the philosophy articulated in the Woods Committee report, that with the CF's screening and individual selection of recruits introduces a presumption of fitness and suitability that should be imposed on the adjudication process. It seems to me that this reversal of rationale has been central to the changes that have been taking for some time now, behind the scenes and unwittingly before our very eyes. There is every reason to believe that things are going to get much worse for our disabled and disadvantaged veterans before they get any better for them. Minister O'Toole might just have been more effective than his predecessors were at concealing that reality from us.

## The People Have Spoken

On October 19, 2015, Canadians saw the departure of the O'Toole presence in Veterans Affairs Canada when Canadians rose up to fire the Harper Government. A landslide election rejected the treachery and deceit that had exploded onto the parliamentary and political landscape over the preceding decade, and the platform of the government-elect for veterans was, predictably, very magnanimous. Only time will tell if we have turned a corner, and the expectation of Canadians that their perceived obligations to those veterans who have served this country so well and their families will, henceforth, be fulfilled. One must remember, however, that it was a government formed by this political party that introduced the New Veterans Charter in the first place.

---

12 https://legionmagazine.com/en/2015/07/cracks-in-the-system/#sthash.4mwq3WBw.dpuf

CHAPTER 12:

# Conclusion

I expect that many Canadians may have a difficult time accepting that the situation I have described hitherto is not an exaggeration, misperception, or outright lie. I certainly understand such a reaction. We Canadians just don't do that kind of thing to others, especially our veterans! If anything, as a society Canadians tend to be a little more communal than might be considered normal for the human race. We live in a climate that is trying to kill us, and if our forefathers and mothers hadn't pitched in and given their neighbours a hand when they needed it, they all would have perished. I believe this has caused the proclivity to help others to become woven into our cultural DNA; and we go about our daily lives instinctively trying to live up to such a tradition. Time and time again, in Bosnia and Afghanistan, I saw that manifest itself in the way Canadian soldiers interacted with local communities.

I think that is why it was so traumatic for me personally to see, as Ombudsman, how selfish and exploitative our government is in their treatment of those Canadians who truly served their country. To me, the behaviour I witnessed in the corridors of power in our nation's capital was anything but community minded. The attitude in the senior echelons of the Government of Canada towards our veterans was so deliberately harmful and seemingly counter-cultural it caused me to wonder what it really means to be Canadian.

I believe, too, that the circumstances of our nation have made Canadians, as a people, a little more optimistic than an "average" demographic of the human race — too damned optimistic for our own good.

My distant relatives who arrived in Canada from Ukraine would certainly testify to that, I think, having settled on the bald-assed prairies in log and sod huts and endured the desperately harsh winters as they did. It must have been akin to torture until spring arrived with the warmth, colour, and majesty that we all know characterizes Canada's wilderness in summer. That must have been a wonderful feeling. Those pioneers probably emerged in the spring having survived the frozen bowels of Hell to look at each other and exclaim, "Aren't things looking up! It's going to be a great summer, and there is no way next winter will be anything like what we just survived!" Once again, I saw that kind of optimism manifest itself in spades in the actions of our soldiers in circumstances where it would have been quite normal to become consumed by pessimism.

As a consequence, even if Canadians are prepared to accept my allegation that the Government of Canada could be so malevolent, there is a very good chance they will not take up the torch to take our democracy back from the parliamentarians and senior bureaucrats who have corrupted it. In the absence of a crisis that affects us all, Canadians will probably just keep going to the polls, hopeful that the system will eventually correct itself.

Let there be no doubt, I truly believe that beneath the visible portion of this iceberg represented by VAC and the VRAB and their gross deliberate mistreatment of our veterans and their families who have served this nation so well, lies a behemoth of institutional incompetence, intransigence, and malfeasance that threatens the very democracy of Canada, the quality of life we enjoy, and our special status in the world as a caring and committed nation. We mistakenly entrust the stewardship of those institutions blindly to the very parliamentarians who have secretly perverted them for their own purposes.

At this point, I am reminded of the creepy comment that Minister Thompson made to me early on equating the Members of Parliament to criminals, musing that they are the only inmates in the world who make the rules for the penitentiary that they are serving their sentences in. In the end, their lot is not about leading a nation; it's about winning in politics. This democracy, however, belongs to us as Canadian citizens, and it is up to us, the electorate, to insist that our government becomes more transparent, responsible and accountable to the people of Canada.

It is darkly ironic that the very people who have made the most significant personal sacrifices to make our country what it is today are being victimized by the very government they served. We can all be very, very sure that this is not the kind of democracy that our veterans fought and so many of their comrades died for. So, it is my hope that:

> *"At the going down of the sun and in the morning,*
> *We will remember them."*

# Epilogue

As I turn the page of my experience as the Veterans Ombudsman, quite literally with the writing of this epilogue, I must say I have mixed emotions. I loved my time serving with Canada's finest, and I would probably do it all over again, but I would never encourage anybody to follow in my footsteps. I am still a proud Canadian, proud of all the great accomplishments the people of Canada can take credit for; at the same time, however, I curse the government for the way they have victimized our citizenry for decades.

I know what it is like to be radicalized, although I hasten to differentiate between that and the criminalization of so many of our frustrated and confused youth today. I would have expected that subsequent to my career in the military I, like so many of my peers, would have moved on to a senior executive position within the defence industry, a jammy second career in some kind of public service job, or taken on the odd contract as a consultant for the CF. That, however, was before our defeat in Afghanistan and my rude awakening as to just how corrupt and ineffective our government truly is. That rude awakening has caused me to take a more radical approach to how I would enjoy my "golden years."

I am so grateful to all of the amazing people I had the privilege to serve with throughout my career. I am very lucky that when I left the OVO that I was mature, secure, relatively stable and had a great support system in place consisting of family, friends, and professional caregivers that kept me, too, from ending up on the scrap heap of lives broken by serving our country. Finally I am thankful for the way mainstream Canadians have rallied thus far to support their veterans.

So despite my erratic sleep patterns, and all the aches and pains that I wake up with every morning — the result of one too many hard landings under a parachute or too much time under a rucksack, I really have nothing to complain about. If being radicalized can mean spending some quality time, finally, with my family and, hopefully, inspiring future leaders as to how they might fix the mess we left our next generation, then I am a happy person.

I wish that for everyone.

# About the Author

During the course of his long and honorable military career, Colonel Pat Stogran served as a United Nations Military Observer in Bosnia, where in 1994, he and his team were instrumental in saving the besieged enclave of Gorazde and its 45,000 inhabitants from a massacre at the hands of the Bosnian Serb Army. In the wake of 9/11, he led the Third Battalion Princess Patricia's Canadian Light Infantry as it spearheaded the Canadian Forces historic mission in Afghanistan, marking the first occasion since the Korean War that Canada committed troops to ground combat operations against a declared enemy. Upon retirement from the military, Colonel Stogran served three years as Canada's first Veterans Ombudsman, the experience he has chronicled in Rude Awakening. Having spent his entire adult life as a soldier, today he is committed to finding out who Pat the civilian is, and to giving back to his family who supported him so faithfully for so long through so much. In his retirement, Colonel Stogran occupies his time reading, writing, and talking about leadership. The Colonel hopes that by telling his story his knowledge and experience might serve to inspire the future leaders of Canada to reverse the alarming trend of corruption and incompetence that seems to have consumed our government. Colonel Stogran lives in Ottawa with his wife and children.